SpringerBriefs in Computer Science

SpringerBriefs present concise summaries of cutting-edge research and practical applications across a wide spectrum of fields. Featuring compact volumes of 50 to 125 pages, the series covers a range of content from professional to academic.

Typical topics might include:

- A timely report of state-of-the art analytical techniques
- A bridge between new research results, as published in journal articles, and a contextual literature review
- A snapshot of a hot or emerging topic
- An in-depth case study or clinical example
- A presentation of core concepts that students must understand in order to make independent contributions

Briefs allow authors to present their ideas and readers to absorb them with minimal time investment. Briefs will be published as part of Springer's eBook collection, with millions of users worldwide. In addition, Briefs will be available for individual print and electronic purchase. Briefs are characterized by fast, global electronic dissemination, standard publishing contracts, easy-to-use manuscript preparation and formatting guidelines, and expedited production schedules. We aim for publication 8–12 weeks after acceptance. Both solicited and unsolicited manuscripts are considered for publication in this series.

**Indexing: This series is indexed in Scopus, Ei-Compendex, and zbMATH **

Poornachandra Sarang • Leena Nadkar

Blockchain Without Barriers

An Authentic Guide to Blockchain Interoperability

 Springer

Poornachandra Sarang ⓘ
ABCOM
Mumbai, India

Leena Nadkar ⓘ
MPSTME NMIMS (Deemed University)
Mumbai, India

ISSN 2191-5768　　　　　　　ISSN 2191-5776　(electronic)
SpringerBriefs in Computer Science
ISBN 978-3-032-03412-0　　　ISBN 978-3-032-03413-7　(eBook)
https://doi.org/10.1007/978-3-032-03413-7

© The Editor(s) (if applicable) and The Author(s), under exclusive license to Springer Nature Switzerland AG 2025

This work is subject to copyright. All rights are solely and exclusively licensed by the Publisher, whether the whole or part of the material is concerned, specifically the rights of translation, reprinting, reuse of illustrations, recitation, broadcasting, reproduction on microfilms or in any other physical way, and transmission or information storage and retrieval, electronic adaptation, computer software, or by similar or dissimilar methodology now known or hereafter developed.
The use of general descriptive names, registered names, trademarks, service marks, etc. in this publication does not imply, even in the absence of a specific statement, that such names are exempt from the relevant protective laws and regulations and therefore free for general use.
The publisher, the authors and the editors are safe to assume that the advice and information in this book are believed to be true and accurate at the date of publication. Neither the publisher nor the authors or the editors give a warranty, expressed or implied, with respect to the material contained herein or for any errors or omissions that may have been made. The publisher remains neutral with regard to jurisdictional claims in published maps and institutional affiliations.

This Springer imprint is published by the registered company Springer Nature Switzerland AG
The registered company address is: Gewerbestrasse 11, 6330 Cham, Switzerland

If disposing of this product, please recycle the paper.

To my late beloved Father, who constantly pushed me to pursue higher education.
Poornachandra Sarang

*To my beloved son, **Dev Raut**, may your curiosity always lead you to build, explore, and connect the worlds around you. This book is for you.*
Leena Nadkar

Preface

Cryptocurrencies have become as widespread as CBDCs (Central Bank Digital Currencies). CBDCs can be exchanged and traded easily through centralized authorities. However, cryptocurrencies built on blockchain technology are not marketable because the platform does not natively support cross-chain authentication and security. In the current circumstance, how can you transfer Bitcoin from your own account to another Ethereum account, or a piece of property registered on a Hyperledger to a possible buyer, without relying on trusted intermediary?

This is exactly where we need interoperability across today's segmented blockchains. If you are a seasoned blockchain user, you would argue that bridges enhance interoperability across various blockchains. A token bridge allows me to move Bitcoin to Ether. Now, the question is whether these transactions are safe and secure. Take a look at infamous hacks like Wormhole and Nomad. These bridges aren't secured. We still need to do a lot of research to make them completely secure.

In addition to bridges, researchers and academics have developed a number of other interoperability solutions. Several protocols have been developed for effective, secure communication between blockchains, including Cosmos IBC (Cosmos Inter-Blockchain Communication Protocol), LayerZero ULN (LayerZero Ultra Light Node), Chainlink CCIP (Chainlink Cross-Chain Interoperability Protocol), and XCM (Cross-Consensus Message Format). These, too, are not without flaw.

Furthermore, because blockchains are scattered across different jurisdictions around the world, interoperability raises significant governance concerns. Every country has its own governance regulations, and meeting those criteria presents a significant barrier to interoperability engineers. The Cross-Domain Trust Mesh (CDTM) was designed to strike a balance between security, scalability, and governance in multi-chain systems.

It is now our vision to establish a truly decentralized world, known as Web 3.0. In this book, we will begin with the current hurdles that we must solve in order to create interoperability between siloed blockchains. We will discuss the many interoperability technologies available today, as well as their drawbacks. Finally, we will discuss the current research areas that are being pursued in order to realize the Web 3.0 vision.

More specifically, this is what the five chapters of this book will discuss.

Chapter 1 establishes the foundations of blockchain interoperability. This chapter lays the groundwork by discussing why interoperability is so important and how existing ecosystems are failing to satisfy demand. It describes the architecture, underlying assumptions, and communication logic of many protocols, such as LayerZero, Chainlink CCIP, Cosmos IBC, and XCM.

In Chapter 2, we discuss the security challenges associated with current implementation approaches and how they might be mitigated. Here, we'll look at replay issues, real-world attacks, and smart contract exploitation. In addition to addressing cryptographic defenses and AI-driven mitigation techniques, it investigates double spending, Oracle manipulation, the Poly Network and Wormhole attacks.

Chapter 3 addresses the essential problem of governance and the role of regulators. This chapter zooms out to look at the governance and legal problems surrounding cross-chain applications. It investigates smart legal contracts, DAO accountability, bridge liability, AML/KYC, and the role of RegTech in achieving institutional alignment in decentralized systems.

Chapter 4 delves into the practical world of developing interoperability tools on your own. This chapter provides a step-by-step guide for developing and testing cross-chain systems, including CCIP communication simulation, lock-mint bridges, and testing of ULN-style messaging. This chapter is your playground, complete with fully functional Truffle projects, deployment walkthroughs, event logging, and retry logic.

Chapter 5 establishes a framework for future research in this field. It summarizes the main takeaways for researchers. The chapter discusses future trends, actionable insights, and a vision for modular systems, smart wallets, governance-aware ecosystems, and interoperable dApps. In addition to making proposals for future research and development, it introduces the Cross-Domain Trust Mesh (CDTM). Blockchains will evolve from competition to collaboration, resulting in a modular mesh rather than a single chain. The boundaries between public, private, on-chain, off-chain, L1s, and L2s will be eliminated soon.

Finally, we'd like to add something. This book is inspired by current research in this field, the growing demand among blockchain users for interoperability and the developer's aim to create a truly interoperable system, a Web 3.0 vision. As a result, the knowledge in this book will be extremely useful to you, whether you are an architect, developer, researcher, or simply an inquisitive student.

Mumbai, India Poornachandra Sarang
Mumbai, India Leena Nadkar

Competing Interests The authors have no competing interests to declare that are relevant to the content of this manuscript.

Contents

1 Blockchain Interoperability—Foundations 1
   1.1 Preamble 2
   1.2 Siloed Blockchain Networks 2
       1.2.1 Blockchain Ecosystems 3
       1.2.2 Network Limitations 5
       1.2.3 Inter-Chain Communication 5
   1.3 Need for Interoperability 6
       1.3.1 Finance Applications 6
       1.3.2 Non-Finance Applications 7
       1.3.3 How to Achieve Interoperability? 7
   1.4 Interoperability Solutions 8
       1.4.1 Atomic Swaps 8
       1.4.2 Bridges 10
       1.4.3 Relays 14
       1.4.4 Interoperability Protocols 17
   1.5 Scalability Issues 22
       1.5.1 Blockchain Trilemma 22
       1.5.2 Security Concerns 24
   1.6 Future Solutions and Innovations 25
       1.6.1 Architectural Enhancements 25
       1.6.2 Adaptive Models 26
   1.7 Web 3.0 27
       1.7.1 Web3 Architecture 28
       1.7.2 Web3 Benefits 28
       1.7.3 What Is Needed? 29
       1.7.4 PoS, PoA, and Trustless Governance 29
       1.7.5 Use Cases 30
   1.8 Summary 30
   References 31

2 Security Challenges... 35
2.1 Introduction... 36
2.2 Key Vulnerabilities... 38
2.3 The Single Point of Failure... 38
   2.3.1 Poly Network Attack... 38
   2.3.2 Wormhole Bridge Exploit... 39
   2.3.3 Oracles and Honeypots... 39
   2.3.4 Mitigations... 39
2.4 Smart Contract Exploits... 41
   2.4.1 The DAO Attack... 42
   2.4.2 Parity Wallet Bug... 42
   2.4.3 Smart Contracts Tools... 42
   2.4.4 Mitigations... 43
2.5 Double-Spending... 44
   2.5.1 What Is Double-Spending?... 44
   2.5.2 How Does it Work?... 45
   2.5.3 Bitcoin Gold Attack... 46
   2.5.4 Mitigations... 47
2.6 Replay Attacks... 47
2.7 Cryptographic Defenses... 48
   2.7.1 Trusted Relays... 48
   2.7.2 Threshold Signatures... 49
   2.7.3 Oracles... 51
2.8 What's Next?... 52
2.9 Future Security Directions... 53
   2.9.1 Quantum-Resistant Cryptography... 53
   2.9.2 AI-Driven Security Models... 54
   2.9.3 AI Benefits... 55
   2.9.4 Reliable Interoperable Smart Contracts... 55
   2.9.5 Cross-Chain Identity... 58
2.10 Summary... 59
References... 61

3 Role of Regulatories... 65
3.1 Introduction... 66
   3.1.1 Need for Regulation... 67
   3.1.2 Innovation and Jurisdiction Conflict... 68
3.2 Industry Regulations... 69
   3.2.1 Finance... 70
   3.2.2 Supply Chain... 70
   3.2.3 Banking... 71
3.3 Compliance... 71
   3.3.1 AML/KYC in Interoperable Apps... 72
   3.3.2 Data Sovereignty... 73
   3.3.3 Token Classification... 73

	3.3.4	Legal Gray Zones	74
	3.3.5	Regulatory Sandboxes	74
	3.3.6	International Collaboration	74
3.4	Jurisdictional Gaps		75
	3.4.1	Bridge Liability	76
	3.4.2	DAO Accountability	77
	3.4.3	Smart Contract Enforcement across Borders	77
	3.4.4	Legal Wrappers	78
	3.4.5	Dispute Resolution	78
	3.4.6	Regulatory Oversight	79
3.5	Governance		79
	3.5.1	Role of DAOs	80
	3.5.2	Meta-Governance	81
	3.5.3	Sybil Resistance	81
	3.5.4	Vote Hijacking	82
	3.5.5	Decentralized Risk Controls	82
3.6	RegTech		83
	3.6.1	AI-Driven Compliance Monitoring	83
	3.6.2	Verifiable Credentials	84
	3.6.3	DID-Based Onboarding	84
	3.6.4	ZKPs for Privacy-Compliance Disclosures	85
	3.6.5	Smart Legal Contracts	85
	3.6.6	Regulatory Oracles	85
3.7	Summary		86
References			86
4	**Developer Guide**		**93**
4.1	Introduction		95
	4.1.1	Cross-Chain Smart Contracts	95
	4.1.2	Scope of Development	96
4.2	Development Environment Setup		96
	4.2.1	Installing Node.js, Truffle and Ganache	97
	4.2.2	`Truffle` Project Creation	98
4.3	Foundations of Interoperability		100
	4.3.1	Programmable Logic for Interoperability	101
	4.3.2	Smart Contracts as Relayers	101
	4.3.3	Execution Boundaries	102
	4.3.4	State Dependencies	102
4.4	Implementing Interoperability		102
4.5	Programming Smart Contracts		103
	4.5.1	Cross-Chain Simulations on EVM	103
	4.5.2	Solidity Syntax Essentials	104
	4.5.3	Design Patterns	106
4.6	Cross-Chain Messaging Patterns		107
	4.6.1	`Lock-Mint`, `Burn-Mint` & Oracle-Based Flows	107
	4.6.2	Simulating Message Flow	108

		4.6.3 Events, Listeners, and JSON-RPC Calls	108
		4.6.4 Retry and Fallback Logic	109
	4.7	LayerZero with Truffle	109
		4.7.1 Trustless Omnichain Communication with ULN	110
		4.7.2 Deployment	111
		4.7.3 Contract Code	111
		4.7.4 Deployment Scripts	112
		4.7.5 Deployment Walkthrough	113
	4.8	Chainlink CCIP	118
		4.8.1 Oracle-Based Routing and Message Reliability	118
		4.8.2 Building with Chainlink CCIP	119
		4.8.3 Contract Code	120
		4.8.4 Deployment Walkthrough	122
	4.9	Token Bridge	124
		4.9.1 Prototype	126
		4.9.2 Security Checklist	130
	4.10	Security Considerations	131
		4.10.1 Replay Protection and Nonce Tracking	132
		4.10.2 Oracle Manipulation and Verifiable Messaging	133
		4.10.3 Circuit Breakers, Pause Mechanisms, and Role-Based Access	133
		4.10.4 Static Analysis and Deployment Verification	133
	4.11	Developer Tooling Summary	134
		4.11.1 Truffle: Foundation for Cross-Chain Simulation	134
		4.11.2 Web3.js for Simulating Cross-Chain Clients	134
		4.11.3 APIs for Modular Testing and Future Upgrades	135
		4.11.4 Project Structure Best Practices	135
	4.12	Summary	136
	References		137
5	**Key Takeaways for Researchers**		143
	5.1	Summary of Key Lessons	145
		5.1.1 Interoperability in Fragmented Ecosystems	145
		5.1.2 Blockchain Interoperability Models	145
		5.1.3 Practical Use Cases	146
		5.1.4 Cross-Chain Security and Tooling	146
	5.2	Best Practices	147
		5.2.1 Trustless Cross-Chain Messaging	147
		5.2.2 Developer Abstraction	147
		5.2.3 Rollup-Aware Interoperability	148
		5.2.4 Enterprise Grade BlockChain Applications	148
		5.2.5 Security Primitives	149
		5.2.6 Governance Alignment	149
	5.3	Future Multi-Chain Ecosystems	149
		5.3.1 Multi-Chain Paradigm	150
		5.3.2 Hiding Complexity	150

	5.3.3	Non-Monetary Applications	151
	5.3.4	Interoperable dApps	151
	5.3.5	DeFi in the Future	152
5.4	The Next Phase of Interoperability		153
	5.4.1	Modularization	153
	5.4.2	Interdisciplinary Collaboration	153
	5.4.3	Seamless Fluidity	155
	5.4.4	Intelligent Wallets	155
	5.4.5	Dynamic dApps	156
	5.4.6	Rise of Supra-DAOs	156
	5.4.7	Interoperability Beyond DeFi	156
	5.4.8	Regulatory Harmonization Across Chains	157
5.5	Final Thoughts		157
	5.5.1	The Interoperability Trilemma	158
	5.5.2	Security at the Crossroads	158
	5.5.3	Reimagining Governance	159
	5.5.4	A Vision: The Cross-Domain Trust Mesh	160
	5.5.5	The Path Ahead: Standards, Verification, and Composability	160
	5.5.6	The Last Word	160
5.6	Conclusion and Future Directions for Research		161
	5.6.1	The Future Is Composable	161
	5.6.2	What Needs Reconsideration?	161
	5.6.3	For the Researchers	162
References			163

About the Authors

Poornachandra Sarang in his IT career spanning four decades, has been consulting large IT organizations on the design and architecture of systems using state-of-the-art technologies. He has authored several books covering a wide range of emerging technologies. Dr. Sarang is a Ph.D. advisor for Computer Science and Engineering and is on the thesis advisory committee for aspiring doctoral candidates. He has designed and delivered courses/curricula for universities at the post-graduate level, including courses and workshops on emerging technologies for industry. He is a known face at technical and research conferences delivering both keynote and technical talks.

Leena Nadkar is a researcher and educator specializing in blockchain. Currently pursuing a Ph.D. in Computer Engineering at MPSTME, NMIMS, Mumbai, she has taught Blockchain Technology, Cryptography and Network Security, Advanced Web Technologies, Database Management Systems, Cloud Computing, and other Computer Engineering subjects as an Assistant Professor and Visiting Faculty. She has authored research papers, Udemy courses, and copyrighted content on blockchain and emerging technologies. A speaker at technical conferences and workshops, she actively shares insights on Udemy, YouTube, LinkedIn, and Medium, contributing to blockchain education and research.

Chapter 1
Blockchain Interoperability—Foundations

Contents

1.1	Preamble	2
1.2	Siloed Blockchain Networks	2
	1.2.1 Blockchain Ecosystems	3
	1.2.2 Network Limitations	5
	1.2.3 Inter-Chain Communication	5
1.3	Need for Interoperability	6
	1.3.1 Finance Applications	6
	1.3.2 Non-Finance Applications	7
	1.3.3 How to Achieve Interoperability?	7
1.4	Interoperability Solutions	8
	1.4.1 Atomic Swaps	8
	1.4.2 Bridges	10
	1.4.3 Relays	14
	1.4.4 Interoperability Protocols	17
1.5	Scalability Issues	22
	1.5.1 Blockchain Trilemma	22
	1.5.2 Security Concerns	24
1.6	Future Solutions and Innovations	25
	1.6.1 Architectural Enhancements	25
	1.6.2 Adaptive Models	26
1.7	Web 3.0	27
	1.7.1 Web3 Architecture	28
	1.7.2 Web3 Benefits	28
	1.7.3 What Is Needed?	29
	1.7.4 PoS, PoA, and Trustless Governance	29
	1.7.5 Use Cases	30
1.8	Summary	30
References		31

© The Author(s), under exclusive license to Springer Nature
Switzerland AG 2025
P. Sarang, L. Nadkar, *Blockchain Without Barriers*, SpringerBriefs in Computer
Science, https://doi.org/10.1007/978-3-032-03413-7_1

Abstract What will happen if blockchains can't exchange data with each other? In order to answer the question, this chapter delves into the crucial topic of blockchain interoperability and how it plays a critical role in the evolution of Web 3.0. Bitcoin, Ethereum and Hyperledger are the three most well-known blockchain networks. This chapter commences with a study of their interoperability.

The need for smooth interoperability is made apparent by the many real-world applications in various industries, including non-financial (supply chain, healthcare, IoT) and financial (DeFi, CBDCs). This chapter looks at a number of solutions, including message-passing protocols, atomic exchanges, relays, and bridges. This chapter also discusses scalability in connection to interoperability. Web 3.0, a user-driven, decentralized, and interoperable ecosystem that permits the safe exchange of identities, assets, and applications among its chains, is discussed at the chapter's conclusion.

Keywords Blockchain Interoperability · Cross-Chain Communication · Web 3.0 · Decentralized Finance (DeFi) · Interoperability Protocols · Cross-Chain Bridges

1.1 Preamble

We are all aware that Blockchain is a decentralized, digital ledger that is immutable, transparent, and completely eliminates the necessity for a centralized authority. The first practical application of the blockchain—Bitcoin, was introduced in January 2009, following the initial outline by anonymous Satoshi Nakamoto in 2008. There are currently over 20000 cryptocurrencies distributed across 1000 blockchains [1, Cryptocurrency, Wikipedia, The Free Encyclopedia]. In addition to cryptocurrencies, asset management and smart contracts now make use of this modern blockchain technology.

Unfortunately, each blockchain operates in complete isolation from other networks due to its inherent nature. This prevents the transmission of assets or the exchange of currencies across these networks. Researchers have devised numerous solutions to facilitate the interoperability of these networks. Nevertheless, we are still a long way from attaining true interoperability in order to establish a decentralized web, which is commonly referred to as Web 3.0. If and when Web3 is successful, it will bring about total decentralization in our centralized world, which is a vision for all of us. When Web3 emerges, the decentralization will shift power from big businesses to individuals.

Let's first examine the development of blockchain technology since its launch in 2009 in order to comprehend the interoperability problems.

1.2 Siloed Blockchain Networks

The working of each blockchain network is inherently independent of other networks. The existence of other networks on the web is not even recognized by each network, let alone the interaction. The assets that are held by each network, which

1.2 Siloed Blockchain Networks

were initially only cryptocurrencies, are valuable and cannot be transferred or exchanged with peers in other networks.

Ecosystems such as Bitcoin [2], Ethereum [2], and frameworks like Hyperledger [3] are typically operated in isolated environments, and we refer to them as siloed networks because they lack native interoperability. Each of the blockchain platforms, Bitcoin and Ethereum, has a primary network, known as the mainnet. Additionally, they can support testnets or sidechains. Developers can establish numerous autonomous permissioned networks with Hyperledger.

The segregated architecture of popular blockchain ecosystems is depicted in Fig. 1.1. We'll now give a quick overview of each environment.

1.2.1 Blockchain Ecosystems

Let us commence with Bitcoin, the initial cryptocurrency and the first blockchain application in the world.

1.2.1.1 Bitcoin

Bitcoin was introduced as a decentralized digital currency and payment system that lacked the native support for sophisticated smart contracts that are found in modern ecosystems. While cryptocurrencies are generally acknowledged in a wide range of

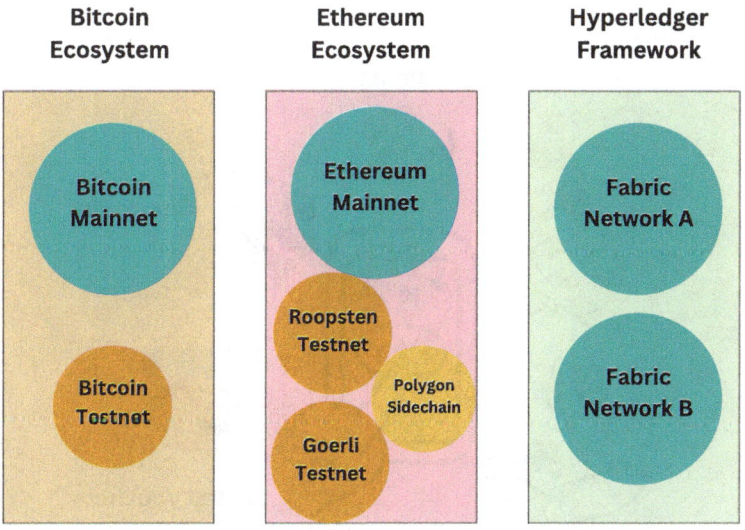

Fig. 1.1 Siloed blockchains

industries, including the purchase of Microsoft credits, gift cards, and even space travel reservations, its use is restricted when users wish to interact with applications or assets on other chains, such as Ethereum.

Figure 1.2 provides a few instances of bitcoin use cases, such as buying meals, playing games, using digital coupons, buying electronics, and booking vacation.

1.2.1.2 Ethereum

In the Ethereum ecosystem, the Mainnet is responsible for the operation of live decentralized applications and transactions that utilize Ether (ETH). Testnets, including Ropsten [4] and Goerli [5], offer developers a testing environment that mimics the main network. A sidechain, Polygon [6], offers transactions that are both quicker and more cost-effective. However, it is self-contained and has its own consensus mechanism.

1.2.1.3 Hyperledger

On the business side, the Hyperledger Fabric framework allows organizations to create their own proprietary permissioned networks. These respective networks may be optimized for supply chain, healthcare, or finance; however, they are not natively interoperable.

Jointly, these three ecosystems lack an inherent mechanism for frictionless, secure communication, necessitating the development of cross-chain interoperability solutions. Bitcoin was initially a fundamental decentralized payment system,

Fig. 1.2 Cryptocurrency purchases

while Ethereum incorporated smart contracts and decentralized applications (dApps). Hyperledger, in contrast, features permissioned networks that were intended for enterprise use in application-level scenarios such as finance and supply chain. It is due to these architectural and historical distinctions that interoperability is not inherent and needs to be engineered.

We will now talk about segregated networks' limitations.

1.2.2 Network Limitations

Blockchain technology is inherently isolated, with each blockchain network operating independently. The majority of networks, whether they are public (such as Bitcoin and Ethereum) or permissioned (such as Hyperledger), operate in isolation, lacking any built in mechanism for interacting with others. This kind of fragmentation results in duplicated efforts, inefficiencies, and acts as barriers to innovation.

Due to vendor lock-ins, an additional type of restriction is introduced. The migration of a network to another network that is more efficient or potentially interoperable is not possible once it has been developed. Also, the interoperability is significantly hampered by the diverse consensus models implemented by various vendors.

Interoperability is important for the unrestricted transfer of assets between national and international digital currencies [7] or for the implementation of smart contracts that span multiple platforms [8]. The blockchain's decentralized potential is unrealized and fragmented in the absence of interoperability. In the absence of an industry-wide standard or inter-chain communication mechanism, developers and businesses continue to operate in isolation, thereby forfeiting the advantages of composable [7] and cross-platform applications [3].

Now, we will examine the advantages of inter-chain communication.

1.2.3 Inter-Chain Communication

Evidently, the industry has prioritized interoperability among isolated networks. In an effort to facilitate inter-chain communication, it is imperative to establish specific mechanisms and standards. Such mechanisms would allow users to transmit assets, access decentralized finance (DeFi) platforms [8], and even participate in governance processes regardless of the blockchain they are on [9]. For instance, token holders on one network could vote on propositions that are being discussed on another, which would enable more inclusive and participatory cross-chain governance [8]. Similarly, the maintenance of multiple wallets, tokens, or identities would be eliminated for users, as digital assets would be free to travel between blockchains [10].

The user experience would be improved by decreasing complexity and increasing transparency as a result of these communication norms. Users could interact with numerous chains through a single interface, which would facilitate simpler asset management [3], reduce friction [9], and increase liquidity [8] by eliminating the need to manually replicate data across chains and juggle broken pools of assets.

Cross-chain functionality also enhances transparency, as all interactions can be traced and verified on-chain. Cross-chain functionality facilitates inclusion, especially for users constrained by costs or access on certain blockchains, and enhances accessibility for decentralized apps (dApps) designed to serve users irrespective of the underlying chain [11].

The necessity of interoperability is not solely theoretical or structural. It is substantially motivated by use cases across a variety of industries. Particularly, the finance sector has emerged as one of the most urgent beneficiaries of cross-chain functionality, as there is an increasing demand for inter-platform liquidity, transparent asset transfers, and the integrated execution of smart contracts.

With this requisite context in place, we will now examine the increasing significance of interoperability in a variety of industries, starting with financial applications and extending to non-financial domains such as healthcare, the Internet of Things (IoT), and others.

1.3 Need for Interoperability

The number of active blockchains is listed on numerous websites. There are likely thousands of blockchains in use now, and the list [12, "List of blockchains," *Wikipedia, The Free Encyclopedia*] is growing every day. It is essential that all of these blockchains, regardless of their financial or non-financial nature, are interoperable in order to establish a decentralized world. We will now address the interoperability requirements of both sectors.

1.3.1 Finance Applications

In order for the financial sector to realize its objectives of enhanced liquidity, decreased transaction fees, and effortless asset transfers, interoperability is indispensable. Investors may seek alternative blockchains to transmit bitcoins in order to capitalize on reduced fees or expedited execution. Operational time and custodial risk are sacrificed in order to prevent interoperability through the transmission of data through centralized exchanges [2].

The necessity for cross-chain liquidity, which refers to the ease of moving assets across chains, is also critical. Solana may be the preferred option for loan settlement for certain users due to its ability to process up to 65,000 transactions per second, ultra-low gas fees (typically below $0.01 per transaction), and integration with bridges such as Wormhole. Some individuals utilize Ethereum to facilitate transactions at a speedier pace, while others may prefer to transfer funds from Avalanche [13] to Fantom [14]. Interoperability is indispensable in these environments to render decentralized finance (DeFi) systems more inclusive and composable [15]. It would enable efficient coordination among a variety of financial networks.

Moreover, interoperable platforms are essential for the implementation of decentralized trading, cross-chain stablecoins, and global financial instruments like CBDCs. While interoperability is desirable, it is essential to utilize these technologies efficiently and securely across various platforms and international boundaries [16].

We now examine the necessity of interoperability in non-financial applications.

1.3.2 Non-Finance Applications

Interoperability in blockchain is a critical factor in industries such as healthcare, supply chain, and the Internet of Things (IoT).

A healthcare provider or hospital that utilizes one blockchain must be capable of securely and promptly accessing patient data that is stored on another blockchain. In the absence of interoperability, patient safety and real-time therapy are compromised by disjointed or delayed access [7]. In the Internet of Things (IoT), the blockchain receives information in real time from the sensors. We can initiate payment or supply order on another blockchain like Hyperledger if blockchain interoperability is achieved. This type of automation necessitates real-time communication across blockchains [10].

NFTs are typically restricted to the native blockchains of the majority of gaming and metaverse platforms. The interoperability of the digital assets enables their use on other platforms without the need for minting or transferring. Automation and cross-chain traceability can also be advantageous for the detection of frauds in supply chain networks [17].

Now that we are aware that interoperability is essential for a variety of purposes, including secure healthcare data sharing and decentralized financial asset transfers, the subsequent logical step is to examine the technical methods used to achieve this.

1.3.3 How to Achieve Interoperability?

The blockchain ecosystem has given rise to a number of innovative protocols and procedures, all of which are designed to eliminate communication barriers between distinct blockchain networks. The fundamental design objectives of these systems are trustlessness, which implies that users should not depend on centralized middlemen; scalability, which refers to their ability to accommodate an increasing network traffic; and security, which implies that they should prevent fraud and attacks.

We will address atomic exchanges in the subsequent sections, which enable decentralized, trustless, peer-to-peer asset transfers across blockchain networks. Using burn-and-mint or lock-and-mint procedures, bridge-based approaches enable the transmission of data and tokens between chains that are incompatible with one another. Relays, which emphasizes cross-chain data validation through cryptographic techniques such as Merkle proofs, enable decentralized and trustless verification of blockchain states. Last but not least, Interoperability Protocols establish standards for interoperability among chains. These protocols are implemented by prominent companies such as Chainlink CCIP [18], LayerZero [18], Cosmos IBC [19], and Polkadot's XCM [20, 21].

These solutions, which provide the technical foundation for enabling decentralized, scalable, and secure cross-chain interactions, are covered in more detail in the following sections.

1.4 Interoperability Solutions

In order to mitigate the fragmentation of blockchain architectures that are heterogeneous, numerous interoperability solutions have been proposed and implemented. From basic token transmission protocols to intricate protocols for decentralized communication and smart contract execution, these have been a diverse range. Each solution responds to the interoperability challenge in its own distinctive manner, with varying degrees of decentralization, security, and scalability.

Numerous protocols and technologies for interoperability have been developed by the researchers over the years. Polkadot's XCM, Cosmos IBC, LayerZero, and Chainlink CCIP are among the protocols, while atomic exchanges, relays, and bridges are among the technologies. The practical implementation of this research has been demonstrated, and we have observed a high level of adoption. Not necessarily, they accomplish the ultimate objective of establishing a fully decentralized world, which is often referred to as a Unified Blockchain Ecosystem or Web3. However, it is evident that they have made a significant stride in this regard.

Next, we'll talk about these technologies. This will be followed by the interoperability protocols in the subsequent section. We start with Atomic Swaps.

1.4.1 Atomic Swaps

Atomic swaps facilitate the trustless exchange of assets between various blockchain networks without the need for a central intermediary. The underlying mechanism is based on Hashed Time-Locked Contracts (HTLCs), which ensure that a trade either succeeds in full or fails completely, thereby eliminating the risk of partial transactions or fund loss [2]. In this framework, one party secures funds by employing a cryptographic hash, while the other party is obligated to submit a preimage (secret)

1.4 Interoperability Solutions

in order to retrieve them. The contract becomes null and void if the agreed-upon conditions are not fulfilled within a designated time frame, triggering an automatic reimbursement to both parties. This ensures mutual compliance without relying on a centralized intermediary.

We will now provide an example to demonstrate how Atomic Swap operates.

1.4.1.1 Functioning

In Fig. 1.3, Atomic Swaps shows how Alice and Bob, two users, can safely exchange cryptocurrency between two distinct blockchains: Blockchain A's Bitcoin (BTC) and Blockchain B's Ether (ETH) without the assistance of a centralized middleman. In order to prevent money loss, this procedure makes use of Hashed Timelock Contracts (HTLCs) [22], a cryptographic technique that guarantees that either both sides finish the trade or neither does.

Here is a concise summary of the events.

When Alice (Step 1) wishes to exchange her Bitcoin for Bob's ETH, the procedure starts. At the same time, Bob (Step 2) wants to exchange his ETH for Alice's Bitcoin. Alice creates a secret hash (Step 3) by locking her Bitcoin in an HTLC on

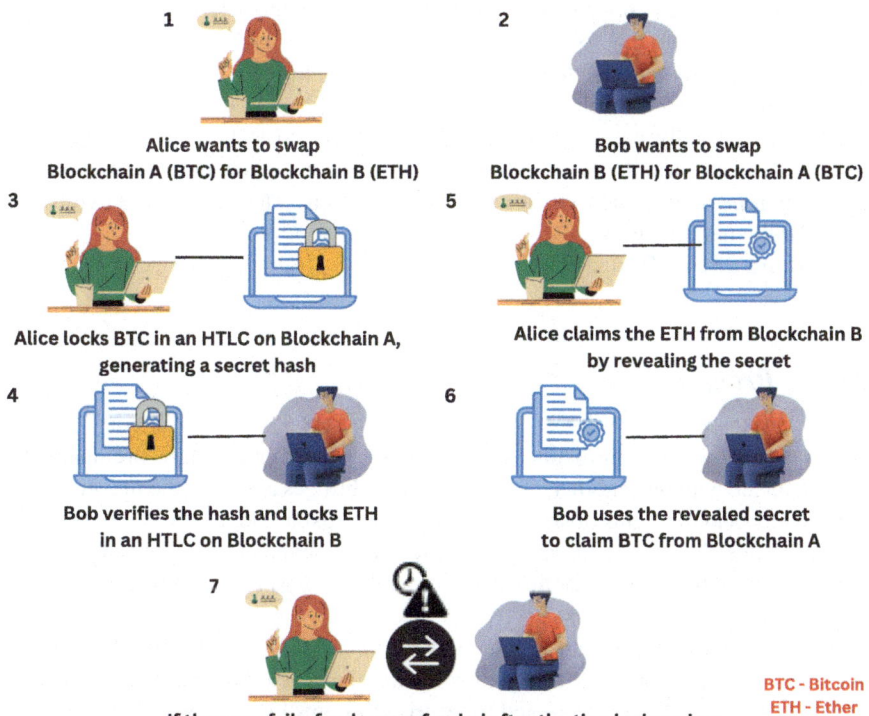

Fig. 1.3 Working of atomic swaps

Blockchain A to start the swap. After confirming the hash, Bob locks his ETH in a matching HTLC on Blockchain B (Step 4). Alice can claim Bob's ETH after it has been locked, but she must first divulge the original secret (Step 5). Bob can see the secret that Alice gave him to claim the ETH, and he uses it to unlock and claim the BTC on Blockchain A (Step 6).

To guarantee that neither Alice nor Bob lose money, the funds are automatically returned to their rightful owners if either participant does not finish their portion of the transaction within the allotted time lock window (Step 7). This guarantees an atomic, trustless transaction in which either party walks away with their initial assets or receives what they desire.

We now examine some of the latest advancements in the field of atomic swaps.

1.4.1.2 Recent Developments

Latest advancements have introduced asynchronous fair exchange protocols that eliminate the need for time constraints and guarantee real-time finality [23]. Furthermore, the implementation of new models allows for multi-asset atomic exchanges, which enable users to trade multiple currencies in a single transaction. These advancements enhance liquidity, reduce transaction costs, and are suitable for high-frequency DeFi applications by maintaining low latency [24].

In spite of the fact that token swapping on centralized exchanges remains one of the most straightforward methods, it is custodial and subject to regulatory risks [10]. Atomic swaps on decentralized exchanges (DEXs) [23] are user-driven and safer, but they are usually chain compatibility-dependent and technically elaborate. In spite of these constraints, atomic swaps remain a fundamental component of blockchain interoperability due to their security, transparency, and ability to circumvent centralized intermediaries.

Next, we discuss Bridge-Based Approaches.

1.4.2 Bridges

When two networks with distinct consensus algorithms and designs are unable to communicate with one another, cross-blockchain bridges allow for the movement of data, assets, and the status of smart contracts. Most token bridges operate by locking tokens on one chain and generating wrapped tokens on the other chain. The bridges act as intermediaries that facilitate interoperability ensuring assets can be used across blockchains.

Bridges address the isolation issue among blockchains by enabling secure and verifiable communication, which in turn enables the development of platforms such as DeFi [9], NFT Markets [10], and Enterprise Systems [3] to operate across a variety of networks.

Let us now look at the bridge design.

1.4 Interoperability Solutions

1.4.2.1 Architecture

A typical blockchain bridge consists of four key parts:

- **Relayers**: Send transaction data to the intended chain.
- **Validators**: Acknowledge completion of transaction.
- **Event storage**: For auditing purposes.
- **Security module**: Guards against malevolent activity.

We shall now describe the operation of a bridge.

1.4.2.2 Functioning

We will use a scenario to demonstrate how Bridges work.

Figure 1.4 depicts the operation of a blockchain bridge, an interoperability device facilitating asset transfer between two distinct blockchains. The illustration depicts a whole cycle of asset depositing, transferring, and redeeming through a wrapped token method. The method operates in a sequential manner as follows:

- **Asset Deposit**—The user commences the cross-chain transfer by depositing assets into a bridge smart contract deployed on Blockchain A.
- **Asset Locking and Proof Generation**—Upon deposit, the bridge smart contract securely locks the assets and produces a cryptographic proof confirming the retention of the funds.
- **Validators Relay Proof**—Validators authenticate the asset lock on Blockchain A and subsequently transmit the proof to Blockchain B.
- **Verification and Token Minting**—On Blockchain B, a bridge contract authenticates the proof (for instance, utilizing Merkle proofs), and upon validation, it mints wrapped tokens that signify the original locked assets.
- **Wrapped Token Receipt**—The user obtains wrapped tokens on Blockchain B, which are tied at a 1:1 ratio with the locked tokens on Blockchain A. These can now be utilized within the ecosystem of Blockchain B.
- **Asset Reclaimation**—The user burns wrapped tokens on Blockchain B to retrieve the original tokens. Burning eliminates the wrapped tokens and instructs the bridge to disburse the original assets.
- **Asset Release**—The bridge contract on Blockchain A authenticates the burn evidence and subsequently returns the previously locked assets to the user's wallet.

This procedure guarantees that the original asset remains on its native chain, hence decreasing the risk of duplication or double-spending. The user consistently possesses either the original asset or its wrapped counterpart, but never both, hence guaranteeing trustless value transfer across chains.

We now examine the many kinds of bridges that are currently in use in this industry.

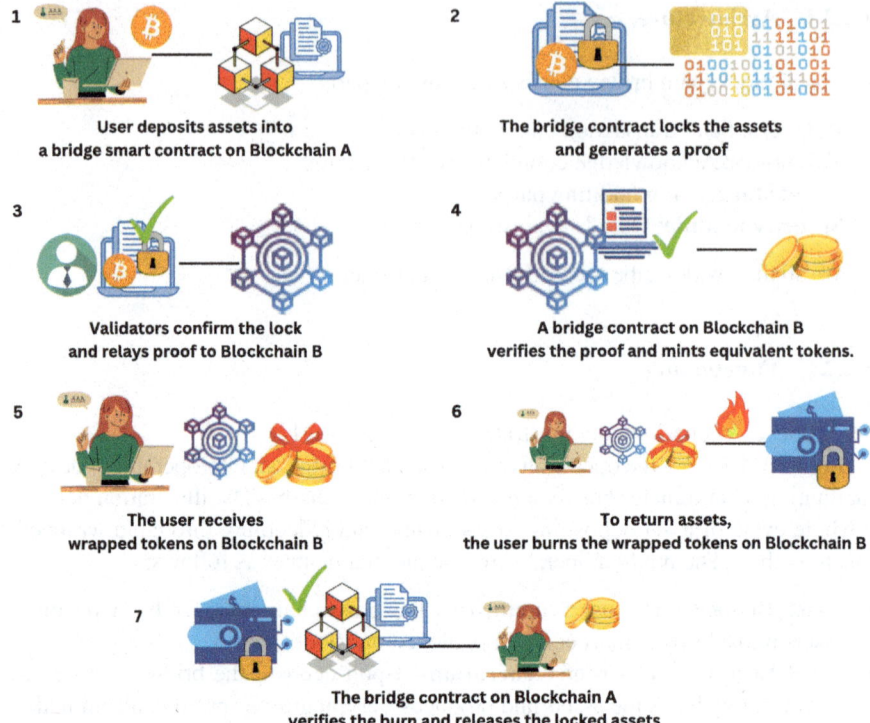

Fig. 1.4 Working of blockchain bridges

1.4.2.3 Types of Bridges

There are numerous blockchain bridges, each of which possesses unique features and functionalities.

- **Token Transfer Bridges**—They are utilized to facilitate the transmission of tokens between chains. They frequently implement Lock-and-Mint or Burn-and-Release patterns, in which tokens are either locked on the origin chain and minted on the destination chain, or they are burned on the origin chain and minted on the destination [18].
- **Message-Passing Bridges**–These bridges extend token transfers to facilitate the transmission of arbitrary data and smart contract state between chains. It enables the execution of dApps in a synchronized manner, the invocation of smart contracts remotely, and the voting on cross-chain governance [9].
- **NFT-Based Identity Bridges**—This type of bridge is the most recent innovation; it employs non-fungible tokens (NFTs) as distinctive identifiers. The NFTs facilitate decentralized authentication and enhance traceability, accountability, and security in cross-chain interactions by validating user identities between chains [7].

- **Multi-Protocol or Hybrid Bridges**—These bridges incorporate a variety of technologies, including relayers, oracles, and threshold signatures, to improve scalability, reduce latency, and increase security, particularly in business environments [25].
- **General Message-Passing Bridges**—Smart contract execution and governance activities between blockchains are both enabled by transit bridges such as LayerZero and Axelar [26]. Although they increase the complexity of developing decentralized applications, they also increase the challenge of maintaining synchronization and security, a significant issue in industries such as healthcare and supply chains that rely on reliable communication between systems.

We will now cite a few implementations of bridges.

1.4.2.4 Implementations

- The **LayerZero** bridge facilitates the seamless operation of dApps on Ethereum, Avalanche, and Arbitrum using an Oracle and Relayer model. As an illustration, a DeFi application may automatically update a user's staking position on Avalanche when a user executes an action on Ethereum, eliminating the need to manually transit between networks.
- **Chainbridge** [25] operates on a relayer-based system, which ensures that transactions are exclusively executed after being verified by a majority of relayers. This approach minimizes single points of failure and enhances security.
- Bridges like the **Eternal Bridge** [9] utilize many bridge protocols alongside one another to improve scalability and reduce latency, hence optimizing cross-chain transactions in speed and cost-efficiency [25].

All these bridges leverage two or more bridging mechanisms (Relayers [9], Oracles [27], Threshold signatures) to provide improved scalability, reduced latency, and gas fees. The majority of their applications are in high-volume cross-chain or enterprise use cases [25].

We now look at some of the weaknesses in this technology.

1.4.2.5 Weaknesses

Bridges between blockchains facilitate compatibility across diverse chains; however, they remain among the most vulnerable components of the decentralized ecosystem. Several high-profile hacks have revealed critical weaknesses in their security architecture and exploitable smart contract vulnerabilities.

The Wormhole [28] bridge hack and the subsequent loss of nearly $320 million were the result of a missing validation phase in the smart contract between Ethereum and Solana in 2022. The Ronin Bridge was utilized by Axie Infinity in March 2022, which resulted in the largest recorded DeFi exploit, a loss of $625 million, due to compromised validator keys that controlled the bridge. Bridges like these are susceptible to vulnerabilities in the absence of decentralized validation or adequate cryptographic protections.

There are numerous industries, such as healthcare, supply chain management, and the Internet of Things (IoT), that require secure, scalable, and general-purpose interoperability between public and private blockchains. Bridge adoption is presently restricted in these industries due to the fact that current solutions are excessively preoccupied with token transfers and fail to address complex data workflows or regulatory compliance frameworks [3].

We next move on to Relays, our next interoperability solution.

1.4.3 Relays

A relay is a communication channel between blockchains that enables one blockchain to query and verify the state of another blockchain. Relays are essential interoperability components that allow blockchains to validate and authenticate data from other networks without the necessity of trusted third parties. Atomic swaps are primarily intended for asset trading, whereas relays facilitate more general cross-chain communication and data transmission.

Cryptographic proofs, including Merkle proofs, are employed by the relay network to verify the integrity and consistency of data in a block by constructing a Merkle Tree [29]. In a Merkle tree, the hash of a data block is stored in a leaf node, while the hash of its child nodes is stored in a non-leaf node. This hierarchical structure facilitates the rapid and secure verification of extensive datasets without necessitating the disclosure or transmission of the entire dataset. Consequently, the efficient and secure validation of data that is transmitted between blockchains guarantees that it remains unaltered during transmission. This mechanism is a fundamental element of secure relay-based interoperability architectures, which enables trustless and verifiable cross-chain transactions [30].

Let's now look at how relays operate.

1.4.3.1 Functioning

We shall provide an example for illustrating relays.

By passing verified data or transaction states via an intermediary process, relay-based mechanisms allow two blockchains (Blockchain A and Blockchain B) to communicate securely, as shown in the schematic in Fig. 1.5.

Let us examine the different steps.

- A user commences a transaction on Blockchain A.
- A relay smart contract on Blockchain A identifies and logs the event initiated by this transaction.

1.4 Interoperability Solutions

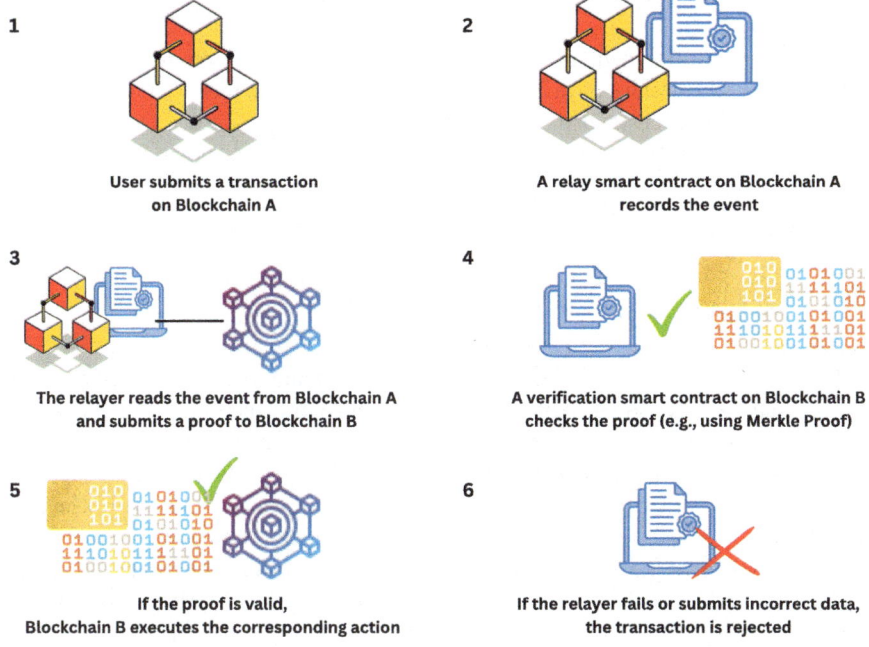

Fig. 1.5 Working of relays

- A relayer, which may be a trusted node or a decentralized consortium of validators, interprets the documented event and produces a proof that the transaction occurred.
- The proof is submitted to Blockchain B, where a verification smart contract checks its authenticity using cryptographic techniques such as Merkle proof, which allows efficient and secure validation of data.
- Upon successful verification, Blockchain B proceeds to execute the relevant action, such as token release, status update, or smart contract execution.
- Nonetheless, if the proof is erroneous or the relayer fails to execute the task correctly, as demonstrated in Step 6, the transaction is rejected.

This approach guarantees trustless communication across blockchains, eliminating the necessity for a central authority. The relay system depends exclusively on coding and cryptographic proofs, guaranteeing integrity and reducing the risk of fraud.

We'll now explore some of the latest developments in relay technology.

1.4.3.2 Validation-on-Demand

A significant development in relay technology is validation-on-demand models [31]. Conventional relays always validate the block headers, thereby increasing the cost of transaction fees and increasing computational expenditure. This burden is diminished by validation-on-demand models, which validate block headers only when necessary, resulting in a significant reduction in costs and enhanced scalability [31].

1.4.3.3 Hybrid Relays

Hybrid relay models include notary-based verification and relay chains. As opposed to traditional notary models that are dependent on centralized bodies for checking, hybrid relay models allow blockchains to verify themselves using cryptographic proofs and employ notaries as a backup measure. This establishes a more flexible and secure system of relays for large-scale, high-frequency cross-chain transactions [31].

Notary-based verification and relay chains are components of hybrid relay models. As opposed to traditional notary models which rely on centralized authorities for verification, hybrid relay models enable blockchains to verify themselves through cryptographic proofs and utilize notaries as a backup. This creates a more secure and adaptable system of relays for high-frequency, large-scale cross-chain transactions [31].

1.4.3.4 Secure Communication

Relays take advantage of more advanced encryption mechanisms. Smart contract-driven encryption integrated within relay protocols secure data integrity and ensure sensitive data is kept confidential during transmission. This integration of encryption, cryptographic verification, and incentive-based architectures creates a robustly secure and scalable cross-chain communication system.

Relays capitalize on more advanced encryption mechanisms. The integration of smart contract-driven encryption into relay protocols guarantees the confidentiality of sensitive data during transmission and ensures the integrity of the data. Through the incorporation of incentive-based architectures, cryptographic verification, and encryption, a cross-chain communication system that is both scalable and robust is established.

Within DeFi, supply chain, and enterprise blockchains, relays are utilized extensively for secure and safe data exchange.

Next, we discuss protocols for blockchain interoperability.

1.4.4 Interoperability Protocols

Interoperability protocols establish common principles and mechanisms that facilitate the execution of smart contracts, asset transfers, and cross-chain communication. They provide features like token mobility, governance voting, and real-time contract invocation, enabling decentralized systems to function seamlessly across several blockchains.

We'll examine a few popular protocols here.

- Polkadot's XCM
- Cosmos IBC
- LayerZero
- Chainlink CCIP
- Twin Token Protocol
- Decentralized Communication Protocols

These protocols have addressed major issues of scalability, security, and finality to enable truly interoperable blockchain ecosystems.

We will now go into greater depth about each of these protocols.

1.4.4.1 Polkadot's XCM

In 2021, Gavin Wood [32], developed Polkadot, a multi-chain structure that allows Parachains which are separate blockchains within the Polkadot network to enjoy the benefits of a shared security model while maintaining their independence. Secure messaging between Parachains and the central Relay Chain is made possible by Polkadot's Cross-Consensus Messaging (XCM) protocol, which is responsible for consensus and coordination.

Figure 1.6 illustrates how Polkadot XCM operates.

Figure 1.6 illustrates the functionality of Polkadot's Cross-Consensus Messaging (XCM), facilitating seamless communication among many chains inside the Polkadot network. Parachains are distinct blockchains that function concurrently on Polkadot, facilitating communication with one another and the Relay Chain via XCM. The Relay Chain functions as Polkadot's core hub, enabling consensus, shared security, and message integrity verification, while facilitating asset transfers among parachains. The ParaSpell SDK enhances this connection by serving as a specialized development toolkit that simplifies low-level complexities, enabling developers to easily compose and transmit cross-chain governance messages affecting both parachains and the Relay Chain.

XCM facilitates essential functionality, including the deployment of smart contracts among parachains, the movement of cross-chain assets, and the ability to vote on multi-chain governance proposals. In order to improve the incorporation of XCM, the ParaSpell SDK was implemented [32]. Pre-built modules are already available to support fungible token transfers and the invoking of smart contracts on

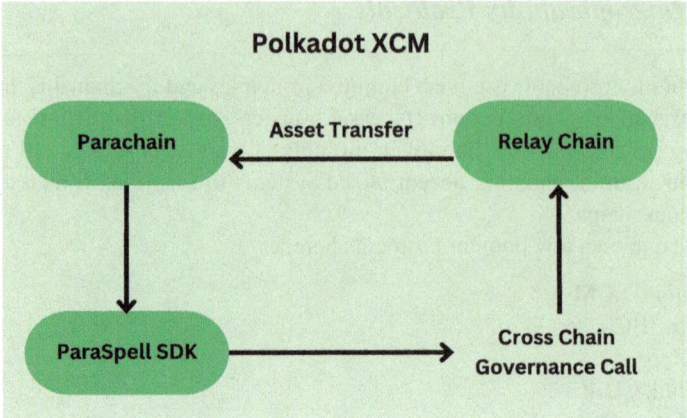

Fig. 1.6 Working of Polkadot XCM

parachains. Configuring and extending XCM (Cross-Consensus Messaging) with custom message formats and execution contexts is also feasible for the purpose of customizing cross-chain logic to meet the unique needs of parachains [33].

Strong security from the Relay Chain, high asset flexibility, and enhanced transaction capacity through parallel processing are among the strengths of XCM. In spite of this, it does possess certain deficiencies. The interoperability of parachains can be impeded by inconsistent governance frameworks and protocol versions, and the Relay Chain can function as a bottleneck in high-load scenarios. To ensure that cross-chain interactions are seamless, it is crucial to have identical versions of XCM across networks.

1.4.4.2 Cosmos IBC

The Cosmos Inter-Blockchain Communication (IBC) protocol enables autonomous blockchains, which are referred to as "zones," to communicate with one another through a hub-and-spoke framework that is facilitated by the Cosmos Hub. IBC is designed to facilitate the secure and verifiable transfer of tokens, smart contract messages, governance votes, and metadata between sovereign chains, with the ultimate goal of facilitating general-purpose blockchain interoperability. Its support for a diverse array of consensus mechanisms, such as Proof-of-Stake (PoS) [34] and Byzantine Fault Tolerance (BFT) [35], is one of its most noteworthy features.

Figure 1.7 illustrates the structure of Cosmos Inter-Blockchain Communication (IBC), a protocol that facilitates the secure and trustless transmission of data and assets between sovereign blockchains, also known as Zone Chains. The two zone chains initiate the procedure by exchanging handshakes in order to communicate. One Light Client on each chain monitors the status of the other chain, while the Relayer, an off-chain mechanism, facilitates the transfer of tokens and smart

1.4 Interoperability Solutions

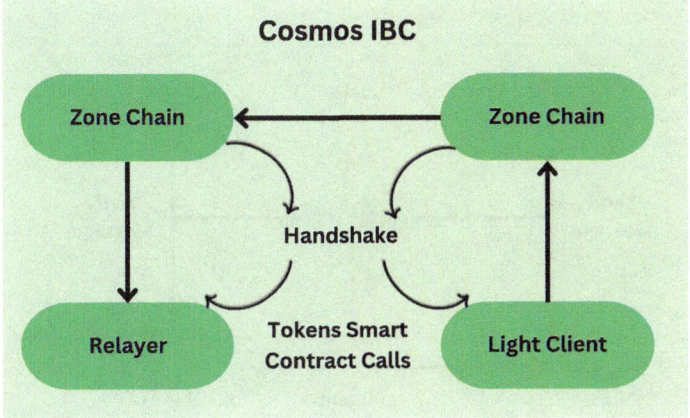

Fig. 1.7 Working of Cosmos IBC

contract calls between chains. This guarantees interoperability without necessitating that chains sacrifice their sovereignty or consensus procedures.

The IBC protocol operates on a coordinated system that includes relayer nodes, light clients, and a handshake protocol. Relayers monitor transactions on a particular chain and transmit them to the destination chain. The state of the counterparty chain is verified by light clients on each chain using Merkle proofs. The handshake procedure ensures secure communication and mutual compatibility among the involved chains [[16]].

The IBC's design is highly modular and adaptable, enabling real-time transfers that enhance asset usability and liquidity. In addition, each zone maintains its own governance framework while simultaneously interfacing with other zones [19].

However, there are also some drawbacks to IBC. Latency and inconsistencies can be the result of synchronization issues between relayers, and failing transactions can be the result of differences in finality models between chains. Additionally, network congestion can significantly affect the efficiency of the protocol by increasing transaction fees and reducing bandwidth availability, especially under high-load conditions.

1.4.4.3 LayerZero

LayerZero is an omnichain interoperability protocol that is designed to facilitate scalable, secure, and lightweight communication between autonomous blockchain networks such as Avalanche, BNB Chain, and Ethereum.

Figure 1.8 presents the working of LayerZero protocol.

The protocol is composed of three primary components: Ultra-Light Nodes (ULNs), Oracles, and Relayers. ULNs are smart contracts on every chain that effectively authenticate the cross-chain state at low computational cost. Oracles acquire

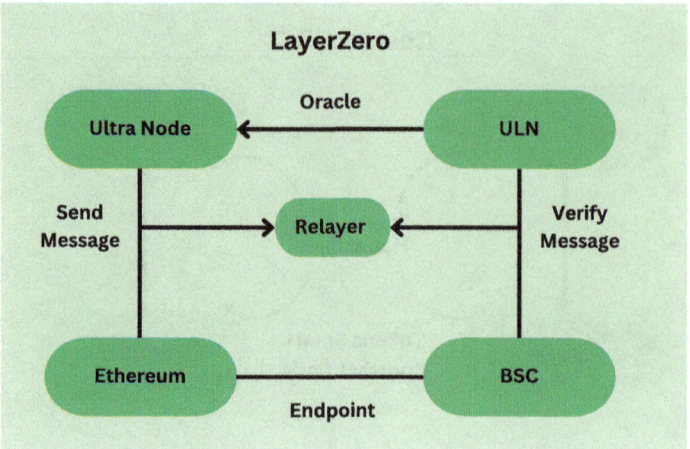

Fig. 1.8 Working of LayerZero

transaction information from the source chain, while Relayers transmit it to the destination chain. An endpoint smart contract decodes the payload and executes the necessary logic on the local chain at the receiving end [20, 21].

The protocol is highly efficient due to the minimal gas consumption that results from the lightweight design of ULNs. LayerZero enables the implementation of complex smart contracts across multiple chains by enabling general-purpose message passing that extends beyond token transfers. Oracles are responsible for verification, while Relayers are responsible for the data transmission. This decentralization of responsibility enhances security [20, 21].

However, the protocol also has certain weaknesses. It is susceptible to single points of failure due to its dependence on trusted Oracle and Relayer pairs. During periods of severe network congestion, transaction processing will be slowed or even rendered unusable. Additionally, the persistence of a consistent consensus among chains with varying finality models remains a significant technical challenge.

1.4.4.4 Chainlink CCIP

Chainlink Cross-Chain Interoperability Protocol (CCIP) is a cross-chain messaging framework that enables secure and verifiable communication between diverse blockchains by leveraging Chainlink's decentralized oracle networks for token transfers and data messaging.

Figure 1.9 presents the working of Chainlink CCIP.

The protocol is operated by a precise mechanism that involves the following: Chainlink Oracles collect and authenticate transaction information from the source chain, a dynamic fee schedule optimizes fees in real time to account for network

1.4 Interoperability Solutions

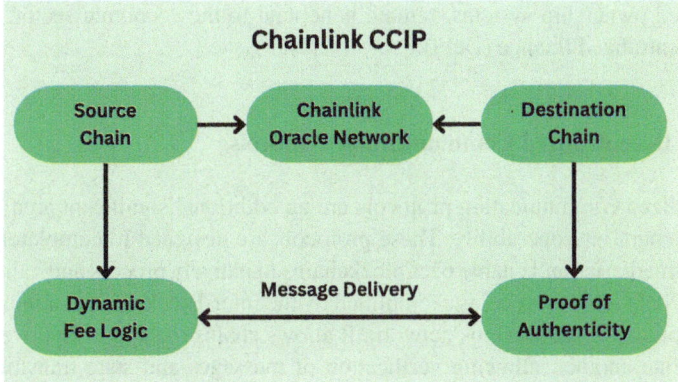

Fig. 1.9 Working of Chainlink CCIP

congestion, and every message is verified through cryptographic Proof-of-Authenticity to ensure its integrity and authenticity [30].

The execution of smart contracts and voting logic on other chains, as well as the cross-chain transfer of both fungible and non-fungible tokens, are among the central features of CCIP. It is supported by the decentralization and reliability of Chainlink's current Oracle infrastructure and offers robust cryptographic guarantees for message integrity. This adaptability renders it suitable for a variety of applications, including DeFi, gaming, and decentralized autonomous organization (DAO) [30].

However, CCIP has its own challenges which affect utilization; gas fees may fluctuate during periods of high network usage. Furthermore, the protocol's reliance on Oracle networks establishes a central point of dependency, necessitating a high level of redundancy to guarantee trust. Ultimately, its architectural intricacy necessitates thorough audits to ensure the security and resilience of smart contract transactions.

1.4.4.5 Twin-Token Protocol

The Twin-Token Protocol is a novel framework that uses synchronized token pairs, each residing on distinct blockchains, to enable secure cross-chain asset transfers. Utilizing cryptographic proofs to authenticate transactions eliminates the necessity for third-party relayers or custodians. Chain-key cryptography and Elliptic Curve Digital Signature Algorithm (ECDSA), which ensure the verifiability and validity of inter-network messages, are fundamental elements of this protocol [10].

Despite providing robust security measures, it remains underutilized beyond banking applications. Due to integration constraints, architectural complexities, and legal obstacles, sectors such as supply chain, IoT, and healthcare have not fully leveraged this infrastructure. Conversely, the low-latency, trustless functionalities for lending, borrowing, and asset exchange inside the protocol, along with

NFT-based ownership systems, remain beneficial to the economic sector, particularly decentralized finance (DeFi).

1.4.4.6 Decentralized Communication Protocols

Decentralized communication protocols are an additional significant area of focus for blockchain interoperability. These protocols are designed to completely eliminate intermediaries and enable peer blockchains to natively process and validate one another's data. This protocol is exemplified by the Inter-Blockchain Communication (IBC) protocol of the Cosmos network. It allows chains to support lightweight clients for one another, allowing verification of messages and state transitions in a trustless environment. This is a lean, transparent, and decentralized system of communications.

The absence of global standards might be the most significant disadvantage of decentralized communication. Therefore, even open protocols are ultimately isolated in small clusters, rather than being integrated into the broader blockchain universe.

In the absence of standardized interoperability protocols, blockchain technology may be restricted to siloed ecosystems, which would restrict its potential and applicability across industries [3]. Despite their incredibly significant advancements, these interoperability protocols have a number of shortcomings, prominent among them being scalability.

The next significant challenge that we will address is scalability, which will inevitably emerge as cross-chain ecosystems continue to grow.

1.5 Scalability Issues

Undoubtedly, you can make the otherwise unique blockchains interoperable with the interoperability methods you have currently examined. These solutions, however, bring up a number of additional issues, leading to the Blockchain Trilemma.

1.5.1 Blockchain Trilemma

The trilemma arises from the difficulty of attaining three essential elements: security, scalability, and decentralization. Enhancing one facet frequently undermines the others. A list of scalability issues is provided here:

- Low TPS—Transactions Per Second
- Finality Delays
- Network Congestions

1.5 Scalability Issues

- Incompatible Consensus Models
- Security Aspect

We will now go over these various challenges.

1.5.1.1 Low TPS

Low transaction throughput is one of the most significant scalability concerns in blockchain interoperability. Blockchains like Bitcoin and Ethereum are unable to handle high transaction volumes due to limited block sizes and delays in their consensus mechanism.

For instance, Bitcoin is capable of processing only approximately 7 transactions per second (TPS), while Ethereum can process approximately 15–30 TPS [36]. Neither of these systems is sufficient to enable widespread cross-chain usage at scale. In periods of high demand, a low throughput results in increased transaction fees and processing time, which poses a challenge in the support of high-frequency trading, decentralized financing (DeFi), and real-time supply chain management.

1.5.1.2 Finality Delays

The finality of a transaction is a critical issue impacting the scalability of blockchain interoperability. Finality ensures that a transaction is final and irreversible. Diverse blockchains employ distinct consensus models, resulting in variations in the timing and mechanisms of finality. For instance, Bitcoin's proof-of-work (PoW) protocol requires approximately six block confirmations to consider a transaction final, which might take up to an hour. In contrast, proof-of-stake (PoS) networks typically achieve deterministic finality within seconds.

The unevenness in finality assurance across blockchains becomes a problem when cross-chain transactions are coordinated. Interoperable blockchain systems may be rendered less reliable due to the incompatibility of confirmation and timing procedures, which can result in delayed settlements and elevated failed transaction rates [36].

1.5.1.3 Network Congestions

Network congestion further increases scalability challenges in blockchain interoperability. Increased cross-chain traffic adds additional demand on blockchain networks, leading to delayed transaction processing and increased gas fees. Congestion escalates with the increasing number of interoperability projects, as multiple transactions compete for the limited network bandwidth.

During the peak DeFi activity on Ethereum in 2020 and 2021, which coincided with the launch of SushiSwap [37] and the emergence of NFT platforms, gas prices experienced a significant increase, with some transactions exceeding $50 per transaction. This compelled numerous users to either postpone transactions altogether or transition to alternative networks, such as Binance Smart Chain [36].

The utilization of adaptive consensus algorithms and enhanced cryptographic protocols can reduce congestion by dynamically modifying network parameters in accordance with real-time traffic conditions [36].

1.5.1.4 Incompatible Consensus Models

One of the fundamental challenges in achieving seamless blockchain interoperability is the mutual incompatibility of consensus models between various networks. The consensus protocols of each blockchain, such as Proof of Work (PoW), Proof of Stake (PoS), Delegated Proof of Stake (DPoS), and Practical Byzantine Fault Tolerance (PBFT), each make their own assumptions about trust, finality, and validator behavior [20, 21]. In particular, when attempting to conduct cross-chain communication or smart contract orchestration, this divergence presents a challenge in establishing a common ground for transaction validation.

In contrast to Ethereum 2.0, which employs PoS with nearly instantaneous finality [33], Bitcoin's PoW consensus is probabilistic and may require up to an hour to achieve final confirmation [2]. Consequently, the synchronization of state across these chains results in latency and consistency issues, for the orchestration of atomic operations and the secure transmission of messages across chains [36]. With the absence of a universal interoperability layer that can abstract away such differences, cross-chain applications remain fragmented and vulnerable to inconsistencies in confirmation guarantees.

Let us now examine the most prevalent security issues that emerge in interoperable blockchains due to scalability constraints.

1.5.2 Security Concerns

Security is a critical concern in the context of blockchain interoperability, as cross-chain communication introduces new attack surfaces and trust assumptions [20, 21] that are not present in single-chain systems [7]. Interoperable systems are susceptible to single points of failure as they rely on bridges, relayers, or validators that can operate off-chain or operate under alternative consensus assumptions. High-profile attacks like the [4] have shown how flaws in bridge logic or improper cross-chain message validation can result in losses of several million dollars.

Furthermore, it is not an easy task to verify the authenticity of a transaction from a foreign chain when that chain employs a consensus model that is either less secure or slower [36]. To address this issue, modern interoperability protocols are utilizing zero-knowledge proofs, threshold signatures, and multi-party computation (MPC) to securely authenticate cross-chain messages. The use of these cryptographic measures, however, adds to protocol complexity and may affect scalability. Thus, interoperability protocol design constitutes a trade-off between trust reduction, performance, and attack tolerance.

We now look up some proposed solutions to mitigate these challenges.

1.6 Future Solutions and Innovations

A number of strategies have been proposed to address these restrictions. Sharding, side chains, and state channels are among the solutions under exploration; however, they are still experimental. We will classify these solutions into following headings:

- Architectural enhancements
- Adaptive models

1.6.1 Architectural Enhancements

1.6.1.1 Sharding

As an improvement to the Layer-1 design, "sharding" divides the blockchain into numerous autonomous chains. Transactions and smart contracts are independently processed by each shard, which significantly enhances overall throughput and decreases latency. The network's burden is distributed among numerous shards in order to increase its scalability without compromising decentralization. The Danksharding phase of Ethereum's roadmap contains plans to employ sharding as a method of scaling the network's base layer [36].

While sharding addresses scalability on a single blockchain, it remains a challenge to ensure interoperability with other external blockchains. When it comes to coordinating state consistency and finality guarantees in various contexts, this is particularly true.

Next, we investigate layer-2 solutions.

1.6.1.2 Layer-2 Solutions

Layer-2 technologies, such as Ethereum's Optimistic Rollups and Bitcoin's Lightning Network, perform off-chain transaction processing as an additional layer. In order to prevent the payment for each Bitcoin transaction on-chain, the Lightning Network employs payment channels to enable quick, cost-effective transactions. Optimistic Rollups, on the other hand, consolidate Ethereum transactions off-chain and submit a single, legitimate proof to the base chain, thereby reducing congestion and maintaining security [36].

In an effort to mitigate the congestion and scalability constraints of base layer blockchains, layer-2 solutions process transactions off-chain or partially off-chain, and only finalize outcomes on the main chain. Plasma, Rollups (Optimistic and ZK), and State Channels are among the technologies that improve throughputs while simultaneously ensuring security through the use of economic incentives or cryptographic proofs. Optimistic Rollups, for instance, aggregate a number of transactions off-chain and present the result to Ethereum with a challenge duration to validate its accuracy [36]. The Lightning Network of Bitcoin, in the same manner, facilitates microtransactions by securing assets in multi-signature wallets, thereby reducing the cost and time of transactions. These systems significantly enhance transaction rates and reduce gas expenses; however, they remain reliant on the underlying base layer for dispute resolution and finality, which restricts the seamless operation of the cross-chains.

1.6.1.3 Parallel Processing

Parallel processing enables blockchains to execute multiple operations simultaneously, thereby reducing latency and substantially increasing throughput. Independent shards or parachains are supported by parallel execution models, such as those in Polkadot and NEAR Protocol, to validate and execute transactions in parallel [20, 21]. Particularly in heterogeneous ecosystems, this design enhances scalability and minimizes congestion by directing a variety of transaction categories (Token transfers, smart contracts) to specialized execution environments. Even so, the primary obstacle to interoperability remains the preservation of atomicity and cross-shard state consistency in transactions.

1.6.2 Adaptive Models

1.6.2.1 Adaptive Consensus Protocols

Adaptive consensus protocols modify their behavior in response to real-time network conditions, such as latency, node participation, or transaction rates [7]. Particularly in situations of volatility or heavy burdens, adaptive behavior enhances scalability and robustness. In protocols like Algorand [38] and Tendermint [39], validator selection and quorum bounds are adjusted in real time to provide tunable finality and quicker block confirmations. Hybrid consensus may also be facilitated by adaptive mechanisms, such as the combination of PoS-PBFT, which allows networks to achieve a balance between performance and security. These protocols are well-suited to interoperable scenarios in which cross-chain operations may fail or be inconsistent due to a delay or disparity in consensus between chains [36].

1.6.2.2 Role of Machine Learning

Machine learning (ML) is demonstrating its potential as a powerful tool for optimizing blockchain interoperability and performance. ML algorithms can be employed to optimize gas prices, identify anomalies in cross-chain communication, forecast congestion patterns, and influence validator behavior. For instance, reinforcement learning models have been proposed [40] as a means of dynamically scheduling transactions across multiple chains in order to achieve efficient load balancing. Furthermore, machine learning (ML) can be implemented to automate the auditing of smart contracts and to identify malicious relayers or bridge contracts by learning from past behavior. Although promising, the integration of ML into blockchain networks is still in its infancy and is accompanied by challenges regarding transparency, auditability, and determinism, all of which are essential attributes of decentralized networks.

Distributed computing architectures can be implemented to parallelize transaction processing across networks, and machine learning models can be implemented to optimize load balancing and transaction routing. This would result in a reduction in latency and an increase in throughput, allowing blockchains to process a greater number of transactions without compromising security or decentralization [36]. In the absence of integration of these technologies into blockchain interoperability platforms, networks will remain bounded by scalability constraints, which will restrict their capacity to facilitate cross-industry, large-scale adoption.

Overall, frictionless blockchain interoperability is anticipated to be most challenging to achieve due to scalability. Blockchain networks are unable to support high-frequency cross-chain transactions due to low rates of throughput, inconsistent transaction finality, and congestion. Incremental workarounds are currently accessible; however, the resolution of the scalability trilemma necessitates the combined efforts of adaptive consensus models, cryptography, and machine learning-powered optimization. This is the point at which blockchain networks will achieve the necessary scalability to facilitate extensive adoption and fully connected ecosystems.

A new Internet known as Web 3.0 is emerging that offers answers to the issues you have explored thus far.

1.7 Web 3.0

Web 3.0 signifies a paradigm shift toward a decentralized, user-owned internet that replaces intermediaries with code-based peer-to-peer interactions. In contrast to Web 2.0, which is characterized by the monopolization of data and digital identity by centralized platforms, Web 3.0 enables individuals to manage their assets, credentials, and interactions through the use of smart contracts and cryptographic primitives. The objective is to establish a digital environment that is censorship-resistant and trustless, in which applications are regulated by communities and protocols rather than corporations.

1.7.1 Web3 Architecture

The architectural framework of Web3 is depicted in Fig. 1.10. Web 3.0 is composed of four distinct layers. Foundational blockchains such as Ethereum, Solana, and Avalanche comprise Layer 1. Interoperability protocols, including IBC, XCM, LayerZero, and Chainlink CCIP, are included in Layer 2. These protocols enable secure cross-chain messaging and token transfers. Decentralized applications (dApps), NFTs, DeFi, and digital identity platforms are all part of Layer 3, which is constructed on interoperable infrastructure. The User Layer provides seamless asset utilization across platforms, self-sovereign identity, and unified wallets. These layers collectively constitute a decentralized and composable Web3 architecture.

1.7.2 Web3 Benefits

Web3 represents a paradigm shift in the operation of digital platforms, placing the user at the core of governance, value creation, and data ownership. In contrast to Web2's dependence on centralized intermediaries, Web3 utilizes blockchain and smart contract frameworks to decentralize authority and distribute control among participants through mechanisms like Decentralized Autonomous Organizations (DAOs). DAOs offer on-chain governance tools that let community members vote on upgrades, funding, and protocol development. Subhashini et al. [41] suggest this paradigm transforms user-platform links by synchronizing infrastructure development with common user inclinations, hence promoting participatory online models.

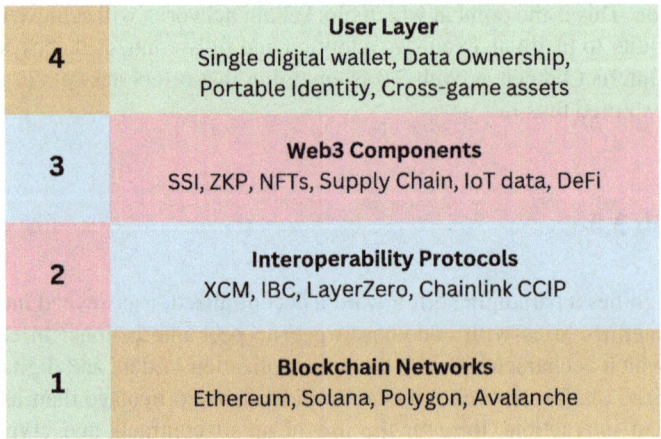

Fig. 1.10 Web3 architecture

A primary benefit of Web3 is in the establishment of tokenized economies that allow users to monetize their attention, behavior, and data while safeguarding their privacy. An example is the Brave browser [42], which compensates users with Basic Attention Tokens (BAT) for opting to see advertisements. According to Virani [11], this approach inverts traditional advertising dynamics: rather than platforms selling user data to third parties, consumers retain their data and receive compensation for their attention. Brave employs local ad matching on users' devices to avoid data leakage, achieving a distinctive equilibrium between monetization and privacy.

Web3 facilitates digital ownership of identity, enabling users to verify and transact without giving up personal data to centralized authority. This is closely linked to self-sovereign identity frameworks and blockchain-based credentials. According to [41], these approaches allow individuals to interact with digital ecosystems while retaining control over their identity metadata, hence reducing vulnerability to the surveillance economy and large-scale data breaches. The identity layer of Web3 is essential for building confidence in peer-to-peer transactions, decentralized finance (DeFi), and cross-chain services.

Finally, as interoperability in blockchain and cross-chain protocols advances (For example, via XCMP, IBC, and eternal bridges), the applicability and accessibility of Web3 platforms expand. The integration of interoperable blockchain infrastructure with user-centric value models ensures that Web3 is not merely a technological revolution, but rather a socio-economic restructuring of the internet. Web3 enhances security, censorship resistance [11], and worldwide accessibility through decentralized consensus and robust cryptographic foundations in a digitally autonomous environment [41].

1.7.3 What Is Needed?

To achieve the Web3 vision, three components are indispensable: semantic validation, distributed ontology, and robust consensus mechanisms. The uniform interpretation of data transmitted across chains is guaranteed by semantic validation. Cosmos IBC and other protocols embed metadata to facilitate this translation, thereby enabling platforms such as Juno and Osmosis to function in a coherent manner [[16]]. Distributed ontologies set up shared vocabularies and frameworks across ecosystems, as seen in Polkadot [20, 21]; they use standard runtime modules to facilitate asset and identity recognition among parachains [33].

1.7.4 PoS, PoA, and Trustless Governance

Consensus models support the integrity of decentralized systems. Proof-of-Stake (PoS) used in Polkadot, depends on validators staking tokens, so aligning their incentives with the security of the network. A staking token is a specialized cryptocurrency that one secures to facilitate blockchain operations, hence earning incentives, similar to receiving additional coins for safeguarding one's assets. Proof-of-Authority (PoA), employed by VeChain [43, 44], provides enterprise-level efficiency through the appointment of trusted validators, rendering it appropriate for regulated sectors such as retail and supply chain. These consensus models also impact governance, as DAOs include token-based voting systems to ratify ideas and allocate resources, promoting decentralized coordination.

1.7.5 Use Cases

Web3 use cases encompass various sectors. In DeFi, interoperable smart contracts facilitate cross-chain lending and token transfers, including the automation of insurance payouts from Hyperledger Fabric to Ethereum [7]. In gaming, assets tokenized as NFTs such as weaponry or avatars can traverse ecosystems, facilitating gameplay across platforms like Decentraland and The Sandbox. Self-sovereign identity (SSI) and zero-knowledge proofs (ZKPs) facilitate user authentication while safeguarding private information, hence enabling decentralized Know Your Customer (KYC) processes. Platforms such as VeChain and ToolChain [43, 44] implement these ideas across global supply chains, ensuring traceability and automating compliance. Technologies such as zk-SNARKs facilitate secure, privacy-preserving interoperability, enabling users to validate data without disclosing it, for instance, confirming wallet balances during transactions [11].

1.8 Summary

Blockchain interoperability has emerged as a crucial foundation in the advancement of decentralized ecosystems. The transition from blockchain silos to the Web 3.0 paradigm of efficient data exchange, asset transfer, and smart contract execution across various contexts has transformed from a theoretical concept into a technological need. We noted that prominent platforms such as Bitcoin, Ethereum, and Hyperledger operate in isolation, and it is essential to integrate these disparate systems for both financial and non-financial applications, including decentralized finance, supply chains, and healthcare.

Recognizing the limitations of these segregated systems, we have explored various interoperability solutions including token exchanges, bridges, relays, and interoperability protocols such as Polkadot's XCM, Cosmos IBC, LayerZero, and Chainlink CCIP. Although each possesses unique capabilities, they also pose issues in implementation related to security, scalability, consensus discrepancies, and semantic interoperability. These issues are being mitigated using adaptive consensus protocols, parallel processing, and machine learning techniques, all designed to establish a scalable and trustless interoperable blockchain network.

Toward the end, we highlighted the Web 3.0 paradigm's objective of integrating user identity, assets, and interactions across domains promoting self-sovereign identification, transferable digital assets, and cross-domain automation. This integrated digital ecosystem, built on trustless, interoperable infrastructures, promises a decentralized internet where people regain ownership of their data and digital footprint.

Blockchain interoperability is not merely a technical aspiration but the foundation of a decentralized digital economy. The convergence of interoperability standards, governance frameworks, and real-world applications signifies the dawn of a new era in blockchain history characterized by diminished silos and flourishing networks.

With a solid basic understanding of blockchain interoperability, its significance, and its applications, we are now prepared to explore its most critical operational aspect that is security. Chap. 2 will examine how the attributes facilitating cross-chain transactions generate novel attack vectors. We will examine the emergence of vulnerabilities in interoperable systems, including bridge hacks, replay attacks, inconsistent consensus assurances, and trust assumptions in relay nodes. We will also discuss the cryptographic and architectural methods to protect against these issues. As the issue of scalability increases, our security models must also evolve. We will explore the intricate security framework of cross-chain blockchain ecosystems in the upcoming chapter.

References

1. Wikipedia contributors: "Cryptocurrency," Wikipedia, The Free Encyclopedia, [Online]. Available: https://en.wikipedia.org/wiki/Cryptocurrency. [Accessed: 18-Jun-2025b]
2. Lys, L., Micoulet, A., Potop-Butucaru, M.: Atomic swapping bitcoins and ethers. In: IEEE International Conference on Blockchain, Paris, France (2024)
3. Kotey, S.D., Tchao, E.T., Ahmed, A.-R., Agbemenu, A.S., Nunoo-Mensah, H., Sikora, A., Welte, D., Keelson, E.: Blockchain interoperability: the state of heterogenous Blockchain-to-Blockchain communication. IET Commun. **17**(8), 891–914 (2023). https://doi.org/10.1049/cmu2.12594
4. Ethereum Foundation: "Ropsten Testnet," Ethereum Documentation, [Online]. Available: https://ethereum.org/en/developers/docs/networks/#ropsten. [Accessed: 14-May-2025a]
5. Ethereum Foundation: "Goerli Testnet," Ethereum Documentation, [Online]. Available: https://ethereum.org/en/developers/docs/networks/#goerli. [Accessed: 14-May-2025b]
6. Polygon Labs: "What is polygon?" Polygon Technology Documentation, [Online]. Available: https://polygon.technology. [Accessed: 14-May-2025]
7. Sizan, N.S., Dey, D., Layek, M.A., Uddin, M.A., Huh, E.-N.: Evaluating blockchain platforms for IoT applications in industry 5.0: a comprehensive review. Blockchain Res. Appl. **100276** (2025). https://doi.org/10.1016/j.bcra.2025.100276
8. Sönmez, F.Ö., Knottenbelt, W.J.: Cross-chain notification and awareness management. In: IEEE International Conference on Blockchain, London, UK, pp. 420–430 (2024). https://doi.org/10.1109/Blockchain62396.2024.00062
9. Mitrović, A., Vukmirović, S., Dalčeković, M., Nedić, N., Čapko, D.: Cross-chain general message passing protocol via eternal bridge. In: IEEE International Conference on Telecommunications Forum (TELFOR), Novi Sad, Serbia (2023). https://doi.org/10.1109/TELFOR2023.00032

10. Kumar, V., Budhiraja, I., Jabbari, A., Garg, D., Singh, D., Mengani, N.: Efficient blockchain interoperability design for cross-chain transactions in future internet-of-value. Peer Peer Netw. Appl. **18**(110), 1–21 (2025). https://doi.org/10.1007/s12083-025-01941-w
11. Virani, S.S.: Blockchain end user adoption and societal challenges: exploring privacy, rights, and security dimensions. IET Blockchain. **4**(S1), 691–705 (2024). https://doi.org/10.1049/blc2.12077
12. Wikipedia contributors: "List of blockchains," Wikipedia, The Free Encyclopedia. [Online]. Available: https://en.wikipedia.org/wiki/List_of_blockchains. [Accessed: 03-Jun-2025a]
13. Gün Sirer, E., van Renesse, R., Miers, I.: Avalanche: a novel metastable consensus protocol family for cryptocurrencies. Team Rocket. (2018) [Online]. Available: https://avalabs.org/whitepapers/avalanche.pdf
14. Fantom Foundation: "Lachesis Consensus Protocol," Fantom Technical Documentation (2020). [Online]. Available: https://fantom.foundation/2020/11/04/lachesis-consensus-algorithm/
15. Wang, Y., Yan, Y., Liu, X., Gao, W., Wang, Z.: A technique for ensured cross chain IBC transactions using TPM. In: IEEE International Conference on Big Data and Privacy Computing (BDPC), Xi'an, China (2024). https://doi.org/10.1109/BDPC59998.2024.10649356
16. Han, J., Kim, J., Youn, A., Lee, J., Chun, Y., Woo, J., Hong, J.W.-K.: Cos-CBDC: design and implementation of CBDC on cosmos Blockchain. IEEE Int. Conf. Blockchain. (2024b). https://doi.org/10.1109/ICBCTIS64495.2024.00014
17. Han, Y., Wang, C., Wang, H.: Research on blockchain cross-chain model based on 'NFT + cross-chain bridge'. IEEE Access. **12**, 77065–77078 (2024a). https://doi.org/10.1109/ACCESS.2024.3401405
18. "Blockchain interoperability guide," Cyfrin, Feb. 2024. [Online]. Available: https://www.cyfrin.io/blog/blockchain-interoperability-guide. [Accessed: 14-Mar-2025]
19. Kim, J., Essaid, M., Ju, H.: Inter-Blockchain communication message relay time measurement and analysis in cosmos. In: The 23rd Asia-Pacific Network Operations and Management Symposium (APNOMS) (2022). https://doi.org/10.1109/APNOMS60508.2022.00231
20. Morháč, D., Valaštín, V., Košťál, K., Kotuliak, I.: Enhancing XCMP interoperability across Polkadot Paraverse. In: IEEE International Conference on Blockchain, Bratislava, Slovakia (2023a). https://doi.org/10.1109/Blockchain50366.2023.00032
21. Morháč, D., Valaštín, V., Košťál, K., Kotuliak, I.: ParaSpell XCM SDK: a new protocol for interoperability in Polkadot Paraverse. In: 2023 Fifth International Conference on Blockchain Computing and Applications (BCCA) (2023b). https://doi.org/10.1109/BCCA58897.2023.10338906
22. Poon, T., Dryja, J.: The bitcoin lightning network: scalable off-chain instant payments. Technical Whitepaper. (2016) [Online]. Available: https://lightning.network/lightning-network-paper.pdf
23. Thyagarajan, S.A., Malavolta, G., Moreno-Sanchez, P.: Universal atomic swaps: secure exchange of coins across all Blockchains. IEEE Symp. Secur. Priv (SP). **2022**, 1299–1314 (2022). https://doi.org/10.1109/SP46214.2022.00063
24. Dwivedi, R., Singla, T., Shukla, S.: Cross-chain atomic swaps without time locks. In: 2023 Fifth International Conference on Blockchain Computing and Applications (BCCA) (2023). https://doi.org/10.1109/BCCA58897.2023.10338878
25. Lisi, A., Lopardo, N., Tortola, D., Mori, P., Ricci, L., Severino, F.: A cross-chain rating system: bridging EVM-based blockchains with Chainbridge. In: 2023 International Conference on Omni-Layer Intelligent Systems (COINS) (2023). https://doi.org/10.1109/COINS57856.2023.10189274
26. Axelar Network: "Axelar documentation: secure cross-chain communication," Axelar Docs (2024). [Online]. Available: https://docs.axelar.dev. [Accessed: Jun. 3, 2025]
27. Vijayalakshmi, C., Florence, S.M.: Flameshift protocol: revolutionizing interoperability with dynamic asset recycling for cross-chain communications. SN Comput. Sci. **5**, 773 (2024). https://doi.org/10.1007/s42979-024-03116-5

References

28. "Blockchain bridge Wormhole loses nearly $320 million in apparent crypto hack," CNBCTV18, 03-Feb-2022. [Online]. Available: https://www.cnbctv18.com/cryptocurrency/blockchain-bridge-wormhole-loses-nearly-320-million-in-apparent-crypto-hack-12343952.htm. [Accessed: 03-Jun-2025]
29. Frauenthaler, P., Sigwart, M., Spanring, C., Sober, M., Schulte, S.: ETH relay: a cost-efficient relay for Ethereum-based blockchains. In: IEEE International Conference on Blockchain, Vienna, Austria (2020). https://doi.org/10.1109/Blockchain50366.2020.00032
30. Yang, S., Zhang, G., Li, Y., Wang, P., Zhao, C., Feng, B., Shen, C., Zhang, Y.: A secure cross-chain mechanism based on relay chain and smart contract encryption scheme. In: 2023 11th International Conference on Information Systems and Computing Technology (ISCTech) (2023). https://doi.org/10.1109/ISCTech60480.2023.00023
31. Yang, S., Zhang, G., Li, Y., Wang, P., Zhao, C., Feng, B., Shen, C., Zhang, Y.: Cross-chain architecture of blockchain integrating notary mechanism and relay-chain technology. In: 2024 4th International Conference on Blockchain Technology and Information Security (ICBCTIS) (2024). https://doi.org/10.1109/ICBCTIS64495.2024.00014
32. Web3 Foundation: "Cross-consensus message format (XCM)," Polkadot Wiki. [Online]. Available: https://wiki.polkadot.network/docs/learn-xcm. [Accessed: 18-Jun-2025]
33. Caprolu, M., Di Pietro, R., Lombardi, F., Onofri, E.: Characterizing Polkadot's transactions ecosystem: methodology, tools, and insights. In: 2024 IEEE International Conference on Decentralized Applications and Infrastructures (DAPPS) (2024). https://doi.org/10.1109/DAPPS61106.2024.00016
34. Saleh, M., Taleb, T., Ksentini, A.: Blockchain with proof-of-stake consensus: a survey. IEEE Access. **9**, 134123–134145 (2021). https://doi.org/10.1109/ACCESS.2021.3116781
35. Zhang, G., Li, Y., Zhang, W.: Reaching consensus in the byzantine empire: a comprehensive review of BFT consensus algorithms. arXiv. *preprint*, arXiv:2203.06979. (2022)
36. Rao, I.S., Kiah, M.L.M., Hameed, M.M., Memon, Z.A.: Scalability of blockchain: a comprehensive review and future research direction. Clust. Comput. **27**, 5547–5570 (2024). https://doi.org/10.1007/s10586-023-04257-7
37. SushiSwap: "What is SushiSwap?" *Sushi Official Docs*, 2022. [Online]. Available: https://docs.sushi.com
38. Chen, J., Micali, S.: Algorand: a secure and efficient distributed ledger. Theoretical Computer Science Group, MIT (2017) [Online]. Available: https://arxiv.org/abs/1607.01341
39. Kwon, J.: Tendermint: consensus without mining. Whitepaper. (2014) [Online]. Available: https://tendermint.com/static/docs/tendermint.pdf
40. Zhao, B., Gao, S., Wang, W.: Reinforcement learning for blockchain cross-chain transaction scheduling. IEEE Trans. Netw. Sci. Eng. **9**(3), 1355–1366 (2022). https://doi.org/10.1109/TNSE.2022.3141382
41. Subhashini, P., Alekhya, J., Rana, A., Lakhanpal, S., Veeresh, G., Al-Allak, M.A.: Navigating Web3 evolution with blockchain's role in shaping next generation internet semantics. In: IEEE International Conference on Communication, Computer Sciences and Engineering (IC3SE), Hyderabad, India (2024). https://doi.org/10.1109/IC3SE62002.2024.10593138
42. Brave Software: Introducing the brave browser. Brave Blog. (2016) [Online]. Available: https://brave.com/blog/
43. VeChain Foundation: "VeChain Whitepaper v2.0," *VeChain Official Documentation*, Dec. (2018). [Online]. Available: https://www.vechain.org/whitepaper/
44. VeChain Foundation: VeChain ToolChain™ overview. VeChain Developer Portal. (2022) [Online]. Available: https://docs.vechain.org/toolchain/

Chapter 2
Security Challenges

Contents

2.1	Introduction	36
2.2	Key Vulnerabilities	38
2.3	The Single Point of Failure	38
	2.3.1 Poly Network Attack	38
	2.3.2 Wormhole Bridge Exploit	39
	2.3.3 Oracles and Honeypots	39
	2.3.4 Mitigations	39
2.4	Smart Contract Exploits	41
	2.4.1 The DAO Attack	42
	2.4.2 Parity Wallet Bug	42
	2.4.3 Smart Contracts Tools	42
	2.4.4 Mitigations	43
2.5	Double-Spending	44
	2.5.1 What Is Double-Spending?	44
	2.5.2 How Does it Work?	45
	2.5.3 Bitcoin Gold Attack	46
	2.5.4 Mitigations	47
2.6	Replay Attacks	47
2.7	Cryptographic Defenses	48
	2.7.1 Trusted Relays	48
	2.7.2 Threshold Signatures	49
	2.7.3 Oracles	51
2.8	What's Next?	52
2.9	Future Security Directions	53
	2.9.1 Quantum-Resistant Cryptography	53
	2.9.2 AI-Driven Security Models	54
	2.9.3 AI Benefits	55
	2.9.4 Reliable Interoperable Smart Contracts	55
	2.9.5 Cross-Chain Identity	58
2.10	Summary	59
References		61

© The Author(s), under exclusive license to Springer Nature
Switzerland AG 2025
P. Sarang, L. Nadkar, *Blockchain Without Barriers*, SpringerBriefs in Computer Science, https://doi.org/10.1007/978-3-032-03413-7_2

Abstract The intricate security issues affecting cross-chain blockchain systems are covered in this chapter. A presentation on historical hacks that reveal system vulnerabilities in smart contracts and inter-chain bridges, including the DAO vulnerability, the Wormhole bridge attack, and the Poly Network exploit, opens up the discussion. This chapter describes how malicious actors exploit differences in consensus and contract enforcement across chains to explain replay vulnerabilities and double-spending attacks in decentralized systems. Particular attention is paid to Oracle manipulation and the shortcomings of existing cryptographic defenses.

Using operational solutions like Thorchain, RenVM and AnySwap, as well as cryptographic techniques like trustworthy relays, threshold signatures, and authenticated data feeds, mitigation options are investigated. Along with providing strong design requirements for compatible smart contracts, this chapter also examines recent developments in AI-based security models and quantum-resistant encryption. The final section provides researchers and developers with a blueprint for safe, compatible systems by describing current risks in identity management, cross-chain governance and oracle trustworthiness.

Keywords Bridge attacks · Oracle manipulation · Replay attack · Double-spending · Cryptographic defenses · Trusted relay · Threshold signature · Cross-chain governance · DAO attack · Cross-chain identity · Secure cross-chain messaging

2.1 Introduction

In the previous chapter, we studied blockchain interoperability, which is the capacity of multiple blockchains to transfer value, exchange data, and facilitate smooth user interfaces. This paradigm is significantly transforming the manner in which identification systems, business applications, non-fungible tokens (NFTs) [1], and DeFi (decentralized finance) [2] operates by facilitating the movement of assets and data across isolated chains. Advancements in interoperability have enabled the development of composable smart contracts, execution of cross-chain token exchanges, and provision of multi-chain liquidity. Protocols such as LayerZero, Wormhole, Polkadot's XCMP, and Cosmos IBC facilitate communication across heterogeneous blockchain networks, each adopting distinct approaches to trust, validation and messaging.

Although interoperability creates new opportunities, it also makes the blockchain more vulnerable to intrusions. As blockchain systems interconnect, the security perimeter also enlarges. A single vulnerability could initiate a cascading series of events. By exploiting the most vulnerable component in a linked ecosystem, such as a bridge, oracle, or relay node, rather than only compromising the foundational layer of a single network, hackers can now orchestrate systematic threats across multiple chains [3].

2.1 Introduction

Interoperable designs create new threats, including bridge vulnerabilities, double-spending across chains, desynchronization of cross-chain smart contracts, and replay attacks. Figure 2.1 depicts the functionality of a blockchain bridge and its attack surface.

The Poly Network exploit in 2021 [4] and the Wormhole attack in 2022 [4] showed that weaknesses in bridge protocols lacking robust multi-party consensus or signature verification might result in substantial financial losses.

Interoperability presents considerable challenges for transaction atomicity, cross-chain finality, and validator consensus. Cross-chain messages typically rely on asynchronous relaying [5, 6], different consensus mechanisms, and state verification methodologies that may be vulnerable to discrepancies; manipulation, or delays, thereby creating possibilities for adverse exploitation [7].

These facts highlight the need for reviewing security protocols in the multi-chain environment. Modern cryptographic and protocol-level safety features are necessary, irrespective of the continued utility of Merkle Proofs, cryptographic hashes, and consensus methodologies. Methods for safeguarding cross-chain links, such as threshold signatures, dependable relays, artificial intelligence-driven auditing tools, and quantum-resistant encryption [8], are currently the focus of significant studies.

The subsequent sections will look at the primary weaknesses present in interoperable blockchain systems, along with a summary of the suggested governance and cryptographic measures. Understanding the evolving threat landscape enables developers and researchers to formulate more resilient and secure cross-chain architectures. By proactively addressing these risks, they can remove redundant security checks, enhance consensus efficiency, and prevent performance bottlenecks, thereby indirectly enhancing scalability, as the system expands over many chains.

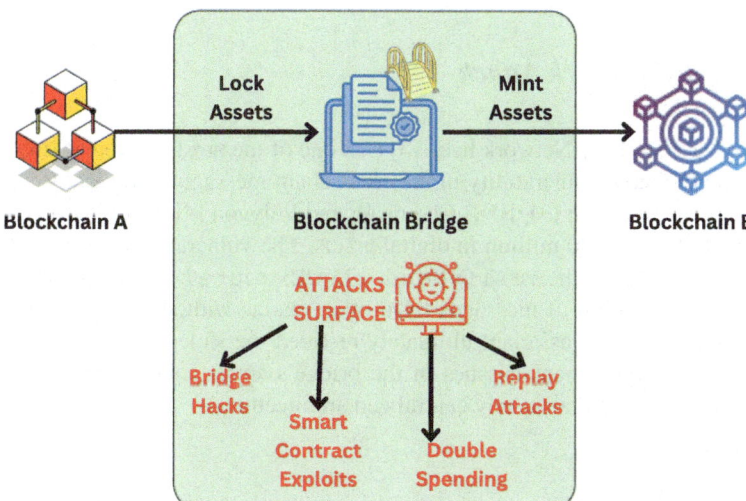

Fig. 2.1 Working of a blockchain bridge and its attack surface

Let us first consider the different kinds of vulnerabilities imposed due to interoperability.

2.2 Key Vulnerabilities

The interoperable systems are vulnerable to several dangers, including single points of failure, smart contract exploits, and double-spending. We shall explain each issue comprehensively, detailing its occurrence, instances where these threats have been seen, and several mitigating strategies to prevent future occurrences.

Let us now consider the first type of vulnerability—the single point of failure.

2.3 The Single Point of Failure

In blockchain interoperability architecture, bridges serve as the crucial connecting element across networks; however, they are the system's most vulnerable point. A blockchain bridge facilitates the transfer of data or assets between incompatible blockchains by protecting assets on the source chain and minting or unlocking equivalent tokens on the target chain. This bridging mechanism, while conceptually straightforward, establishes a singular point of failure at the intersection of asset custody, signature verification, and state synchronization.

This kind of threat has been repeatedly observed in some of the biggest hacks in blockchain history. We will now cite a few examples of attacks in the recent past.

2.3.1 Poly Network Attack

The August 2021 Poly Network hack [3] was one of the most severe hacking, as an attacker exploited a vulnerability in the cross-chain messaging protocol to redirect funds around Ethereum [3], BNB Chain [4], and Polygon [4], resulting in an illicit transfer of almost $600 million in digital assets. The vulnerability originated from the improper usage of the `verifyHeaderAndExecuteTx` function, which permitted the verification of messages from other chains without the validation of a trusted state root. The assailant ultimately restored the stolen funds; however, the attack exposed fundamental issues in the bridge's smart contract logic [3], poor access control [8], and an overly centralized architecture.

2.3.2 Wormhole Bridge Exploit

A major case occurred in February 2022 with the Wormhole bridge attack [4] that connected Solana to Ethereum. The attacker bypassed signature verification protocols, enabling the minting of 120,000 wrapped ETH (wETH) without depositing genuine ETH, resulting in a loss over $320 million. The attack occurred due to a failure in the guardian signature verification included in Wormhole's consensus mechanism [3]. These attacks demonstrate how unaudited message verification protocols, absence of cryptographic safeguards, and centralized validator groups can evolve into catastrophic flaws.

2.3.3 Oracles and Honeypots

A small group of off-chain validators, sometimes called oracles, transmit and attest to cross-chain events in most blockchain bridges instead of certifying transactions. These oracles become high-value targets because they are important points of trust in the system that could be compromised by outside manipulation, malicious attacks, or mistakes in configuration.

Honeypots are vulnerabilities in systems using single-signature or centralized-relay authorization, which allows attackers to manipulate or alter assets to tempt humans or automated agents into engaging with a compromised contract or address. Due to their excessive dependence on a limited number of trusted entities, these systems are vulnerable to attacks such as DNS hijacking, oracle manipulation, and front-running [4].

More recent bridge designs use distributed security methods to reduce these hazards.

2.3.4 Mitigations

Let us now review some of the techniques used by modern bridges.

2.3.4.1 Thorchain

ThorChain [9] is a decentralized liquidity protocol that facilitates native cross-chain swaps without the necessity of wrapping tokens or relying on centralized exchanges. To protect cross-chain transactions, ThorChain uses a Threshold Signature Scheme (TSS) [10], in which the private key is never completely created or kept in one place. Rather, the signing procedure is dispersed among several nodes, who work together to produce a legitimate signature without ever disclosing the entire key. A valid signature can be produced only when the majority of nodes reach consensus. This method mitigates single-point-of-failure vulnerabilities by preventing any legitimate validator from independently transferring assets. TSS introduces operational complexity, including potential liveness issues during validator transitions and node synchronization, while simultaneously enhancing security.

2.3.4.2 RenVM

RenVM [9] employs a different yet comparably secure approach utilizing Multi-Party Computation (MPC). It is designed as a virtual machine that executes scripts to lock, mint, and burn digital assets across blockchains, with security dependent on the collaboration of Darknodes. In a multiparty computation (MPC) deployment, each node possesses a fragment of the private key, which is never entirely reassembled. Instead, cryptographic operations are conducted collaboratively across nodes without disclosing the complete key at any time. This guarantees both decentralization and confidentiality.

RenVM enables the seamless movement of assets like BTC, BCH, and ZEC [11] between Ethereum and other blockchains. MPC [4] schemes, while advantageous, require effective coordination and economic incentives to guarantee honest participation and are susceptible to collusion if the set of validators are not highly decentralized [9].

2.3.4.3 AnySwap

AnySwap [9] (now Multichain) features a modular architecture with a strong emphasis on validators. It employs light-client verification, reliable relayers, and Merkle proof techniques to ensure secure cross-chain communication. Unlike RenVM and ThorChain, which rely on distributed key management, Multichain uses Merkle Proof and enhanced verification clients on destination chains to cross-validate state updates. Initial versions of Multichain had problems with validator centralization; by 2023, a serious security breach was caused by compromised access credentials [3]. This shows the trade-offs in bridge design concerning operating complexity, speed, and decentralization. The protocol now utilizes zero-knowledge proofs (ZKPs) and decentralized governance layers [9] to enhance trust-minimized interoperability.

Offering multi-layered security, these defenses integrate distributed trust with cryptographic proofs. Among the drawbacks are additional complexity, delays, and gas expenses. Moreover, recent audits demonstrate that even TSS-based systems are prone to logical flaws and financial attacks. This points out to the need of dynamic threat modeling, consistent security audits, and formal verification for any cross-chain architecture.

Until bridges are entirely decentralized, formally verifiable, and fault-tolerant, developers must see all of them as a high-risk domain and provide strict testing, fallback mechanisms, and multilayer cryptographic validation in their designs.

In the next section, we will discuss Smart Contract Exploits.

2.4 Smart Contract Exploits

Smart contracts are the foundation of blockchain automation, offering self-executing, tamper-proof agreements between participants. Their self-governing characteristics and deterministic reasoning have led to advancements such as automated lending, decentralized exchanges, and tokenized government [12]. The immutability that provides robustness to smart contracts is, nonetheless, a double-edged sword once deployed, erroneous code cannot be rectified without forking the chain or initiating entirely new contracts. This immutability worsens the adverse effects of coding errors, logical fallacies, and unforeseen interactions.

Figure 2.2 illustrates several critical weaknesses in immutable smart contracts, including logic errors, reentrancy attacks, and unanticipated interactions, and emphasizes how these flaws may result in money loss, governance failure, and system risk.

We will now cite two examples of such attacks.

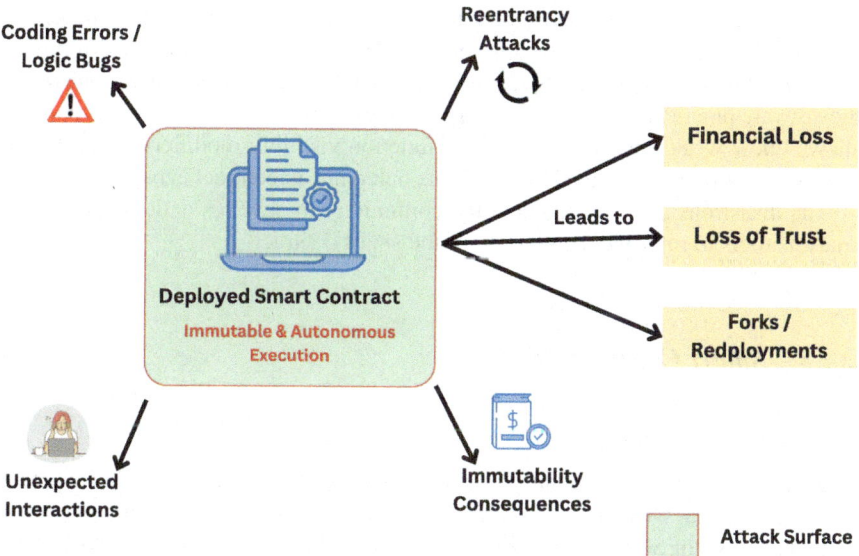

Fig. 2.2 Smart contract exploits

2.4.1 The DAO Attack

The 2016 DAO hack [13] is one of the most notable examples in blockchain history that showed the vulnerability of smart contracts. The Decentralized Autonomous Organization (DAO) was an investor-driven venture capital fund established on Ethereum, with over $150 million in ETH contributed at that time. The attacker exploited a reentrancy vulnerability in the contract's withdrawal mechanism, allowing recursive calls before internal balance modifications. The attacker exploited this situation to the amount of almost $60 million by making multiple calls to the withdrawal function without making the required state modification [14].

The hack significantly split the Ethereum community on the right path of action. This ultimately led to Ethereum's hard fork, splitting the network into Ethereum (ETH) and Ethereum Classic (ETC). While ETC adhered to the principle of "code is law" and preserved the modified chain state as a historical reference, Ethereum opted to revert the hack.

2.4.2 Parity Wallet Bug

Another notable instance is the Parity Wallet bug in 2017, which impacted a widely utilized multi-signature wallet used by various ICO companies like Golem, Polkadot, and Basic Attention Token (BAT) [4]. A user accidentally invoked the `initWallet` function on a deployed library contract, thereby taking up the ownership. In an effort to revoke ownership subsequently, the user unintentionally deleted the wallet library code, making over $150 million in ETH permanently unusable [14]. More than $150 million in ETH, including contributions from significant ICOs such as Polkadot [15], was irrevocably frozen, representing one of the most severe practical consequences of poor smart contract design [14]. This episode showed how weak initialization, lack of function visibility modifiers, and reliance on common libraries can lead to disastrous outcomes in contract ecosystems.

The disastrous attacks prompted the community to develop static and dynamic analysis tools to improve the security of the smart contracts.

2.4.3 Smart Contracts Tools

Let us explore a few tools.

- **Zeus**: Zeus [16] is a formal verification and symbolic execution platform that detects critical weaknesses in Ethereum smart contracts. Zeus conducts conceptual analysis of Solidity code, identifies prevalent flaws such as integer overflow, unsafe access, and reentrancy, and generates brief vulnerability reports [16]. It additionally facilitates white-box testing.

2.4 Smart Contract Exploits

- **ContractFuzzer**: ContractFuzzer [17] identifies runtime issues and logic flaws in smart contracts by subjecting them to fuzz testing regimens with random and unpredictable inputs. It assists in identifying security vulnerabilities such as reentrancy, assertion errors, and inadequate access control checks [17]. It is suited well for composability risk testing since it mimics calls from malicious users and external contracts.
- **MythX**: MythX is a powerful security analysis tool that delivers complete vulnerability detection through combining fuzzing with static and conceptual analysis. It evaluates contracts for reentrancy, arithmetic errors, transaction order dependence, and denial-of-service vulnerabilities, and is integrated into development workflows [16]. It is cloud-based and facilitates DevSecOps [4] interaction with Truffle Suite and RemixIDE [4].
- **Slither**: Slither [4] assesses Solidity contracts for documented security vulnerabilities and anti-patterns, including exposed functions, reentrancy, and uninitialized storage pointers [16]. It offers call and inheritance graphs and data flow analysis, enabling understanding and optimization of smart contracts during development.
- **Securify**: Securify [16], created by the ETH Zurich team [16], uses security patterns and compliance rules to evaluate smart contracts. It categorizes contract activity into safe, warning, or violation categories according to an established set of security criteria [16]. Securify is appropriate for developers seeking formal assurance of contract logic and auditors in need of compliance verification.

Although technologies such as Securify provide significant static analysis and formal verification, they cannot completely eradicate vulnerabilities that occur at runtime or through complex contract interactions. This is particularly applicable in the area of decentralized finance (DeFi), where the interoperability of smart contracts brings additional levels of risk.

2.4.4 Mitigations

A significant cause for the continual existence of these vulnerabilities is the openness of decentralized finance (DeFi), where contracts often engage with or invoke other contracts.

External code may generate incorrect assumptions on its functionality, resulting in security vulnerabilities. For example, flash loan arbitrage swiftly obtains significant capital without the collateral, performs transactions across multiple protocols, and subsequently repays the loan in a single atomic transaction. Improperly secured flash loans can be exploited to manipulate pricing or exploit temporal disparities. One significant category of these vulnerabilities arises from external dependencies that provide smart contracts with vital data. Oracle manipulation is changing the source data that gives a smart contract real-world information in order to fraudulently manipulate the logic of the contract and make it function improperly.

Similarly, front-running reasoning attacks happen when an attacker monitors the transaction pool and preemptively submits a transaction with increased fees to leverage the visibility of unconfirmed transactions, such as executing a trade immediately before a significant swap to benefit from price fluctuations [3].

Therefore, developers must comply with secure development protocols, which include upgradability frameworks with stringent access constraints, timelocks for privileged activities, comprehensive behavior definitions, and unit testing. Furthermore, third-party audits and bug bounties have become integral components of the security lifecycle for leading DeFi protocols.

Poorly drafted smart contracts, without vision, impart irrevocable vulnerabilities suited for exploitation, especially in cross-chain contexts where flaws are able to expand throughout ecosystems. The lessons from the DAO and Parity [4] serve as enduring reminders of the necessity for diligence, appropriate tools, and community vigilance in the development of smart contracts.

Having discussed Smart Contract exploits let us have a look at the Double-Spending threat.

2.5 Double-Spending

Double-spending is likely the most fundamental and fatal threat to blockchain networks. It is the opposite of the concept of digital scarcity, wherein each token or unit of bitcoin is distinct and can be utilized just once.

2.5.1 What Is Double-Spending?

Double-spending refers to a user's attempt to utilize the same digital asset twice by exploiting weaknesses in a blockchain's consensus or transaction finality processes. This defect can undermine the blockchain economy, exchanges, and decentralized apps by diminishing trust and causing financial loss [18].

Double-spending occurs when the attacker sends a payment to a recipient, such as a merchant, and subsequently invalidates the original transaction by broadcasting an alternate version of the blockchain that eliminates the payment. The attacker successfully retains both the digital currency and the commodity or service acquired, thereby duplicating value.

We will now explain to you how double-spending occurs with a detailed illustration.

2.5 Double-Spending

2.5.2 How Does it Work?

Consider a Double-Spending Success Scenario. The attacker uses the same coins on two occasions: initially to acquire commodities (through Tx1), and subsequently to reclaim them (through Tx2) by overriding the original transaction with a longer chain.

Figure 2.3 illustrates how double-spending attacks occur. The attacker prepares two conflicting transactions.

The following steps explain how a Double Spending attack happens:

1. Two Contradictory Transactions Initiated by the Attacker.

   (a) The attacker initiates the attack by creating two contradictory transactions using the identical coins:
   - Tx1 is a transaction that sends coins to a merchant.
   - Tx2 is a hidden transaction that transfers identical coins to the attacker.

   (b) Tx1 (To Merchant) is Recorded on the Blockchain.

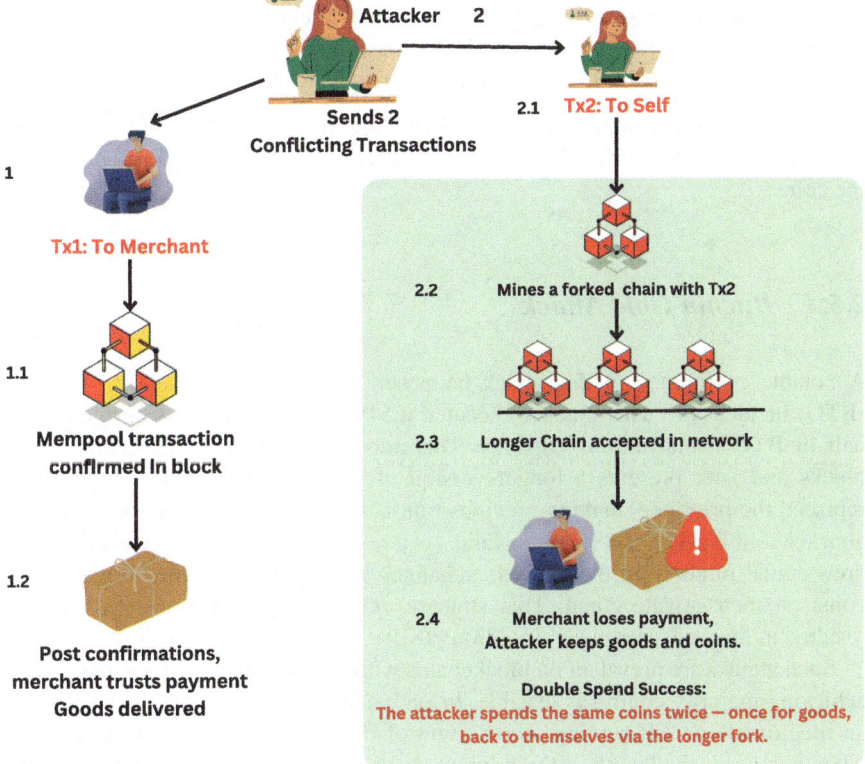

Fig. 2.3 Double-spending attack

- Tx1 is broadcast on the blockchain network and included into the mempool, a repository for unconfirmed transactions.
- It is obtained by miners and subsequently confirmed within a block.

  (c) Merchant Authenticates and Delivers Merchandise.

- After one to two blocks, the merchant considers the payment as received.
- Presuming the blockchain's integrity, the merchant hands over the products to the attacker.

2. Attacker Triggers the Fork with Tx2.

   (a) Simultaneously, the attacker secretly mines an alternative version of the blockchain, prior to the inclusion of Tx1. In this forked chain, Tx1 is excluded, whereas Tx2 (to self) is included.
   (b) Forked Chain Grows with Tx2. The attacker continues to add to the forked chain, extending it beyond the legitimate chain. This is feasible in Proof of Work systems if the attacker possesses adequate mining power.
   (c) The Network Acknowledges the Longer Chain. When the attacker's fork constitutes the longest legitimate chain, it propagates throughout the network. According to Nakamoto consensus, nodes select the longest valid chain, thereby overriding the original chain that includes Tx1.
   (d) Tx1 is Orphaned and Double-Spending is successful. Tx1 is discarded and is no longer part of the official blockchain history.

Consequently, the merchant has dispatched the products, although the payment is no longer visible on the blockchain. The attacker retains both the products and the coins.

2.5.3 Bitcoin Gold Attack

A notable occurrence of this attack happened in 2018 during the Bitcoin Gold (BTG) incident [4]. The attacker executed a 51% attack by possessing more than half of BTG's total mining capacity. This allowed the attacker to secretly mine blocks and later presents a longer version of the blockchain. The longer chain replaced the prior one, making previous transactions, including those in which the attacker sold BTG to exchanges, invalid. As a result, the attacker successfully withdrew actual funds from the hacked exchanges while preserving the original BTG coins on their private chain. This strategy, referred to as chain reorganization, resulted in losses exceeding $18 million [18].

Such attacks are prevalent on blockchains with low hash power, when the cost of achieving majority control is feasible. In such a network, an attacker may develop an illegitimate or self-serving secret chain of transactions and release it publicly when it exceeds the length of the original chain. According to protocol, the longest chain is deemed valid within the network, hence nullifying prior transactions [14].

To avoid duplicate spending, large blockchains have employed multiple mitigations. We are going to look at various mitigations.

2.5.4 Mitigations

Ethereum's transition to Ethereum 2.0 and Proof-of-Stake (PoS) [4] adds finality checkpoints at specific places in the chain, beyond which blocks cannot be reversed without significant economic cost. In Proof of Stake, validators must stake assets, which are slashed if they validate false transactions, making attacks excessively expensive [19].

Furthermore, Layer 2 solutions [4] like payment channels and optimistic or zk-Rollups reduce the susceptibility of base layer chains to double-spend attacks. They finalize a group of off-chain transactions in a cryptographically verifiable manner, committing only the final state to Layer 1. This makes the system resistant to on-chain tampering and consensus challenges [14].

Recent consensus mechanisms, such as Avalanche [20] and Algorand [7], achieve rapid or deterministic finality. These guarantee that a transaction is irreversible once recorded, preserved in the unlikely scenario of extensive network dominance—far exceeding the economic or logistical capabilities of attackers.

Despite the persistent vulnerability of double-spending, blockchain technologies have seen substantial advancements to mitigate its likelihood. Improved consensus, financial penalties, cryptographic finality, and scalable Layer 2 infrastructures guarantee transaction integrity even in adverse conditions. Such solutions are essential in cross-chain networks where transaction states require synchronization and double-spending must be averted across all [9].

Having acquired knowledge on the nature and avoidance of double-spending, we will now proceed to look into another significant threat—Replay Attacks, which use the structural consistency of transactions across chains to inappropriately duplicate valid transactions.

2.6 Replay Attacks

A similar and significant problem in the cross-chain and multi-chain ecosystem is replay attacks. Such situations involve a legitimate transaction propagated on one chain being maliciously replicated on another chain, particularly when different networks utilize similar transaction frameworks or cryptographic primitives. This issue is particularly severe during hard forks or chain splits, when both chains may initially accept and validate identical transaction signatures.

A relevant real-world example is the 2016 DAO hard fork [13], during which the Ethereum (ETH) and Ethereum Classic (ETC) chains split about a strategy to address stolen funds from a faulty DAO contract. Consequently, both chains utilized identical transaction formats and encryption algorithms, allowing a transaction broadcasted on Ethereum to be replicated on Ethereum Classic (and vice versa), thereby enabling users or malicious actors to potentially duplicate transactions across networks [21].

To mitigate this problem, Ethereum implemented EIP-155 [4], which incorporated an additional `chainId` argument in every transaction. This innovation made the transaction legitimate solely on the designated chain for which it was transmitted, hence invalidating attempts to replay the transaction on connected chains [22]. In addition, modern systems employ session keys, unique nonces, and time-limited commitments to link a transaction's context to a specific network, session, or temporal window, therefore mitigating possible replay vulnerabilities in advanced cross-chain systems.

In interoperable systems, especially those involving wrapped tokens, bridge protocols, or forked decentralized exchanges [4], it is increasingly crucial to ensure that transaction authenticity is connected to the originating chain. In the absence of such security, a single signature could permit several transfers across chains, resulting in a hazardous scenario for financial transactions.

Replay protection has therefore emerged as a crucial necessity in multi-chain designs, commonly executed via middleware relayers, on-chain chainID verifiers, or cryptographic message attestation layers [4] integrated into bridge protocols. These mechanisms guarantee that cross-chain interactions are atomic, context-aware, and immune to replay attacks.

We will now discuss the development of cryptographic countermeasures to protect interoperability against these increasing risks.

2.7 Cryptographic Defenses

The cryptographic defenses represent innovative techniques for improving cross-chain security. These defenses comprise trusted relays, threshold signatures, and decentralized oracles. We will now study each one in more depth.

2.7.1 Trusted Relays

As interoperability across blockchain networks increases, the reliability of cross-chain communication becomes essential. Trusted relays serve as essential mechanisms for conveying authenticated state updates between blockchains, hence removing reliance on a sole source of truth. Trusted relays operate as intermediaries, overseeing occurrences on the source chain and transmitting authenticated proofs to the destination chain.

To ensure message authenticity, relays commonly utilize Merkle Proofs, a cryptographic data structure that validates certain bits of data as part of an authentic

2.7 Cryptographic Defenses

transaction history. This eliminates the need to recreate the entire transaction history by enabling the receiving chain's smart contracts to independently verify that a message corresponds to a validated transaction on the original chain. This method enables rapid, verified state transfers and significantly decreases computing burden. Reliable relays operate through a multi-party consensus mechanism, wherein designated nodes or validators must agree on a state transition before it is relayed. This improves the system's robustness against faulty participants while reducing the probability of isolated disruptions.

The relay chain of Polkadot guarantees the transfer of finalized and acceptable state transitions across the network while validating the blocks generated by parachains. Protocols like ChainBridge and AnySwap [4] utilize multi-signature relayers to facilitate secure asset transfers across numerous blockchains [9]. Relay mechanisms are crucial for preserving message consistency and integrity in dynamic multi-chain systems.

We will now briefly describe a few relay techniques.

- **Light Client Relay** [12]: A lightweight client of another chain is operated on one chain in order to check block headers and transaction proofs directly on-chain; Cosmos IBC and Near Rainbow Bridge [4] use this technology for trustless communication.
- **External Relayer with Proof Verification** [4]: A relayer is used in protocols like LayerZero and Axelar for safe and quick delivery; it listens on one chain and transmits messages with cryptographic proofs to another.
- **Notary-Based Relay** [10]: Cross-chain events are validated by verified validators or multisig notaries; they are less complicated but more common in older bridges like Wanchain and Multichain.
- **Cross-Chain Message Bus** (CCMP) [5, 6]: A standardized protocol-based relay system that relays and authenticates structured packets with predetermined state and ordering, across chains (XCMP, IBC).
- **Semantic Relay Techniques** [23]: Relays that understand the message's intent and validation history are essential for building cross-domain logic in smart contract orchestration frameworks.

In the next part, we will look at another essential safety mechanism: Threshold Signatures, which increase cryptographic resilience by decentralizing signing authority.

2.7.2 Threshold Signatures

Threshold signature schemes (TSS) provide a significant advancement in safe cross-chain key management. Traditional signatures utilize a single private key to authenticate a transaction, whereas threshold signatures split the signing key into segments and allocate them to various validators or nodes. A designated subset (the 'threshold') of the fragments must work together to reconstruct the signature to authorize the transaction.

Figure 2.4 illustrates the concept of Threshold Signatures, wherein a requisite minimum of participants (3 out of 5 in this instance) must collaboratively generate a valid digital signature. Each selected participant (P1, P3, and P5) produces a partial signature utilizing their secret share, which is then collected and merged to form a whole threshold signature. It is impossible to distinguish this final signature from a standard digital signature, and any external verifier node can validate it. This technology enhances security and decentralization by ensuring that no single entity holds complete signing power, making it appropriate for secure cross-chain validation and multi-party computation.

This approach has two notable benefits. Firstly, it eliminates singular points of failure. As no node possesses the complete private key, an attacker cannot disable the system by compromising a single participant. Secondly, it facilitates fault tolerance and decentralization, as the protocol may reliably operate even if some participants are unavailable or compromised.

For example, with bridge protocols like ThorChain and RenVM [8], threshold signatures enable asset issuance and custody across several chains. A minimum

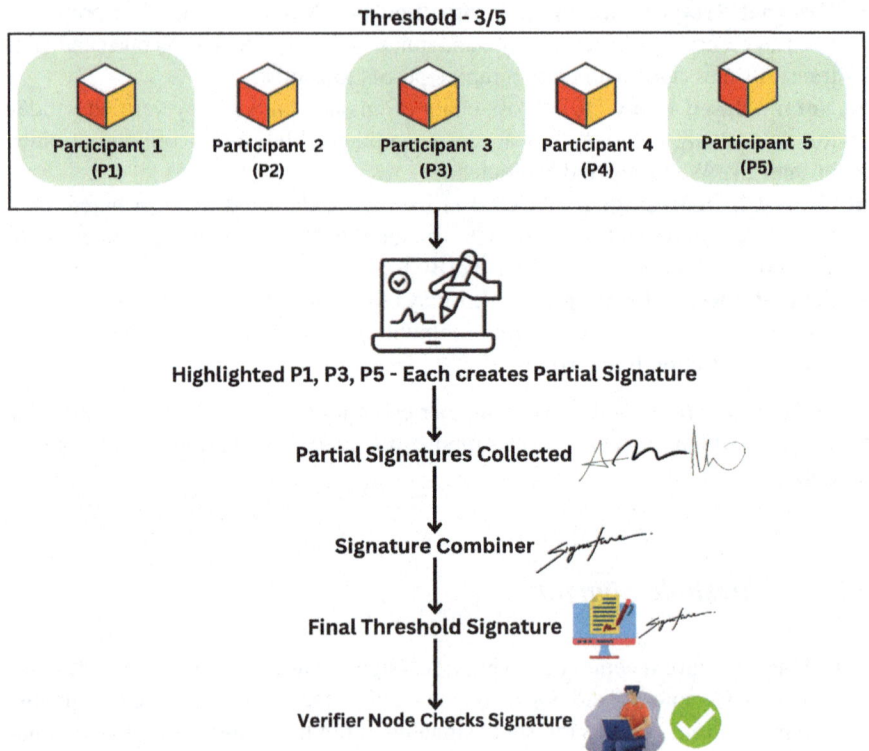

Fig. 2.4 Threshold signatures

2.7 Cryptographic Defenses

amount of validator signatures must be acquired before the minting or transfer of a new token, ensuring security and decentralized trust [8].

Threshold cryptography facilitates dynamic validator sets and secures key rotation, making it especially appropriate for decentralized systems where participants may enter or exit over time. One essential step in building a tamper-evident infrastructure—systems that can identify and document any unwanted activity or data tampering—is the incorporation of threshold cryptography into cross-chain protocols. In tamper-evident systems, cryptographic processes, including digital signatures, are both traceable and verifiable, ensuring that malicious behavior leaves a detectable trace. A significant practical use of this is the implementation of a Threshold BLS Signature Scheme by the Binance Smart Chain Bridge.

In contrast to conventional multisig, which involves passing in and verifying each signature separately, threshold-signing systems allow groups of participants to create a single, compact signature without ever having to reconstruct the complete private key. This enhancement strengthened accountability and decentralization. In this architecture, the signing key is never fully reconstructed; instead, a group of nodes collaboratively generates a signature, with each validator's contribution being cryptographically verifiable. This design provides a strong basis for safe cross-chain asset transfer by avoiding single points of failure and making any deviation or effort at collusion publicly visible [11].

We are going to look at another pillar of decentralized infrastructure, Oracles that connect smart contracts with off-chain and real-world data.

2.7.3 Oracles

Smart contracts are proficient at enforcing on-chain logic; yet, they are unable to natively access external data like price, weather, or real-world events. This is the role of oracles. Oracles are reliable data sources that acquire, authenticate, and provide external information to smart contracts, facilitating the full functionality of decentralized applications.

Figure 2.5 illustrates the concept of Oracles.

However, oracle systems naturally pose a significant risk of intrusion, particularly when they lack redundancy or are centralized. A compromised oracle can

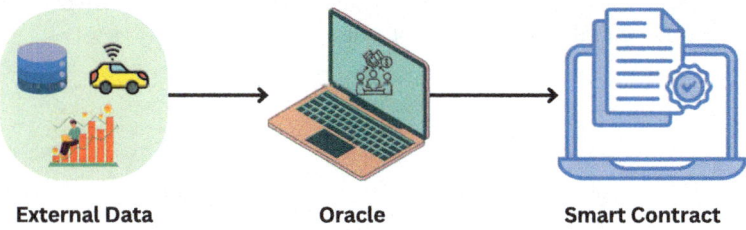

Fig. 2.5 Concept of Oracles

deliver distorted data to smart contracts, resulting in significant financial losses, illustrated by the bZx [24] protocol hack, when the attacker altered an oracle-supplied price to exploit the protocol through a flash loan attack.

In response, modern decentralized oracle networks like Chainlink [24] aggregate data from multiple sources and employ consensus processes to generate tamper-proof outputs. To guarantee robustness, Chainlink nodes query several data sources, obtain a majority consensus, and subsequently report to the blockchain, even in the presence of fraudulent or biased sources.

To improve reliability, innovative oracle solutions like Chainlink employ fallback sources, data deviation assessments, and machine learning-driven anomaly detection methods, all complemented by decentralization. Additional solutions encompass staking-based slashing incentives (used in Witnet [25]), cryptographic promises (applied in Band Protocol [10]), and permissionless oracle registries to enable dynamic source onboarding. To mitigate manipulation and uphold data integrity, several cross-chain bridges and DeFi protocols employ multi-layered oracle systems, validating data from multiple sources and networks before acceptance.

2.8 What's Next?

We discussed the role of cryptographic tools in protecting the functionalities of interoperable systems through the implementation of Trusted Relays, Threshold Signatures, and Oracles.

Cryptographic protection protocols serve as the primary defense against the majority of challenges associated with blockchain interoperability. Trusted relays play a vital role in enabling authenticated cross-chain state transfers by leveraging Merkle Proofs and validator consensus. Authenticated cross-chain state transfers are made easier through trusted relays utilizing Merkle Proofs and validator consensus. Threshold signatures facilitate decentralized key management to prevent single-node failure or compromise, while Oracles bridge the gap between blockchains and external data through many stages of validation.

These cryptographic primitives collectively enhance the security, stability, and decentralization of cross-chain systems, providing a foundation for robust multi-chain applications.

The next section will look at future security directions, focusing on cutting-edge methodologies such as Quantum-Resistant Cryptography, AI-Driven Security Models, and Decentralized Identity Protocols.

2.9 Future Security Directions

In the previous section, we examined major weaknesses impacting cross-chain networks, including replay attacks, bridge attacks, smart contract exploitation, and double-spending. Consequently, we now direct our attention to proactive measures aimed at ensuring security of blockchain interoperability in future. New security paradigms are emerging to address the intricate issues of data integrity and cross-network communication as the ecosystem evolves into a highly interconnected, multi-chain framework.

The future of cross-chain security is being shaped by several groundbreaking technologies.

2.9.1 Quantum-Resistant Cryptography

We now address Quantum-Resistant Cryptography, a crucial defense for the future of blockchain systems against potential quantum attacks.

Quantum computing presents a significant risk to the existing cryptographic framework of blockchains. The majority of modern blockchain protocols employ traditional cryptographic methods, like Rivest–Shamir–Adleman (RSA), Elliptic Curve Digital Signature Algorithm (ECDSA), and Elliptic Curve Cryptography (ECC) for the security of digital signatures and key exchange management. Although these algorithms are immune to classical computer attacks, they are vulnerable to quantum attacks, especially those employing Shor's algorithm, which can factor big integers and compute discrete logarithms at an exponentially faster rate than classical methods. Such capability will allow quantum-powered attackers to reverse-engineer secret keys or fabricate signatures, hence compromising transaction integrity and identity within blockchain systems.

This vulnerability primarily affects cross-chain interoperability, as message-passing protocols, token wrapping, and bridges heavily rely on signature verification to provide authenticity across networks. A quantum attacker could enable widespread exploitation or systemic financial loss across interconnected networks if they manage to compromise a single cryptographic key in such a system.

To tackle this difficulty, researchers developed post-quantum cryptography (PQC) [26], the forthcoming generation of cryptographic algorithms anticipated to be immune to quantum attacks. The most promising candidates among the post-quantum cryptography schemes encompass lattice-based cryptographic systems such as CRYSTALS-Dilithium (Cryptographic Suite for Algebraic Lattices) [26], which provide strong safety for digital signatures and are being evaluated for standardization by NIST (National Institute of Standards and Technology). These issues depend on the difficulty of problems like the Shortest Vector Problem (SVP) [26] and the Learning With Errors (LWE) problem, both of which are considered quantum-resistant. Furthermore, hash-based signature schemes such as SPHINCS+

(Stateless Practical Hash-based Incredibly Nice Cryptographic Signature) [26] and XMSS (eXtended Merkle Signature Scheme) [26] have been proposed for post-quantum lightweight security with minimal computational overhead and are very easy to implement in blockchain applications with limited resources.

Numerous blockchain initiatives and research organizations have commenced the integration of quantum-resistant algorithms into their platforms to guarantee lasting strength. Kumar et al. [26, 27] emphasized that the use of such cryptographic primitives is not optional but essential to provide trust, immutability, and the long-term viability of Web3 ecosystems.

As blockchain networks evolve into multi-chain value-transfer systems, failure to transition to quantum-safe security models may introduce catastrophic risk. Thus, standardizing and implementing PQC is a strategic requirement for every forward-thinking blockchain project, not only an academic one, in order to prepare for post-quantum times.

The second major innovation that will shape the future of secure interoperability is AI-Driven Security Models.

2.9.2 AI-Driven Security Models

As pointed out in the previous part on Quantum-Resistant Cryptography, the future of blockchain security consists of not only countering quantum computer attacks but also proactively preventing and detecting risks. This can be accomplished by using the capabilities of artificial intelligence (AI). AI can revolutionize blockchain security with adaptive, dynamic, and contextual security frameworks that can identify, learn from, and respond to real-time attacks in interoperable systems.

In contrast to traditional rule-based security protocols, AI utilizes machine learning (ML), natural language processing (NLP), and deep neural networks (DNN) to automate the identification of patterns, detect anomalies, and find new vulnerabilities in blockchain protocols and smart contracts. In cross-chain contexts, where message relaying, asynchronous execution, and validator heterogeneity expand the attack surface for advanced attacks, this is particularly crucial.

Several AI-driven methods and technologies have been suggested to enhance the security of decentralized applications and smart contracts.

We will now discuss a few AI-driven models.

- **S-gram**: S-gram is a semantically-aware auditing tool that detects vulnerabilities in Ethereum smart contracts through analyzing code semantics in addition to control flow, hence identifying anomalous behaviors that deviate from standard execution patterns [24]. It has been effective in exposing zero-day vulnerabilities that standard static analysis techniques cannot detect.
- **ContractFuzzer**: ContractFuzzer [17] is a notable software application that uses fuzz testing, a method of automatically adding erroneous or incorrect data into smart contracts to simulate various attack vectors. Utilizing the approach to

identify reentrancy flaws, overflows, and access control vulnerabilities before release is particularly crucial [17].
- **Graph Neural Networks**: The application of a graph neural network (GNN) [28] enhances vulnerability identification. GNNs analyze Abstract Syntax Trees (ASTs) and control flow graphs of smart contracts to enable the detection of security vulnerabilities using graph pattern matching. The method has proven to be more effective than previous machine learning-based classifiers [28] in detecting exploit-vulnerable behavior.

We now look at some of the benefits offered by these AI-driven models.

2.9.3 AI Benefits

AI models assist in real-time security monitoring for cross-chain asset transfers in addition to vulnerability discovery. The systems supervise validator activity and mempool saturation; mempool is a temporary repository for unverified blockchain transactions prior to verification, and event emissions to detect front-running attacks, liquidity manipulations, or inconsistent state changes between bridges.

AI predicts the effectiveness of governance proposals in decentralized autonomous organizations (DAOs) by analyzing sentiment, voting history, and stakeholder alignment. The AI employs natural language processing (NLP)—a domain of AI that allows computers to perceive, comprehend, and analyze human language—and clustering models to identify patterns of analogous voting behavior and sentiments.

DataHarbour [25] and Advanced eHealth [29] exemplify the integration of blockchain and AI to secure decentralized data exchanges. These solutions employ AI as a threat detection mechanism and for adaptive authentication, privacy protection, and access regulation based on anomalies in multi-party data-sharing contexts.

As blockchain networks expand in size and complexity, the necessity for AI-powered security solutions will further escalate. AI-driven models represent an advancement from traditional defensive solutions to proactive, intelligent protective layers that can react to evolving threats in real time—ensuring that interoperability does not compromise safety.

We will now address the challenges of Smart Contract Interoperability, focusing on how executing logic across several chains introduces new risks related to consensus divergence, asynchronous state, and partial transaction failures.

2.9.4 Reliable Interoperable Smart Contracts

The previous part on AI-Powered Security Paradigms highlighted that the integration of blockchain technology with advanced computational intelligence facilitates the integration of additional automation layers and real-time threat detection to security. However, the complexity of smart contract transactions across several blockchains presents new and highly technical issues as we move from centralized to interoperable decentralized applications. These issues now emerge at the convergence of many protocols, consensus algorithms, and trust boundaries, rather within the framework of an isolated chain.

The next section addresses the challenges of smart contract interoperability, concentrating on three key areas: cross-chain contract execution risks, oracle manipulation, and governance vulnerabilities.

2.9.4.1 Cross-Chain Contract Execution Risks

Smart contracts were initially intended to operate inside the deterministic boundaries of a single blockchain. When designed to function across various chains, whether through relayers, bridges, or interoperability protocols, they adopt the architectural variances among the networks. Consensus mechanisms, block finality guarantees, and message propagation delays frequently result in desynchronization between contracts, potentially leading to inconsistent or insufficient outcomes.

A single logical transaction may involve one contract on Ethereum and another on Solana. When the Ethereum contract is finalized and the Solana contract remains incomplete due to network congestion or consensus lag, the system can fall into an incomplete commit state. This violates the idea of atomicity, which states that a transaction must either completely succeed or entirely fail. The finality latency of Ethereum can result in timeouts on fast chains such as Avalanche or Solana, leaving coins or state changes in a transient state.

Furthermore, data inconsistencies may arise from varying state visibility across chains, especially when implementing sequential contract logic dependent on instant balances, rights, or proofs. In some cases, asynchronous state updates can result in logical errors or financial losses.

Researchers have proposed semantic validation frameworks and inter-chain transaction coordination protocols as solutions to these problems [30]. They also have investigated multi-task learning models and semantic-aware smart contract architectures to enhance consistency in cross-chain executions. This involves the implementation of consensus-aware scheduling, fallback conditions, and checkpointing in inter-chain transactions to improve consistency and recoverability across several chains.

We will now focus on another related risk factor Oracle Manipulation, which is among the most often exploited vulnerabilities in smart contract environments.

2.9.4.2 Oracle Manipulation

Oracles play a vital role in bridging on-chain smart contracts with off-chain data, like asset prices, weather conditions, and event results. Oracles improve the functionality of blockchain applications but simultaneously introduce a potential point of failure, particularly in cross-chain scenarios where a single oracle may receive queries from many networks that offer varying latency and consensus constraints.

An exemplary case is the bZx protocol exploit [24] in 2020, wherein a flash loan attack used an oracle-reported price feed to exploit uncollateralized borrowing, resulting in a loss of roughly $one million USD for the protocol. The attacker borrowed a large flash loan, altered the price that the oracle reported on Uniswap, and then took advantage of the false pricing to drain money from bZx's smart contracts.

Decentralized systems use decentralized oracle networks (DONs), like Chainlink, to address these weaknesses. These DONs compile responses from several sources and then input the data into smart contracts [24], but the bulk of the sources should be reliable. The decentralization of oracles, node rotation, reputation-based voting, and backup mechanisms (such as human mediation or off-chain notifications) significantly improve reliability, ensuring the network's resilience against deceit even in the event of widespread oracle failure.

Additionally, redundancy and deviation checks are employed to detect differences in the provided values. These are further enhanced by artificial intelligence-driven anomaly detection systems employing pattern recognition algorithms to detect statistically unlikely alterations or correlation disruptions in oracle data sources [29].

Despite these advancements, oracle systems continue to be susceptible to data delaying, data integrity attacks, and bridge oracle manipulation, especially in protocols reliant on a single chain's oracle for cross-chain price estimations or governance metrics.

Having addressed data integrity challenges, we will now proceed to the third major challenge: Governance Vulnerabilities in cross-chain smart contract systems.

2.9.4.3 Governance Vulnerabilities

In the Web3 ecosystem, governance is predominantly executed through Decentralized Autonomous Organizations (DAOs), wherein token holders vote on proposals, parameter modifications, and system enhancements. In cross-chain implementations, the voting infrastructure frequently shows flaws in synchronization, consistency, and security assurances, rendering protocols vulnerable to manipulation.

A significant threat is vote hijacking by flash loans. In this type of attack, an attacker momentarily acquires a substantial amount of governance tokens through a flash loan, manipulates protocol parameters by voting, and subsequently repays the loan without incurring long-term exposure or interest. In the absence of sufficient mitigations, such as vote-escrowed tokens or mandatory holding periods, this type of economic vulnerability may compromise the validity of the DAO.

A further challenge pertains to the synchronization of cross-chain voting. A DAO may operate on Ethereum, while its execution targets could reside on sidechains like Arbitrum [20] or Avalanche [7]. If voting results are not accurately relayed and verified across chains, proposals may fail or be performed based on outdated assumptions.

Furthermore, Sybil attacks where a single entity creates multiple pseudonymous identities to gain voting power continue to represent a risk, especially in governance systems with limited liquidity. In contrast, ZKPs are being used to offer anonymous yet verifiable identities in voting systems, enhancing voter privacy and providing resistance to Sybil attacks [2].

Emerging frameworks such as Snapshot [2], Tally [25], and ZK-governance [29] models aim to standardize cross-chain governance. These frameworks aim to ensure that DAO votes are cryptographically legitimate, resistant to replay attacks, and transparently documented across many chains, all while preserving voter anonymity and minimizing gas fees.

In conclusion, smart contract interoperability introduces a range of subtle and complex vulnerabilities that extend well beyond single-chain architecture. Cross-chain execution vulnerabilities arise from finality, latency, and inconsistencies in consensus logic. Oracle manipulation attacks compromise network data integrity, particularly when interacting with mismatched or asynchronous pricing systems. Governance issues arise when DAOs lack a secure and coordinated decision-making mechanism across chains. As cross-chain decentralized applications continue to proliferate, these issues must be addressed by a combination of architectural design, cryptographic security measures, and AI-driven monitoring to ensure the reliability and resilience of multi-chain systems.

Following a review of the concerns linked to governance synchronization, oracle dependencies, and execution logic in cross-chain environments, we explore identity, a fundamental aspect of trust. The next part discusses how interoperable blockchain platforms must manage identity authentication, privacy protection, and revocation across several networks.

2.9.5 Cross-Chain Identity

As discussed in the previous section, cross-chain systems introduce complexities in the execution of smart contracts, management of oracle data, and governance protection. A critical element frequently ignored in this paradigm is identity. In decentralized and interoperable contexts, identity has evolved from a mere verification step to a fundamental infrastructure element that must be securely transferred, authenticated, and revoked across several networks. Self-sovereign identity (SSI) systems and decentralized identity (DID) frameworks are advantageous in this scenario. SSI empowers individuals and institutions to autonomously generate, maintain, and present cryptographically signed credentials, independent of centralized authority. DID is a framework that empowers people to manage and administer their digital identities, facilitating verifiable and privacy-preserving exchanges across many platforms without reliance on a central authority.

These systems encounter considerable challenges inside the multi-chain ecosystem.

A significant challenge is the absence of schema standardization; various blockchains may document and transmit identity information in different manners, limiting the uniform exchange or resolution of credentials across networks. This unpredictability obstructs the interoperability of identity assertions, especially in cross-chain governance, DeFi onboarding, and compliance evaluations [2].

The second issue is metadata disclosure, wherein user interactions on one blockchain may inadvertently disclose user data when replicated or mirrored on another. In systems that aggregate on-chain behavior to generate trust ratings or user profiles, data leakage would lead to privacy violations and risks of deanonymization. Privacy concerns intensify in cross-jurisdictional contexts, where regulations like GDPR require meticulous handling of personal data [25].

The third issue is inconsistency in revocation. If an identity credential is revoked or altered on one chain, the modification may not be directly or potentially observable on other chains utilizing the same credentials. This generates weakened trust assumptions and may facilitate the exploitation of revoked or obsolete credentials across interconnected networks.

Diverse technologies and protocols are emerging to achieve these objectives. DIDComm [2] is a secure messaging protocol that enables cross-chain identity exchange via standards-based, encrypted frameworks. The previously mentioned protocols, when used with Universal Resolver, an identification resolver software for diverse DID techniques, establish the foundation for a multi-chain identity architecture [2]. Moreover, ZKPs are progressively integrated to enable users to verify identity attributes (age, nationality, or KYC status) without disclosing excessive personal information—thereby enhancing both privacy and interoperability.

Platforms like DataHarbour demonstrate the capabilities of AI and blockchain in safeguarding identification. DataHarbour facilitates a decentralized and secure exchange of identity-related information utilizing AI and blockchain-based auditable rules to prevent the diversion or misuse of sensitive credentials throughout transfer [25].

Decentralized identity solutions are essential for facilitating secure, privacy-preserving, and compliant interactions within multi-chain ecosystems. These systems must handle interoperability, standardize credential management, and offer cryptographic protections that satisfy user and international regulatory standards in order to reach full maturity.

We will now conclude this chapter by providing a summary of the most significant points learnt about cross-chain system security flaws and countermeasures against them.

2.10 Summary

In this chapter, we discussed the security challenges in cross-chain blockchain systems. The emergence of interoperability protocols like Cosmos IBC, Polkadot XCMP, and LayerZero has made robust, multi-layer security architectures not merely desirable but viable. We discussed fundamental vulnerabilities including bridge hacks, smart contract attacks, double-spending, and replay attacks, as well as the propagation of problems across networks due to their interconnection [3].

Incidents like the Wormhole bridge and Poly Network hacks have demonstrated the vulnerabilities stemming from centralized governance and insufficient validation, resulting in significant financial losses. Deficiencies in smart contracts, highlighted by the Parity wallet vulnerability and the DAO reentrancy hack, exposed the dangers associated with immutable code, whereas the 51% attack on Bitcoin Gold highlighted the vulnerability of Proof-of-Work consensus in low-hash networks.

Further, we examined security strategies like trusted relays for authenticated communication, threshold signature systems for sharing signing authority, and tamper-resistant decentralized oracles such as Chainlink using diverse data sources [8].

We also analyzed upcoming security advancements, including Quantum-Resistant Cryptography—specifically algorithms such as CRYSTALS-Dilithium and SPHINCS+—to counter the risks posed by quantum computers compared with traditional cryptographic techniques like RSA and ECDSA [26]. Real-time vulnerability identification has been demonstrated to be improved by tools such as S-gram, ContractFuzzer, and Graph Neural Networks (GNNs) [25].

This chapter addressed weaknesses in smart contract interoperability, including atomicity failure and latency incompatibility, alongside oracle manipulation shown by attacks like the bZx flash loan exploit, for which redundancy and anomaly detection have been suggested as mitigation [30].

Governance-layer threats, such as vote hijacking using flash loans and Sybil attacks on DAOs, were examined with potential solutions, including ZKPs for secure voting [2].

After analyzing the increasing attack surface introduced by cross-chain interoperability, including bridge vulnerabilities, smart contract exploits, and the development of defenses like threshold cryptography, decentralized oracles, and quantum-resistant algorithms, we now proceed to Chap. 3, which transitions from technological security to the institutional and policy-oriented aspects of trust.

The next chapter addresses governance and regulatory challenges of interoperable blockchain networks, including compliance in cross-border operations, the evolving legal status of DAOs, and KYC/AML compliance within a decentralized framework. Chapter 3 will provide a comprehensive overview of the impact of interoperability on real-world markets such as DeFi, CBDCs, and enterprise banking, as we transition from code-level protection to institutional accountability frameworks. It will also address legal ambiguity, governance transparency, and the convergence of AI, decentralized identity, and Web3-native financial infrastructure.

References

1. Han, Y., Wang, C., Wang, H.: Research on blockchain cross-chain model based on 'NFT + cross-chain bridge'. IEEE Access. **12**, 77065–77078 (2024a). https://doi.org/10.1109/ACCESS.2024.3401405
2. Virani, S.S.: Blockchain end user adoption and societal challenges: exploring privacy, rights, and security dimensions. IET Blockchain. **4**(S1), 691–705 (2024). https://doi.org/10.1049/blc2.12077
3. Hirai, Y.: "Defining the ethereum virtual machine for interactive theorem provers," Financial Cryptography and Data Security: FC 2017 International Workshops, WAHC, BITCOIN, VOTING, WTSC, and TA, Sliema, Malta, Apr. 7, 2017, pp. 520–535
4. "Blockchain Interoperability Guide," Cyfrin, Feb. 2024. [Online]. Available: https://www.cyfrin.io/blog/blockchain-interoperability-guide. [Accessed: 14-Mar-2025]
5. Morháč, D., Valaštín, V., Košťál, K., Kotuliak, I.: Enhancing XCMP interoperability across Polkadot Paraverse. In: IEEE International Conference on Blockchain, Bratislava, Slovakia (2023a). https://doi.org/10.1109/Blockchain50366.2023.00032
6. Morháč, D., Valaštín, V., Košťál, K., Kotuliak, I.: ParaSpell XCM SDK: a new protocol for interoperability in Polkadot Paraverse. In: 2023 Fifth International Conference on Blockchain Computing and Applications (BCCA) (2023b). https://doi.org/10.1109/BCCA58897.2023.10338906
7. Lepore, C.: A survey on blockchain consensus with a performance comparison of PoW, PoS and pure PoS. Mathematics. **8**(10), 1782 (2020)
8. Lattner, C., Adve, V.: LLVM: a compilation framework for lifelong program analysis & transformation. In: International Symposium on Code Generation and Optimization, pp. 75–86. IEEE (2004. (CGO 2004))
9. Kolluri, A., Nikolic, I., Sergey, I., Hobor, A., Saxena, P.: Exploiting the laws of order in smart contracts. In: 28th ACM SIGSOFT International Symposium on Software Testing and Analysis, pp. 363–373 (2019)
10. Yang, S., Zhang, G., Li, Y., Wang, P., Zhao, C., Feng, B., Shen, C., Zhang, Y.: Cross-chain architecture of blockchain integrating notary mechanism and relay-chain technology. In: 2024 4th International Conference on Blockchain Technology and Information Security (ICBCTIS) (2024). https://doi.org/10.1109/ICBCTIS64495.2024.00014
11. Thyagarajan, S.A., Malavolta, G., Moreno-Sanchez, P.: Universal atomic swaps: secure exchange of coins across all blockchains. In: 2022 IEEE Symposium on Security and Privacy (SP), pp. 1299–1314 (2022). https://doi.org/10.1109/SP46214.2022.00063
12. Kim, J., Essaid, M., Ju, H.: Inter-blockchain communication message relay time measurement and analysis in cosmos. In: The 23rd Asia-Pacific Network Operations and Management Symposium (APNOMS) (2022). https://doi.org/10.1109/APNOMS60508.2022.00231
13. Juels, A., Kosba, A., Shi, E.: The ring of gyges: investigating the future of criminal smart contracts. In: 2016 ACM SIGSAC Conference on Computer and Communications Security, pp. 283–295 (n.d.)
14. Huang, Y., Bian, Y., Li, R., Zhao, J.L., Shi, P.: Smart contract security: a software lifecycle perspective. IEEE Access. **7**, 150184–150202 (2019)
15. Caprolu, M., Di Pietro, R., Lombardi, F., Onofri, E.: Characterizing Polkadot's transactions ecosystem: methodology, tools, and insights. In: 2024 IEEE International Conference on Decentralized Applications and Infrastructures (DAPPS) (2024). https://doi.org/10.1109/DAPPS61106.2024.00016
16. Kalra, S., Goel, S., Dhawan, M., Sharma, S.: Zeus: analyzing safety of smart contracts. In: Ndss, pp. 1–12 (2018)
17. Jiang, B., Liu, Y., Chan, W.K.: Contractfuzzer: fuzzing smart contracts for vulnerability detection. In: 33rd ACM/IEEE International Conference on Automated Software Engineering, pp. 259–269 (2018)

18. Hu, K., Lei, L., Tsai, W.T.: Multi-tenant verification-as-a-service (VaaS) in a cloud. Simul. Model. Pract. Theory. **60**, 122–143 (2016)
19. King, S., Nadal, S.: Ppcoin: peer-to-peer crypto-currency with proof-of-stake. Self-Published Paper. **19**, 1 (2012)
20. Lashkari, B., Musilek, P.: A comprehensive review of blockchain consensus mechanisms. IEEE Access. **9**, 43620–43652 (2021)
21. Ibba, G.: A smart contracts repository for top trending contracts. In: 2022 IEEE/ACM 5th International Workshop on Emerging Trends in Software Engineering for Blockchain (WETSEB), pp. 17–20. IEEE (n.d.)
22. Idé, T.: Collaborative anomaly detection on blockchain from noisy sensor data. In: 2018 IEEE International Conference on Data Mining Workshops (ICDMW), pp. 120–127. IEEE (n.d.)
23. Mitrović, A., Vukmirović, S., Dalčeković, M., Nedić, N., Čapko, D.: Cross-chain general message passing protocol via eternal bridge. In: IEEE International Conference on Telecommunications Forum (TELFOR), Novi Sad, Serbia (2023). https://doi.org/10.1109/TELFOR2023.00032
24. Liu, H., et al.: S-gram: towards semantic-aware security auditing for ethereum smart contracts. In: 33rd ACM/IEEE International Conference on Automated Software Engineering, pp. 814–819 (2018)
25. Sengupta, A., Ranjan, R., Ghosh, A., Wang, L., Zomaya, A., Buyya, R.: DataHarbour: enabling decentralized AI data marketplace using blockchain. In: IEEE Transactions on Services Computing, Early Access (2023). https://doi.org/10.1109/TSC.2023.3256086
26. Kumar, N., Hossain, M.S., Jolfaei, A., Sangaiah, A.: Building resilient web 3.0 infrastructure with quantum information technologies and Blockchain: an ambilateral view. IEEE Internet Things J. **10**(2), 1082–1090 (2023). https://doi.org/10.1109/JIOT.2022.3224343
27. Kumar, V., Budhiraja, I., Jabbari, A., Garg, D., Singh, D., Mengani, N.: Efficient blockchain interoperability design for cross-chain transactions in future internet-of-value. Peer Peer Netw. Appl. **18**(110), 1–21 (2025). https://doi.org/10.1007/s12083-025-01941-w
28. Liu, Z., et al.: Combining graph neural networks with expert knowledge for smart contract vulnerability detection. IEEE Trans. Knowl. Data Eng. **35**(2), 1296–1310 (2021)
29. Shukla, M., Verma, A., Kumar, N., Sharma, S.K., Hossain, M.S.: Advanced eHealth with explainable AI secured by blockchain with AI-empowered block sensitivity for adaptive authentication. IEEE Trans. Industr. Inform. **19**(9), 9809–9817 (2023). https://doi.org/10.1109/TII.2022.3228264
30. Huang, J., Zhou, K., Xiong, A., Li, D.: Smart contract vulnerability detection model based on multi-task learning. Sensors. **22**(5), 1829 (2022)

Further Readings

Dwivedi, R., Singla, T., Shukla, S.: Cross-chain atomic swaps without time locks. In: 2023 Fifth International Conference on Blockchain Computing and Applications (BCCA) (2023). https://doi.org/10.1109/BCCA58897.2023.10338878

Frauenthaler, P., Sigwart, M., Spanring, C., Sober, M., Schulte, S.: ETH relay: a cost-efficient relay for Ethereum-based blockchains. In: IEEE International Conference on Blockchain, Vienna, Austria (2020). https://doi.org/10.1109/Blockchain50366.2020.00032

Han, J., Kim, J., Youn, A., Lee, J., Chun, Y., Woo, J., Hong, J.W.-K.: Cos-CBDC: design and implementation of CBDC on cosmos blockchain. In: IEEE International Conference on Blockchain (2024b). https://doi.org/10.1109/ICBCTIS64495.2024.00014

Hook, T.B., Brown, J.S., Breitwisch, M., Hoyniak, D., Mann, R.: High-performance logic and high-gain analog CMOS transistors formed by a shadow-mask technique with a single implant step. IEEE Trans. Electron Devices. **49**(9), 1623–1627 (2002)

Kotey, S.D., Tchao, E.T., Ahmed, A.-R., Agbemenu, A.S., Nunoo-Mensah, H., Sikora, A., Welte, D., Keelson, E.: Blockchain interoperability: the state of heterogenous Blockchain-to-

Blockchain communication. IET Commun. **17**(8), 891–914 (2023). https://doi.org/10.1049/cmu2.12594

Kolvart, M., Poola, M., Rull, A.: Smart contracts. In: The Future of Law and Etechnologies, pp. 133–147. Springer (2016)

Hsien-De Huang, T., Kao, H.Y.: R2-d2: color-inspired convolutional neural network (cnn)-based android malware detections. In: 2018 IEEE International Conference on Big Data (Big Data), pp. 2633–2642. IEEE (n.d.)

Li, Z., et al.: MuSC: a tool for mutation testing of ethereum smart contract. In: 34th IEEE/ACM International Conference on Automated Software Engineering, pp. 1198–1201. IEEE (2019)

Liao, Z., et al.: Large-scale empirical study of inline assembly on 7.6 million ethereum smart contracts. IEEE Trans. Softw. Eng. **49**(2), 777–801 (2022)

Liao, J.W., et al.: Soliaudit: smart contract vulnerability assessment based on machine learning and fuzz testing. In: 6th International Conference on Internet of Things: Systems, Management and Security (IOTSMS), pp. 458–465. IEEE (2019)

Lin, S.Y., et al.: A survey of application research based on blockchain smart contract. Wirel. Netw. **28**(2), 635–690 (2022)

Lisi, A., Lopardo, N., Tortola, D., Mori, P., Ricci, L., Severino, F.: A cross-chain rating system: bridging EVM-based blockchains with Chainbridge. In: 2023 International Conference on Omni-Layer Intelligent Systems (COINS) (2023). https://doi.org/10.1109/COINS57856.2023.10189274

Liu, L., et al.: Blockchain-enabled fraud discovery through abnormal smart contract detection on Ethereum. Futur. Gener. Comput. Syst. **128**, 158–166 (2022)

Lys, L., Micoulet, A., Potop-Butucaru, M.: Atomic swapping bitcoins and ethers. In: IEEE International Conference on Blockchain, Paris, France (2024)

Rao, I.S., Kiah, M.L.M., Hameed, M.M., Memon, Z.A.: Scalability of blockchain: a comprehensive review and future research direction. Clust. Comput. **27**, 5547–5570 (2024). https://doi.org/10.1007/s10586-023-04257-7

Sizan, N.S., Dey, D., Layek, M.A., Uddin, M.A., Huh, E.-N.: Evaluating blockchain platforms for IoT applications in industry 5.0: a comprehensive review. Blockchain Res. Appl. **100276** (2025). https://doi.org/10.1016/j.bcra.2025.100276

Sönmez, F.Ö., Knottenbelt, W.J.: Cross-chain notification and awareness management. In: IEEE International Conference on Blockchain, London, UK, pp. 420–430 (2024). https://doi.org/10.1109/Blockchain62396.2024.00062

Subhashini, P., Alekhya, J., Rana, A., Lakhanpal, S., Veeresh, G., Al-Allak, M.A.: Navigating Web3 evolution with blockchain's role in shaping next generation internet semantics. In: IEEE International Conference on Communication, Computer Sciences and Engineering (IC3SE), Hyderabad, India (2024). https://doi.org/10.1109/IC3SE62002.2024.10593138

Vijayalakshmi, C., Florence, S.M.: Flameshift protocol: revolutionizing interoperability with dynamic asset recycling for cross-chain communications. SN Comput. Sci. **5**, 773 (2024). https://doi.org/10.1007/s42979-024-03116-5

Wang, Y., Yan, Y., Liu, X., Gao, W., Wang, Z.: A technique for ensured cross chain IBC transactions using TPM. In: IEEE International Conference on Big Data and Privacy Computing (BDPC), Xi'an, China (2024). https://doi.org/10.1109/BDPC59998.2024.10649356

Chapter 3
Role of Regulatories

Contents

3.1	Introduction		66
	3.1.1	Need for Regulation	67
	3.1.2	Innovation and Jurisdiction Conflict	68
3.2	Industry Regulations		69
	3.2.1	Finance	70
	3.2.2	Supply Chain	70
	3.2.3	Banking	71
3.3	Compliance		71
	3.3.1	AML/KYC in Interoperable Apps	72
	3.3.2	Data Sovereignty	73
	3.3.3	Token Classification	73
	3.3.4	Legal Gray Zones	74
	3.3.5	Regulatory Sandboxes	74
	3.3.6	International Collaboration	74
3.4	Jurisdictional Gaps		75
	3.4.1	Bridge Liability	76
	3.4.2	DAO Accountability	77
	3.4.3	Smart Contract Enforcement across Borders	77
	3.4.4	Legal Wrappers	78
	3.4.5	Dispute Resolution	78
	3.4.6	Regulatory Oversight	79
3.5	Governance		79
	3.5.1	Role of DAOs	80
	3.5.2	Meta-Governance	81
	3.5.3	Sybil Resistance	81
	3.5.4	Vote Hijacking	82
	3.5.5	Decentralized Risk Controls	82
3.6	RegTech		83
	3.6.1	AI-Driven Compliance Monitoring	83
	3.6.2	Verifiable Credentials	84
	3.6.3	DID-Based Onboarding	84
	3.6.4	ZKPs for Privacy-Compliance Disclosures	85
	3.6.5	Smart Legal Contracts	85

© The Author(s), under exclusive license to Springer Nature
Switzerland AG 2025
P. Sarang, L. Nadkar, *Blockchain Without Barriers*, SpringerBriefs in Computer
Science, https://doi.org/10.1007/978-3-032-03413-7_3

3.6.6 Regulatory Oracles	85
3.7 Summary	86
References	86

Abstract In this chapter, we look at the relationship between blockchain interoperability and regulatory frameworks in an increasingly decentralized digital world. It depicts the constant battle between technical advancement and the power of jurisdiction, beginning with the fundamental demand for regulation in interchain networks. This chapter assesses the impact of industry-specific laws in banking, supply chains, and finance, focusing on compliance issues such as data sovereignty, AML/KYC, and token classification.

The chapter addresses novel methods such as regulatory sandboxes, international collaboration, and legal wrappers, thereby clarifying legal uncertainties and jurisdictional gaps in smart contract enforcement. The topic focuses on governance models, specifically responsibility for DAOs and bridge operators, as well as metagovernance challenges such as vote hijacking and Sybil attacks.

This chapter finishes with an introduction to the emerging domain of RegTech, which encompasses decentralized identity onboarding, AI-powered compliance, and the use of verifiable credentials and zero-knowledge proofs (ZKPs) for privacy-protecting disclosures. The use of smart legal contracts and regulatory oracles as programmable enforcement instruments is also discussed. Overall, this chapter gives a detailed path for combining cross-chain innovation with institutional and regulatory requirements.

Keywords Blockchain regulation · Cross-chain compliance · DAO accountability · Regulatory sandbox · International legal frameworks · RegTech · Decentralized governance · Smart legal contracts · Regulatory oracles · Meta-governance · Zero-knowledge proofs

3.1 Introduction

In previous chapters, we explored how blockchain interoperability is transforming our digital ecosystem from isolated, centralized systems to a decentralized, interconnected reality. This emerging sector is already influencing numerous verticals, including banking, logistics, governance, and identity. This shift raises a significant question: Does decentralization necessitate modifications of our current regulatory framework? Is it possible for decentralization to comply with existing regulations? The legal frameworks, regulatory requirements, and jurisdictional borders that define today's centralized society are becoming increasingly fragile, as blockchain networks grow more global and begin operating outside conventional trust and enforcement mechanisms.

This chapter looks at scenarios where interoperability is revolutionizing sectors such as finance, supply chains, and digital identity, while regulators are lagging behind in addressing the swift advancements, especially concerning compliance, cross-border data governance, and legal accountability for decentralized protocols. We will talk about the regulatory and governance gaps that must be addressed as well as the technological limitations that make the shift to decentralization inevitable. In a multi-chain economy, how can regulators adapt to preserve financial integrity, consumer protection, and security? What policy-driven or technical tools are being proposed to strike a balance between innovation and compliance?

3.1.1 Need for Regulation

Blockchains, as a decentralized and globally distributed ledger system, are neither constrained by geographical locations nor regulated by any single authority. A significant regulatory concern emerges when interoperability facilitates communication among various chains. Decentralized transaction processing reduces the effectiveness of territorially based national legal standards [1]. Enforcing financial laws was the responsibility of banks, custodians, and central exchanges under the old system. These entities provide checkpoints for Know-Your-Customer/Anti-Money Laundering compliance, transaction monitoring, and asset classification. Regulatory arbitrage and illegitimate financial transfers may present challenges in a cross-chain system, as value can migrate from a compliant chain to a permissionless one through bridges or relays without compliance checks [2].

Furthermore, several countries have differing terminology when referring to tokens and smart contracts. A coin's classification as a security or commodity in one nation may vary from its classification as a utility asset in another. The absence of legal recognition for smart contracts generated and maintained in a cross-chain scenario by DAOs or decentralized entities makes them unenforceable in instances of disputes or failures. [3].

Who is liable when an interoperable system fails in the absence of a definite legal agreement or a recognized legal entity? In the occurrence of a bridge exploit or a failure of a multi-chain protocol, it is probable that no one can be held liable. This is particularly true when these systems are managed by anonymous DAOs, leading to jurisdictional ambiguity for regulators and judges [4]. We must revise our regulations for this purpose. Composable DeFi platforms, decentralized identities, and programmable money are products of cross-chain technologies; therefore, the legal frameworks overseeing these developments must likewise adapt to be dynamic, flexible, and composable. Legal initiatives in the UK [5], Singapore [6], and the UAE [7] established regulatory sandboxes; [8] has formulated standards for blockchain governance; and Decentralized Identifiers (DIDs) [9] have implemented privacy-preserving Know-Your-Customer (KYC) protocols [10].

Interoperability allows for swift innovation; but traditional legal systems have been reluctant to evolve due to jurisdictional apprehensions. The next section examines the conflict between innovation and jurisdiction.

3.1.2 Innovation and Jurisdiction Conflict

The remarkable pace of advancement in blockchain interoperability is driven by decentralized communities, open-source innovation, and composable protocol stacks. However, this occurs in direct contradiction to the established jurisdictional frameworks of common law. In an ideal scenario, individuals would adhere to the laws within their respective regions, trust centralized intermediaries, and have their disputes resolved by authoritative institutions. On the contrary, traditional regulatory frameworks are not ideal for interoperable blockchain networks due to their decentralized, borderless, and pseudonymous nature [1].

A considerable regulatory backlog has emerged due to this gap, as lawmakers are unable to keep pace with innovations emerging across supply chains. Using DeFi enables the elimination of regulatory intermediaries, permitting the borrowing of funds on one blockchain and repayment on another. The challenges of investor protection, tax law enforcement, and asset flow monitoring worsen as a result [11]. Issues emerge when regulated gateways are completely bypassed, leading to financial transactions being executed through bridges or cross-chain smart contracts. In such scenarios, AML/KYC enforcement becomes significantly more difficult due to the absence of centralized exchanges or custodial intermediaries [2]. The Financial Action Task Force (FATF) [12] has opted to broaden its criteria to include Virtual Asset Service Providers (VASPs) [12] that enable cross-chain transactions, irrespective of their decentralized or non-custodial nature.

Furthermore, there is currently no international standard for the classification of tokens. Certain nations perceive a token as a utility, while others classify it as a security. For cross-chain protocols and their developers, this has unanticipated legal ramifications [3]. A cross-chain smart contract, especially one regulated by a decentralized autonomous organization (DAO), is unlikely to be a legally binding contract or to be attributed to any one jurisdiction. In these situations, legal responsibility is not always obvious [13]. Despite its empowering attributes, the DAO's decentralized governance model complicates the enforcement of jurisdiction. Who would be liable for user damages if a DAO ran a bridge that was compromised or failed? Victims often find themselves uncertain concerning legal recourse [4] as most DAOs are not recognized as registered legal bodies. Debate exists on the allocation of responsibility amidst this legal ambiguity as well as the regulation of DAO treasuries and the potential liability of open-source developers for protocol exploits. The variations in governmental responses and enforcement strategies intensify the issues. There is considerable discussion over the governance of immutable, permissionless smart contracts following the US Treasury's classification of Tornado Cash as a privacy-enhancing mixer contract [2].

Bridging this gap will require future regulations that are technologically proficient, flexible, and capable of integrating with decentralized infrastructure while maintaining security, compliance, and trust. Without change, regulatory ambiguity could lead to limiting innovation, discouraging acceptable development, and pushing development into unregulated, dark pools.

3.2 Industry Regulations

Now, let us look at industry regulation for the industries where these changes and conflicts are already noticeable.

3.2 Industry Regulations

At the moment, blockchain interoperability is enabling decentralized systems to replace traditional centralized ones, resulting in significant changes across numerous industries. Decentralization and interoperability have been adopted, but businesses are finding it increasingly difficult to adapt since they can't get beyond the existing regulatory frameworks. As interoperability increases, so does the need for adaptable, cross-border regimes that can guarantee financial stability, consumer protection, and legal compliance across interdependent networks.

Figure 3.1 shows the evolution of the regulatory landscape across industries due to increasing interoperability. In addition to their technical and commercial dimensions, these innovations have significant implications for governance, requiring the establishment of innovative legal frameworks, compliance standards, and monitoring mechanisms to facilitate decentralized operations and the interchain transfer of assets. In the absence of innovative regulation, legal ambiguity and systemic risk may simultaneously jeopardize the potential for interoperability.

The subsequent sections examine three significant industries undergoing regulatory changes or trials: finance, supply chain, and banking.

Layers			
1	**Blockchain Interoperability** Central Enabler		
2	**Industries Transformed**		
	Finance Sector (DeFi) Multi-chain, DEXes, Liquidity	**Supply Chain & Logistics** Asset tracking, Anti-counterfeit	**Banking & Business Systems** CBDCs, Remittance, Programmable Money
3	**Governance and Regulatory Evolution** Compliance frameworks, Cross-border regulations, Decentralized governance models (DAOs)		
4	**Outcomes** Global Decentralized Transformation		

Fig. 3.1 Decentralized transitions and regulatory impacts across key industries

3.2.1 Finance

The finance industry is expecting an immediate and potentially significant impact. Modern Decentralized Financial (DeFi) services rely on multi-chain financial systems enabled by blockchain interoperability. Decentralized Exchanges (DEX) facilitate lending, borrowing, and liquidity aggregation across numerous chains through cross-chain connectivity. Therefore, capital efficiency has increased, gaps have diminished, and liquidity may be observed between networks such as Polkadot, Binance Smart Chain, and Ethereum [14].

Regulatory scrutiny has increased with the emergence of decentralized and tokenized asset transfer systems such as Chainlink CCIP [15], ThorChain [16], and Cosmos IBC [16]. Smart contract frameworks have made it possible for smart contracts to function across networks, which has expanded the market and allowed for the development of innovative financial products [17].

Despite enhancing market efficiency and reducing operating expenses, this decentralized innovation challenges established financial regulation. Given that these networks operate decentralized and without middlemen, regulators must reevaluate their approaches to risk assessment, anti-money laundering promises, and know-your-customer protocols [17]. Certain nations are exploring regulatory sandboxes, while others are implementing new global compliance regulations to govern the global adoption of DeFi tools.

3.2.2 Supply Chain

In supply chain and logistics, multi-chain interoperability systems are used to solve crucial problems including vendor accountability, data silos, and counterfeiting prevention. In supply chain and logistics, multi-chain interoperability technologies address critical challenges such as vendor accountability, data silos, and counterfeiting prevention. These systems enable secure and verifiable asset tracking, thereby improving transparency and efficiency in global trade. Privacy-preserving smart contracts and multi-channel access control are additional methods to improve data security in blockchain-based tracking systems [18].

These developing technologies are giving rise to regulatory concerns about data privacy, cross-border documentation, and compliance with trade standards. Regulators are drafting standards for e-BL [19], blockchain traceability, and digital customs to match the growing digitization of logistics [18].

3.2.3 Banking

Real-time remittance solutions, interoperable Central Bank Digital Currencies (CBDCs), and programmable money are a few instances of how interoperability is causing a paradigm shift in the banking industry. Blockchain-native infrastructures are being used in initiatives like Cos-CBDC (Cosmos CDBC) [20] and Hyperledger Fabric-based CBDC bridges [21] to enable final settlement and cross-border value exchange while adhering to regulatory standards [22].

These developments represent an enormous shift in the interoperability revolution; regulators are now actively driving integration strategies and compliance laws rather than being passive onlookers. The Financial Stability Board's [23] report [24] on the regulation, supervision, and oversight of crypto-asset markets set supervisory standards for digital assets, and the Bank for International Settlements' July 2022 report [23] on access and interoperability of CBDCs described interoperability frameworks for cross-border CBDCs.

When considered collectively, these stories show how regulatory constraints have made interoperability a need rather than a technological issue. The new approaches that attempt to solve the governance and compliance issues brought on by these industry-wide linkages are examined in the sections that follow.

We will first take a look at the compliance aspects of interoperability, specifically at how decentralized, cross-chain ecosystems are reshaping AML/KYC enforcement, data sovereignty, token classification, and international coordination.

3.3 Compliance

With the aid of bridges, relayers, and cross-chain message protocols, blockchain ecosystems are starting to take shape, posing a threat to the fundamentals of regulatory compliance. Interoperable blockchain designs decentralize transactions, remove identifiable intermediaries, and automate tasks using smart contracts, in contrast to traditional systems that rely on centralized institutions such as banks, custodians, and government-regulated exchanges to maintain compliance. A reassessment of decentralized methodologies to guarantee compliance, security, and legal accountability is essential given this evolving ecosystem.

As shown in Fig. 3.2, compliance in interoperable blockchain networks is challenging. AML/KYC, data sovereignty, token classification, and legal gray zones are important regulatory dimensions. Due to the interrelated nature of these elements, robust, cross-jurisdictional governance solutions that can adapt to decentralized, multi-chain architecture are required.

Fig. 3.2 Compliance for blockchain interoperability

3.3.1 AML/KYC in Interoperable Apps

The implementation of Know-Your-Customer (KYC) and Anti-Money Laundering (AML) regulations in a cross-chain, permissionless environment is one of the most critical regulatory challenges. These standards are met in the institutional financial industry by implementing identity requirements at onboarding nodes, like banks or exchanges. Nonetheless, with interoperable DeFi systems, a user can execute a transaction on one blockchain (Ethereum), transfer it through a bridge, and then obtain an asset on another blockchain (Avalanche) without engaging with a regulated intermediary or disclosing the self-identity.

AML/KYC enforcement across chains is almost impossible due to user anonymity. The Financial Action Task Force (FATF) has sought to tackle this issue by expanding the definition of Virtual Asset Service Providers (VASPs) to encompass cross-chain service providers, irrespective of their decentralization status. Enforcement is nonetheless challenging because this kind of formal registration is often lacking when these services are provided by decentralized autonomous organizations (DAOs) and smart contracts.

Ecosystems with weak compliance enforcement are susceptible to regulatory arbitrage, illegal financial activity, and the transfer of funds into unidentified entities. Therefore, researchers are examining regulatory-compliant bridge protocols and decentralized identity systems to integrate KYC layers while maintaining decentralization.

3.3.2 Data Sovereignty

The frequent cross-border transfers of data and digital assets made possible by cross-chain systems give rise to legitimate concerns over data sovereignty and user privacy. According to traditional regulatory norms, such as the European Union's General Data Protection Regulation (GDPR), personal data must be processed and maintained within predetermined geographic boundaries and in accordance with strict confidentiality requirements.

When user metadata, transaction history, or identity verifications are sent across multiple chains, each of which may be subject to various regulatory regulations, it becomes very difficult, if not impossible, to identify the location or ownership of the data. This may lead to scenarios where interoperable applications could unintentionally violate data localization regulations [1].

Companies are therefore developing privacy-enhancing technologies such as zero-knowledge proofs (ZKPs) and anonymous verified credentials [25]. By employing these capabilities, users can verify regulatory compliance without disclosing personal information, allowing applications to achieve both sovereignty and privacy objectives concurrently [25].

3.3.3 Token Classification

The laws governing the use of a single token in an interoperable environment can vary from one state to another. Some jurisdictions may view a token that is classified as a utility token on Ethereum as an uncontrolled asset, a security under US law, or a form of currency under EU law. The transfer of tokens across chains with differing legal definitions exposes developers and consumers to legal concerns stemming from these classification differences [3].

The fact that these tokens can be exchanged and moved between parties only adds complexity to things. The possibility of security tokens, governance tokens, and wrapped assets experiencing regulatory identity alterations during transfers prompts apprehensions over custody, taxation, and legal investor protection. In the absence of appropriate regulatory frameworks, these disparities may result in enforcement proceedings or noncompliance, regardless of the absence of malevolent intent.

Although frameworks such as the Token Taxonomy Framework (TTF) [26] strive to offer uniform classifications and descriptions, they have not garnered widespread support across many jurisdictions.

3.3.4 Legal Gray Zones

Decentralized autonomous organizations (DAOs) are another complex issue. Numerous interoperability protocols are governed by DAOs or open-source developer entities that do not possess formal incorporation or centralized supervision. In the occurrence of a protocol failure, bridge hack, or user loss, the legal obligations of several parties become ambiguous [13].

If a user loses money because of a DAO's untrustworthy cross-chain bridge, who is legally liable? It is difficult to settle a smart contract or an opaque coalition of token holders using traditional contract law.

One of the few jurisdictions which has given DAOs legal wrappers (like DAO LLCs) formal legal standing and restricted liability is Wyoming (USA) [27]. The majority of DAOs are now functioning without a formal incorporation and without clarification regarding their legal status, despite this promising development [4]. Legal risk becomes increasingly evident with the increased use of interoperability protocols in the lack of clear governance frameworks or mechanisms for dispute resolution.

3.3.5 Regulatory Sandboxes

Several regulatory agencies have set up regulatory sandboxes to address these rapid advancements. These are regulated environments where blockchain-based financial goods, including cross-chain services, can be evaluated under the supervision of regulators.

Regulatory sandboxes for interoperable finance have been established by nations such as Singapore, the United Kingdom, and the United Arab Emirates. These sandboxes allow developers to test technologies such as automated smart contracts, cross-border asset transfers, and compliance procedures in a non-production environment [1].

These sandboxes can help regulators and innovators alike. The former can better understand new technologies before enforcing strict regulations, while the latter can collaborate with legislators to develop norms. Nonetheless, they remain limited in scope and inconsistent between jurisdictions, resulting in a fragmented array of experimental laws rather than uniform industry standards.

3.3.6 International Collaboration

International collaboration is necessary to achieve genuine standardization in interoperable blockchain networks. Because cross-chain networks span boundaries, regulation based on the laws of a single nation is inadequate. Various institutions have begun working on frameworks for blockchain governance, smart contract interoperability, and decentralized identity, notably the International Organization for Standardization (ISO) through ISO/TC 307 [10].

The Financial Action Task Force (FATF) [12], the Organization for Economic Cooperation and Development (OECD) [28], and the International Monetary Fund (IMF) [29] are among the supranational policy initiatives that are now concentrating on regulating digital assets across borders. Harmonizing travel rules, regulatory passporting, and around the globe KYC registries are some of the ideas being examined [30] to make compliance operations across jurisdictions easier to coordinate.

In spite of this, global regulatory convergence is still a distant objective. Lack of it would hinder the development of interoperable blockchain technologies since developers and customers would have to deal with a patchwork of outdated, conflicting, and increasingly disruptive rules.

Ensuring compliance inside interoperable blockchain systems is therefore the biggest issue for global regulatory frameworks. While technological improvements facilitate cross-border transfers and decentralized coordination, they simultaneously compromise traditional legal foundations, including accountability, jurisdiction, and identification. Patches are available through solutions such as DIDs, legal wrappers, privacy-preserving compliance proofs, and sandbox environments; however, the development of a cohesive, interoperable global regulatory platform is still in development. The future of blockchain compliance should focus on creating programmable, adaptive, and standards-based governance frameworks to ensure decentralized, cross-chain functionality rather than enforcing centralization.

Legal complexities, particularly those related to jurisdiction, liability, and enforcement, persist as challenges for compliance frameworks attempting to adapt to decentralized technologies. Next, we explore these jurisdictional gaps by analyzing how cross-chain systems complicate conventional ideas of decentralized governance accountability, contract enforceability, and legal jurisdiction.

3.4 Jurisdictional Gaps

Even when there are concerted efforts to decentralize compliance processes, interoperability concerns present more complex legal issues than the mere existence of regulatory gaps. When the idea of legal personhood is ambiguous or nonexistent, issues with jurisdiction, contract enforceability, responsibility attribution, and accountability for governance occur. As blockchain applications get increasingly multi-chain and autonomous, these risks are becoming more pertinent to real users, developers, and organizations.

The legal risk associated with blockchain has its foundation in a fundamental issue: the absence of an appropriate territorial jurisdiction for blockchain systems that are incompatible with one another. In the case of a failure or dispute, it is unclear which national legal system would be applicable when a smart contract operates across many blockchains, each governed by its own legal framework. For

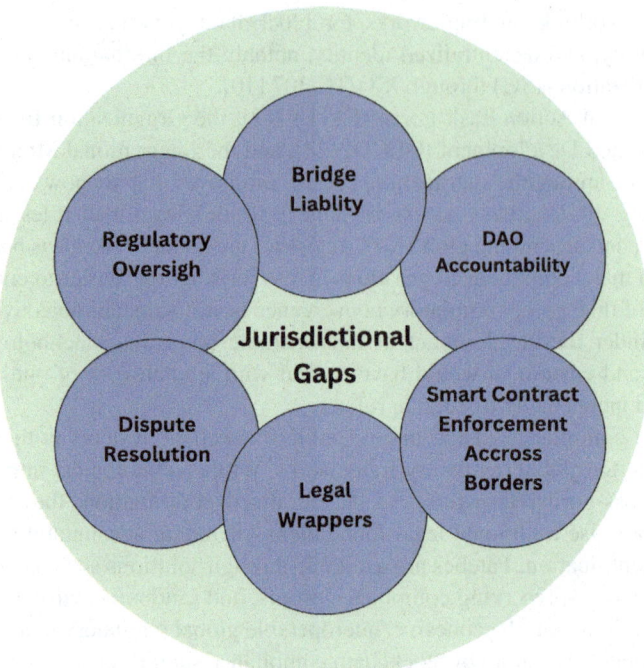

Fig. 3.3 Jurisdictional gaps for blockchain interoperability

example, legal exposure across multiple domains can arise by creating a DeFi loan on Ethereum, collateralizing it on Avalanche, and subsequently settling it over a bridge on Cosmos [1].

In contrast to traditional systems where each actor has a physical residence and every transaction is governed by a specific set of regulations, decentralized and pseudonymous entities might not necessarily have a traceable relationship. This complicates the ability of courts and regulators to assert their power, leaving consumers with limited options for assistance when dissatisfied [11].

Figure 3.3 illustrates the fundamental legal ambiguities that emerge in interoperable blockchain systems, categorized under the concept of jurisdictional gaps. It brings focus to significant topics including cross-border enforcement, legal wrappers, bridge liability, and DAO accountability, emphasizing the urgent requirement for legal frameworks that can manage decentralized and multi-chain operations.

3.4.1 Bridge Liability

Bridges are at the forefront of interoperability, enabling chains to exchange state data, messages, and assets. Furthermore, these attack surfaces are critical since, in the last 3 years, exploits have caused losses totaling billions of dollars [15]. Whether a cross-chain bridge is broken due to validator collusion, signature fraud, or oracle failure, who bears the cost?

The entity that is hidden behind the bridge is usually not the one that is formally registered. A decentralized autonomous organization (DAO), token holders, or anonymous contributors may operate the application. Victims of bridge hacks have little legal recourse because of lack of jurisdiction [13].

Even if a centralized organization or foundation can be identified, they may still refuse to take responsibility because the system is decentralized. The fact that smart contract errors or misconfigurations would not be considered negligence in situations where there is no explicit agreement between the developer and the user further increases the ambiguity in this area of the law.

3.4.2 DAO Accountability

The de-facto governance layer of DAOs is present in many interoperable systems, such as bridges, DEXs, and cross-chain liquidity networks. However, based on current architectures, the majority of decentralized autonomous organizations (DAOs) do not have the legal personhood to be sued, taxed, or held accountable. This brings up more legal concerns [4].

A regulatory conundrum results from this. On one side, DAOs have enormous power in terms of managing treasury funds, choosing validators, and improving the protocol. Conversely, they operate as decentralized, anonymous collectives, wherein victims of exploits governed by DAOs have no direct accuser and lack legal recourse.

As a solution to this, we will discuss DAO legal wrappers shortly. Currently, there exists significant systemic risk stemming from the absence of a legal framework for DAOs, especially in cross-chain contexts with varied user funds.

3.4.3 Smart Contract Enforcement across Borders

The globally autonomous fulfillment of smart contracts adds another level of complexity to the legalities. Smart contracts are distinct from traditional contracts [31] in that they generally do not necessitate the signatures of both parties, do not conform to established legal definitions, and fail to undergo judicial scrutiny prior to execution. They can also function in cross-chain environments between nations with regulations that conflict with digital contracts, financial services, or data processing.

Imagine that a smart contract on Chain A misinterprets an event on Chain B, causing a cross-chain escrow arrangement to fail. What legal framework governs the output? In what situations can a court enforce this agreement? In legal terminology, is a smart contract classified as a contract of any nature?

The answer differs significantly from one jurisdiction to another. There is currently no precedent in most modern courts regarding autonomous, irrevocable, cross-chain smart contracts. Legal ambiguity heightens the probability of unenforceable contracts, unacknowledged claims, and recoverable losses for users [32, 33].

3.4.4 Legal Wrappers

A number of initiatives are exploring the usage of legal wrappers, which are formal legal organizations that "wrap" a decentralized autonomous organization (DAO) or protocol to enhance tax compliance, enforceability, and legal resilience in order to reduce these risks. For instance, DAOs with smart contract-based agreements for operation [4] are able to lawfully register as limited liability businesses (LLCs) in Wyoming [27].

In order to legally represent dispersed entities, foundation models or special purpose corporations are being tested in several jurisdictions. These comprise Singapore [34], Switzerland [35], and several states in the United States of America [36]. These valid frameworks enable DAOs to:

- Finalize legal contracts
- Execute tax remittances
- Limit the individual liability of contributors

These models are not flawless. According to some, the decentralization ideal is too strongly opposed to the additional centralization that legal wrappers offer. Legal registration does not address the problem of cross-chain enforcement of DAO resolutions.

3.4.5 Dispute Resolution

In cross-chain systems, there are issues unique to disputes. Financial losses may arise from deficiencies in smart contracts, governance weaknesses, bridge failures, or oracle attacks, and victims may lack avenues for legal recourse. Judicial litigation is inadequate to address problems in decentralized systems due to its inefficiency, high expenses, and geographical constraints.

Decentralized arbitration technologies are meeting this demand. The Kleros [37] and Aragon [38] Court systems employ game theory and token-weighted juries to facilitate decision-making in decentralized environments. These mechanisms are largely unacknowledged by national legal frameworks, and their decisions lack significant authority in enforced judicial proceedings.

Alternatively, one may utilize smart legal contracts, which integrate mutually executable code with off-chain provisions that can be upheld in a court of law. The enforceability of hybrid contracts remains controversial in many jurisdictions, despite their promise to enhance transparency and facilitate dispute resolution in both on-chain and off-chain scenario [32, 33].

3.4.6 Regulatory Oversight

Governments and regulators are taking the lead in negotiating interoperability agreements. Several authorities are trying to mitigate systemic risk linked to bridges [2] by implementing legislation concerning audits, AML/KYC standards for relayer services and custody. Whether DAOs and bridge operators are considered money transmitters, VASPs [12], or financial intermediaries is still up for debate among some organizations [12]. The FATF [12] and the SEC [39] are among the entities evaluating this matter.

Since the majority of cross-chain operations are anonymous or globally dispersed and frequently lack official incorporation or explicit regulatory permission, it might be challenging to stop regulators from claiming authority. Regulators are progressively becoming aware and advocating for:

- Analyzing protocols across various blockchains
- Disclosures of user risk
- The procedure for token registration
- Guarantee of treasury management

The lack of anticipatory legal adaptation makes it possible for regulators to overreach or become ineffective as a result of restrictions on specific activity. We might be able to reach a compromise by developing interoperable regulatory frameworks in collaboration with the blockchain community and international organizations.

Legislative and jurisdictional challenges are making the use of centralized control in distributed systems increasingly challenging. DAOs are the most well-known governance mechanism that is being developed to address this issue. The following section explores the approaches by which decentralized administration (DAO), meta-governance (MG), sybil resistance (SR), and cross-chain risk management have been modified to address interoperability.

3.5 Governance

The scope and complexity of decentralized systems are increasing, making centralized governance models inadequate. For decentralized coordination, trustless execution, and resistance to manipulation, cross-chain ecosystem governance needs to

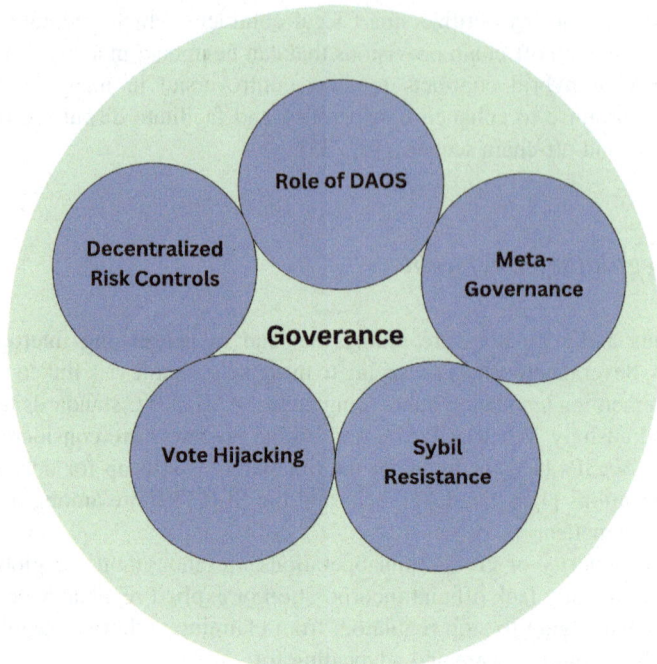

Fig. 3.4 Governance for blockchain interoperability

develop. In this context, DAOs have shown to be the principal entity accountable for administering protocols, executing updates, and enforcing regulations across chains. Nonetheless, this new paradigm introduces governance challenges, including Sybil attacks, vote hijacking, and a lack of frameworks that mitigate risks.

Figure 3.4 illustrates the solutions for cross-chain governance. Mentioned are: decentralized autonomous organizations (DAOs), DAO meta-governance coordination, safeguards against vote hijacking, sybil resistance techniques, and risk control frameworks incorporated into the governance layer.

3.5.1 Role of DAOs

Among the numerous elements of multi-chain ecosystems run by decentralized autonomous organizations (DAOs) are bridge protocols and liquidity distribution. Through their on-chain governance mechanisms, DAOs facilitate community-driven cooperation on networks like Polkadot and Cosmos, which are facilitated by the Interchain Foundation. Furthermore, protocols such as Uniswap and Aave [16] employ DAO frameworks to implement token-weighted voting and treasury-supported smart contracts.

In cross-chain settings, DAOs handle security flaws, modify fees, apply protocol modifications, and maintain validator sets. Bridge contracts are temporarily suspended during exploitation as a result of a collaborative effort that involves DAOs. Many DAOs operate anonymously and lack formal legal recognition, which raises questions about legal accountability, and the irrevocability of decisions.

3.5.2 Meta-Governance

Meta-governance is now crucial as DAOs spread throughout ecosystems. A DAO on Chain A can utilize meta-governance mechanisms to transfer decisions regarding liquidity sharing, fee structures, and bridge improvements to Chain B. In a decentralized autonomous organization (DAO) governing a multi-chain protocol, token holders may vote on decisions affecting subnetworks for which they lack direct authority.

Meta-governance delegation, a mechanism where DAOs pool their voting power to influence protocol-wide decisions, is being experimented with by several protocols. These encompass Curve [40], Balancer [41], and Yearn [42]. The risk of governance centralization emerges when substantial DAOs start to control the outcome of cross-chain votes [43].

Despite providing off-chain or hybrid solutions, meta-governance systems like Tally [44] and Snapshot [45] depend on centralized data feeds or scripts, thereby compromising trust assumptions.

3.5.3 Sybil Resistance

In open, token-governed systems, Sybil resistance is the foundation of good governance. Malicious individuals can acquire numerous addresses or identities without facing Sybil resistance and exploit them to manipulate governmental decisions. In cross-chain scenarios, when DAO proposals may impact assets or bridges on other chains, this becomes much riskier.

As a countermeasure, DAOs are testing Decentralized Identifier (DID)-based voting, Proof-of-Humanity protocols, and reputation systems [37]. These systems seek to link voting power to authenticated, non-falsifiable identities while maintaining anonymity using zero-knowledge proofs [10].

Sybil-proof identity models, which meet FATF's VASP standards, are becoming DAO-compatible KYC systems that assist ensure jurisdictional compliance without compromising user privacy [9].

3.5.4 Vote Hijacking

In vote hijacking, an attacker or significant token holder temporarily acquires governance tokens during pivotal proposal windows and utilizes flash loans to manipulate the voting outcome. This may result in catastrophic outcomes in cross-chain protocols when proposals influence the distribution of assets, protocol parameters, or validator configurations.

Vote-locking DAOs are one way to prevent flash loan hijacks by locking tokens prior to the voting process getting started. Others employ quorum limits, snapshot validation, or postponing voting to guarantee authenticity [15].

Capitalism is still a major issue with DAOs, since token ownership is directly correlated with voting power. Concerns about inclusion and the use of multi-class governance tokens, delegated staking, or quadratic voting are philosophical issues with cross-chain protocols [43].

3.5.5 Decentralized Risk Controls

Risk controls are mainly implemented by DAOs in systems that oversee liquidity pools, wrapped assets, or cross-chain bridges. Examples of risk controls include real-time risk dashboards, automatic circuit breakers, insurance reserves, and penalties for failed validators. One option involves DAOs allocating funds to reimburse users in the event of smart contract failure or bridge exploitation; this is referred to as on-chain governance for treasury distribution. Nexus Mutual [46] is one of several decentralized insurance schemes that employs token weights to determine who gets the insurance claim.

DAO-controlled cross-chain bridges employ threshold cryptography, time-delayed upgrades, or multi-sig security councils to prevent rollback vulnerabilities and governance takeovers. Effective risk management in DAO-governed models necessitates not only technical tools but also active engagement. Voter apathy, inadequate participation, and governance fatigue afflict even the most sophisticated DAOs, rendering this a persistent challenge [4].

The field of Regulatory Technology (RegTech) is experiencing a related evolution as decentralized governance systems and DAOs mature to the point where they can handle interoperability. RegTech is developing solutions, such as AI-powered compliance software, verifiable credentials, and privacy-enhanced identity management systems, to help decentralized ecosystems comply with real regulatory requirements.

In the next section we will address the role of RegTech in transforming compliance within blockchain-based infrastructure.

3.6 RegTech

As interoperable blockchain ecosystems disrupt established regulatory patterns, a new class of technology-based compliance solutions known as regulatory technology, or RegTech, is emerging to solve accountability, identification, and compliance challenges in decentralized contexts. RegTech for blockchain seeks to fundamentally transform compliance by directly integrating intelligence, privacy, and automation into on-chain systems, surpassing mere digitization of documentation.

Figure 3.5 illustrates the six primary components of blockchain RegTech: Regulatory Oracles, Zero-knowledge Proofs, Legal Smart Contracts, Validated Credentials, Onboarding Decentralized Identifiers (DID), and AI-driven Compliance Monitoring. When combined, these resources enable decentralized blockchain systems that are nonetheless aware of legal requirements.

3.6.1 AI-Driven Compliance Monitoring

Artificial intelligence (AI) is becoming more and more important in decentralized networks for real-time anomaly identification, risk grading of transactions, and policy enforcement. By monitoring wallet and bridge activity, AI agents can

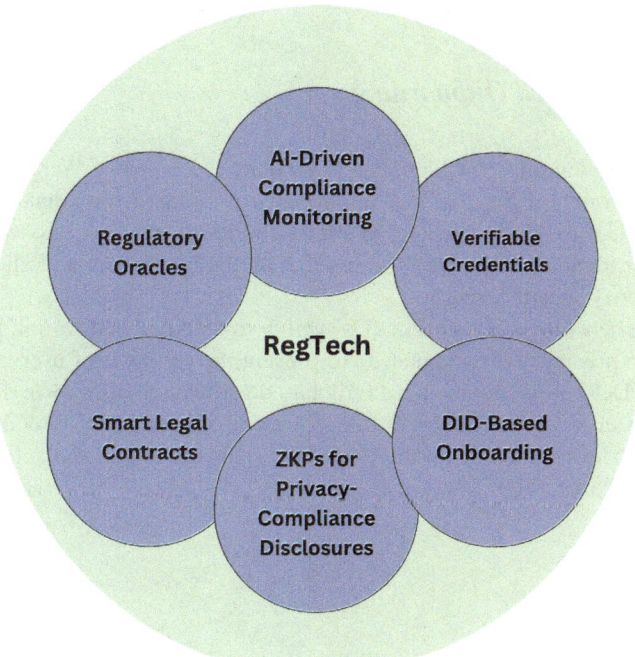

Fig. 3.5 Role of RegTech for blockchain interoperability

identify suspect trends in cross-chain DeFi protocols, including token exchanges, wash trading, insider governance manipulation, and non-compliant asset movements.

Machine learning classifiers are being used by projects like Chainalysis [47] and Solidus Labs [48] to alert users to any non-compliant conduct on DEXs and bridges [26]. AI can act as a continuous regulatory co-pilot when included into interoperable chains, alerting, freezing, or requesting human-in-the-loop authorization for high-risk processes.

3.6.2 Verifiable Credentials

Verifiable credentials (VCs) are tamper-proof, cryptographically signed statements that can be used to make claims about identity, license validity, jurisdictional conformity, and professional qualification. When issued by trustworthy organizations, governments, or exchanges, they go through on-chain validation to verify their legitimacy without revealing the essential details of the credential.

To enable permissioned DeFi, compliance-aware bridges, or region-specific governance rights, VCs in cross-chain protocols can act as digital passports. A credential may show that an individual is above 18 years of age or that they are an EU-licensed broker, without disclosing their name, address, or other supporting documentation.

3.6.3 DID-Based Onboarding

Decentralized Identifiers for Identities (DIDs) are the center of Web3 identity and are utilized for onboarding. DIDs facilitate self-sovereign identity management and are resolvable through blockchain, in contrast to usernames and passwords. Users control their identities; they can secure them on the blockchain and allow apps to access or verify specific criteria.

RegTech benefits greatly from DIDs' ability to facilitate onboarding procedures that balance privacy and compliance. To prevent the retention of user information on-chain, a DeFi protocol may need DID-based verification to confirm that the user is located in an approved country or has undergone off-chain KYC procedures. This objective is being realized with the W3C DID standard and related solutions, such as Civic and Polygon ID [37].

3.6.4 ZKPs for Privacy-Compliance Disclosures

Zero-Knowledge Proofs (ZKPs) serve as the cryptographic basis for privacy-centric compliance. Users can assert claims such as "I am not a sanctioned party" or "My revenues surpass a regulatory threshold" without disclosing the precise amount by utilizing ZKPs, thereby protecting their personal information.

This is particularly useful for cross-chain protocols when disclosure rules vary between jurisdictions. The implementation of ZKPs facilitates regulatory compliance while preserving data localization and privacy standards. Teams such as kSync [49], Aztec [50], and Semaphore [51] are engaged in the study and implementation of zk-SNARKs, zk-STARKs, and zk-KYC [37].

3.6.5 Smart Legal Contracts

As an extension of regular smart contracts, smart legal contracts incorporate legally binding clauses into their executable code. Arbitration regulations, conflict timelines, and payment enforcement timelines exemplify how hybrid contracts can align on-chain and off-chain obligations.

Leading projects in this area are attempting to incorporate blockchain technology with current regulatory frameworks, such the Accord Project [52] and OpenLaw [53]. In terms of interoperability, these contracts are crucial in ensuring that asset swaps and loan settlements, which involve several chains of custody, adhere to all regulations simultaneously [32, 33].

Furthermore, intelligent legal contracts facilitate conflict resolution or legal recourse within DAO-governed systems by aligning code-is-law frameworks with actual legislation.

3.6.6 Regulatory Oracles

DeFi receives compliance-focused data from regulatory oracles for smart contracts. Financial data from Oracles like sanctions lists, tax rates, residency verification, and GDPR flags lets contracts adjust seamlessly.

If a token has failed a compliance audit or if the destination address is in a sanctioned state, a bridge may deny a token transfer request. Systems such as Chainlink are exploring regulatory oracle networks with the aim of decentralizing and standardizing these feeds [15]. Regulatory oracles could be used in the future to programmatically enforce policy changes, check audit trails, and make sure decisions made in cross-chain governance don't go beyond jurisdictional boundaries.

3.7 Summary

This chapter explored the ways in which blockchain interoperability is going beyond being a mere technological advancement and is instead altering global sectors, regulatory standards, and governance structures. Industries such as central banking, logistics, and finance are benefiting greatly from interoperability since it allows for the instantaneous transfer of funds, the exchange of data in real time, and the composable execution of smart contracts across systems that were previously separated.

Recent developments in cross-chain liquidity and protocol composability have made decentralized finance (DeFi) a viable option for those seeking to increase capital efficiency. Supply chains are undergoing a makeover to incorporate verifiable, interoperable ledgers, which will automate compliance and enable real-time asset monitoring. At the same time, the broad acceptance of interoperability between financial systems and CBDCs is enabling programmable finance and international money transfers. Technical obstacles, such as synchronization lag and network congestion, are being overcome by new technologies such as adaptive routing, proxy re-signatures, and multi-channel relayers.

Responsibility and compliance in a globalized, borderless world are being revolutionized by decentralized designs like DAOs, legal wrappers, and DID-based systems inside the realm of regulations. Regulation technology (RegTech) solutions including regulatory oracles, zero-knowledge proofs, and AI-driven compliance are bridging the gap between policy enforcement and centralization.

The next chapter shifts from the theoretical foundations to the actual creation of cross-chain smart contracts. You'll learn how to design, model, and execute multi-chain applications using Solidity in a Truffle and Ganache setting. Using protocols like LayerZero and Chainlink CCIP, we will guide you through the full development process, from modeling cross-chain flows and building EVM-compatible contracts to deploying them. Useful topics such as lock-mint bridges, retry mechanisms, contract upgrades, and oracle-based messaging will be covered. Additionally, you will learn how to minimize cost, improve security, and organize your software for scalable interoperability.

References

1. Virani, S.S.: Blockchain end user adoption and societal challenges: exploring privacy, rights, and security dimensions. IET Blockchain. **4**(S1), 691–705 (2024). https://doi.org/10.1049/blc2.12077
2. Sizan, N.S., Dey, D., Layek, M.A., Uddin, M.A., Huh, E.-N.: Evaluating Blockchain platforms for IoT applications in industry 5.0: a comprehensive review. Blockchain Res Appl. **6**, 100276 (2025). https://doi.org/10.1016/j.bcra.2025.100276
3. Kumar, V., Budhiraja, I., Jabbari, A., Garg, D., Singh, D., Mengani, N.: Efficient blockchain interoperability design for cross-chain transactions in future internet-of-value. Peer Peer Netw Appl. **18**(110), 1–21 (2025). https://doi.org/10.1007/s12083-025-01941-w

4. Lisi, A., Lopardo, N., Tortola, D., Mori, P., Ricci, L., Severino, F.: A cross-chain rating system: bridging EVM-based Blockchains with Chainbridge. In: 2023 International Conference on Omni-Layer Intelligent Systems (COINS) (2023). https://doi.org/10.1109/COINS57856.2023.10189274
5. Financial Conduct Authority (FCA): Regulatory Sandbox Lessons Learned Report, United Kingdom. FCA (2017) https://www.fca.org.uk/publication/research-and-data/regulatory-sandbox-lessons-learned-report.pdf
6. Monetary Authority of Singapore (MAS): FinTech Regulatory Sandbox Guidelines, Singapore Government. (2018). https://www.mas.gov.sg/regulation/sandbox
7. Dubai Financial Services Authority (DFSA): Innovation Testing Licence (ITL) Programme, UAE, (2022). [Online]. https://www.dfsa.ae/innovation/itl-programme
8. International Organization for Standardization (ISO): ISO/TC 307: Blockchain and Distributed Ledger Technologies, ISO, (2020). [Online]. https://www.iso.org/committee/6266604.html
9. W3C: Decentralized Identifiers (DIDs) v1.0: Core Architecture, Data Model, and Representations, World Wide Web Consortium (W3C). (2022). [Online]. https://www.w3.org/TR/did-core/
10. Sengupta, A., Ranjan, R., Ghosh, A., Wang, L., Zomaya, A., Buyya, R.: DataHarbour: enabling decentralized AI data marketplace using Blockchain. In: IEEE Transactions on Services Computing (2023). https://doi.org/10.1109/TSC.2023.3256086
11. Kotey, S.D., Tchao, E.T., Ahmed, A.-R., Agbemenu, A.S., Nunoo-Mensah, H., Sikora, A., Welte, D., Keelson, F.: Blockchain interoperability: the state of Heterogenous Blockchain-to-Blockchain communication. IET Commun. **17**(8), 891–914 (2023). https://doi.org/10.1049/cmu2.12594
12. Financial Action Task Force (FATF): Second 12-Month Review of the Revised FATF Standards on Virtual Assets and Virtual Asset Service Providers, FATF, July (2021). [Online]. https://www.fatf-gafi.org/media/fatf/documents/recommendations/Second-12-Month-Review-Revised-FATF-Standards-Virtual-Assets-VASPs.pdf
13. Sönmez, F.Ö., Knottenbelt, W.J.: Cross-chain notification and awareness management. In: IEEE International Conference on Blockchain, London, UK, pp. 420–430 (2024). https://doi.org/10.1109/Blockchain62396.2024.00062
14. Caprolu, M., Di Pietro, R., Lombardi, F., Onofri, E.: Characterizing Polkadot's transactions ecosystem: methodology, tools, and insights. In: 2024 IEEE International Conference on Decentralized Applications and Infrastructures (DAPPS) (2024). https://doi.org/10.1109/DAPPS61106.2024.00016
15. Choi, N., Kim, H.: Decentralized commit-reveal scheme to defend against front-running attacks on decentralized exchanges. In: IEEE International Conference on Blockchain and Cryptocurrency (ICBC) (2024). https://doi.org/10.1109/ICBC59979.2024.10634344
16. Trozze, A., et al.: Detecting DeFi securities violations from token smart contract code. Financ. Innov. **10**, 78 (2024). https://doi.org/10.1186/s40854-023-00572-5
17. Thyagarajan, S.A., Malavolta, G., Moreno-Sanchez, P.: Universal atomic swaps: secure exchange of Coins across all Blockchains. In: 2022 IEEE Symposium on Security and Privacy (SP), pp. 1299–1314 (2022). https://doi.org/10.1109/SP46214.2022.00063
18. Cai, J., et al.: A Blockchain-based privacy protecting framework with Multi-Channel access control model for asset trading. Peer Peer Netw Appl. **17**, 2810–2829 (2024). https://doi.org/10.1007/s12083-024-01732-9
19. International Chamber of Commerce (ICC): Digitalisation of Trade Finance: Electronic Bills of Lading (e-BL), ICC Digital Standards Initiative, (2021). [Online]. https://www.iccwbo.org/digital-trade/initiatives/electronic-bill-of-lading/
20. Augusto, A., et al.: CBDC bridging between Hyperledger fabric and permissioned EVM-based Blockchains. In: IEEE International Conference on Blockchain and Cryptocurrency (ICBC), pp. 1–8 (2023). https://doi.org/10.1109/ICBC56567.2023.10174953
21. Tsai, W.-T., et al.: A multi-chain model for CBDC. In: 5th International Conference on Dependable Systems and their Applications (DSA), pp. 1–8 (2018). https://doi.org/10.1109/DSA.2018.00016

22. Han, J., Kim, J., Youn, A., Lee, J., Chun, Y., Woo, J., Hong, J.W.-K.: Cos-CBDC: design and implementation of CBDC on cosmos Blockchain. In: IEEE International Conference on Blockchain (2024b). https://doi.org/10.1109/ICBCTIS64495.2024.00014
23. Financial Stability Board: "Regulation, Supervision and Oversight of Crypto-Asset Activities and Markets," October 2022. [Online]. https://www.fsb.org/2022/10/regulation-supervision-and-oversight-of-crypto-asset-activities-and-markets/
24. Bank for International Settlements, "Options for access to and interoperability of CBDCs for cross-border payments," BIS Report. (2022). [Online]. Available: https://www.bis.org/publ/othp52.htm
25. Ding, D., et al.: Privacy protection for Blockchains with account and multi-asset model. China Communications. **16**(6), 69–78 (2019)
26. Shukla, M., Verma, A., Kumar, N., Sharma, S.K., Hossain, M.S.: Advanced eHealth with explainable AI secured by Blockchain with AI-empowered block sensitivity for adaptive authentication. IEEE Trans. Industr. Inform. **19**(9), 9809–9817 (2023). https://doi.org/10.1109/TII.2022.3228264
27. Wyoming State Legislature: Decentralized Autonomous Organizations Supplement—Wyoming Senate Bill SF0038, State of Wyoming, (2021). https://wyoleg.gov/Legislation/2021/SF0038
28. Organisation for Economic Co-operation and Development (OECD): The Tokenisation of Assets and Potential Implications for Financial Markets, OECD Blockchain Policy Series, (2020). [Online]. Available: https://www.oecd.org/finance/The-Tokenisation-of-Assets-and-Potential-Implications-for-Financial-Markets.pdf
29. International Monetary Fund (IMF). The Rise of Crypto Assets: Implications for Financial Stability, IMF Blog. (2021). [Online]. https://www.imf.org/en/Blogs/Articles/2021/08/05/blog-the-rise-of-crypto-assets-implications-for-financial-stability
30. Sonkamble, R.G., Bongale, A.M., Phansalkar, S., Dharrao, D.S.: A secure interoperable method for electronic health records exchange on cross platform Blockchain network. MethodsX. **13**, 103002 (2024). https://doi.org/10.1016/j.mex.2024.103002
31. World Economic Forum: "Advancing Digital Currency for Inclusive Growth in Emerging Economies," January (2021). [Online]. https://www.weforum.org/reports/advancing-digital-currency-for-inclusive-growth-in-emerging-economies/
32. Morháč, D., Valaštín, V., Košťál, K., Kotuliak, I.: Enhancing XCMP interoperability across Polkadot Paraverse. In: IEEE International Conference on Blockchain, Bratislava, Slovakia (2023a). https://doi.org/10.1109/Blockchain50366.2023.00032
33. Morháč, D., Valaštín, V., Košťál, K., Kotuliak, I.: ParaSpell XCM SDK: a new protocol for interoperability in Polkadot Paraverse. In: 2023 Fifth International Conference on Blockchain Computing and Applications (BCCA) (2023b). https://doi.org/10.1109/BCCA58897.2023.10338906
34. Dev Academy: The legal frameworks for DAOs from around the world. Noting Singapore's use of Swiss Association and Private International Act (PILA) models, and Switzerland's Swiss Foundation. (2023). wrapperjulianivaldy.medium.com+14devacademy.org+14mirror.xyz+14
35. Verzun, E.: Switzerland Launches Legal Framework for DAOs: A New Era for Decentralized Organizations, LinkedIn, Oct. 18, 2024, detailing Switzerland's "Blockchain Act" enabling DAOs to register as legal entities
36. Blockchain Association: "Understanding DAO Legislation in the U.S. and Globally," Policy Brief. (2024). [Online]. https://theblockchainassociation.org/policy/dao-legislation
37. Lesaege, C., Ast, N., Georges, F.: Kleros: Short Paper v1.0, (2019). [Online]. https://kleros.io/whitepaper.pdf
38. Aragon Association: Aragon Court Documentation, Aragon Project, (2020). [Online]. https://aragon.org/blog/aragon-court-launches-on-mainnet
39. U.S. Securities and Exchange Commission (SEC): Framework for "Investment Contract" Analysis of Digital Assets, SEC Strategic Hub for Innovation and Financial Technology. (2019). [Online]. https://www.sec.gov/corpfin/framework-investment-contract-analysis-digital-assets

40. Curve Finance: Curve DAO Documentation, Curve Finance, (2024). [Online]. https://resources.curve.fi
41. Balancer: Balancer Governance Overview, Balancer Labs, (2024). [Online]. https://docs.balancer.fi/concepts/governance/overview
42. Yearn Finance: Governance and Voting Documentation, Yearn, (2024). [Online]. https://docs.yearn.finance/governance/overview
43. Vijayalakshmi, C., Florence, S.M.: Flameshift protocol: revolutionizing interoperability with dynamic asset recycling for cross-chain communications. SN Comput. Sci. **5**, 773 (2024). https://doi.org/10.1007/s42979-024-03116-5
44. Kim, J., Essaid, M., Ju, H.: Inter-Blockchain communication message relay time measurement and analysis in cosmos. In: The 23rd Asia-Pacific Network Operations and Management Symposium (APNOMS) (2022). https://doi.org/10.1109/APNOMS60508.2022.00231
45. Lepore, C., et al.: A survey on blockchain consensus with a performance comparison of PoW, PoS and pure PoS. Mathematics. **8**(10), 1782 (2020)
46. de Kruijff, J., Weigand, H.: Understanding decentralized insurance: the case of nexus mutual. In: Proceedings of the 2020 IEEE International Conference on Decentralized Applications and Infrastructures (DAPPCON), pp. 1–8 (2020). https://doi.org/10.1109/DAPPCON49260.2020.00007
47. Chainalysis: NFTs and Wash Trading: Tracking the Rise of Fraudulent Activity in the Digital Art Market, Chainalysis Blog. (2022). [Online]. https://www.chainalysis.com/blog/nft-wash-trading/
48. Solidus Labs: Crypto Market Manipulation Report: The Scale of On-Chain Wash Trading, (2022). [Online]. https://www.soliduslabs.com/news/solidus-labs-reveals-scale-of-crypto-wash-trading
49. Matter Labs: "zkSync: Scalable and Privacy-Preserving Payments on Ethereum," (2024). [Online]. https://zksync.io/. Accessed 27 May 2025
50. Aztec Network: "Aztec Protocol: Enabling Private DeFi on Ethereum," (2024). [Online]. https://aztec.network/. Accessed 27 May 2025
51. Bünz, B. et al.: "Semaphore: A Privacy-Preserving Protocol for Anonymous Signaling," Applied ZK Research. [Online]. https://semaphore.appliedzkp.org/. Accessed 27 May 2025
52. Accord Project, "Accord Project: Open Source Framework for Smart Legal Contracts," Linux Foundation, 2023. https://www.accordproject.org/. Accessed 27 May 2025
53. OpenLaw: "OpenLaw: Automating Legal Agreements Using Smart Contracts," (2023). https://openlaw.io/. Accessed 27 May 2025

Further Readings

"Blockchain Interoperability Guide": Cyfrin. (2024). [Online]. https://www.cyfrin.io/blog/blockchain-interoperability-guide. Accessed 14 Mar 2025

Dwivedi, R., Singla, T., Shukla, S.: Cross-chain atomic swaps without time locks. In: 2023 Fifth International Conference on Blockchain Computing and Applications (BCCA) (2023). https://doi.org/10.1109/BCCA58897.2023.10338878

Frauenthaler, P., Sigwart, M., Spanring, C., Sober, M., Schulte, S.: ETH relay: a cost-efficient relay for Ethereum-based Blockchains. In: IEEE International Conference on Blockchain, Vienna, Austria (2020). https://doi.org/10.1109/Blockchain50366.2020.00032

Han, J., et al.: Cos-CBDC: design and implementation of CBDC on cosmos Blockchain. In: APNOMS 2021, Showcases Asset Mobility Via Cosmos IBC for Multi-Chain Integration (2021)

Han, Y., Wang, C., Wang, H.: Research on Blockchain cross-chain model based on 'NFT + cross-chain bridge'. IEEE Access. **12**, 77065–77078 (2024a). https://doi.org/10.1109/ACCESS.2024.3401405

Hirai, Y.: Defining the ethereum virtual machine for interactive theorem provers. In: Financial Cryptography and Data Security: FC 2017 International Workshops, WAHC, BITCOIN, VOTING, WTSC, and TA, Sliema, Malta, pp. 520–535 (2017)

Hook, T.B., Brown, J.S., Breitwisch, M., Hoyniak, D., Mann, R.: High-performance logic and high-gain analog CMOS transistors formed by a shadow-mask technique with a single implant step. IEEE Trans. Electron Devices. **49**(9), 1623–1627 (2002)

Hsien-De Huang, T., Kao, H.Y.: R2-d2: color-inspired convolutional neural network (cnn)-based android malware detections. In: IEEE International Conference on Big Data (Big Data), pp. 2633–2642. IEEE (2018)

Hu, K., Lei, L., Tsai, W.T.: Multi-tenant verification-as-a-service (VaaS) in a cloud. Simul. Model. Pract. Theory. **60**, 122–143 (2016)

Huang, Y., Bian, Y., Li, R., Zhao, J.L., Shi, P.: Smart contract security: a software lifecycle perspective. IEEE Access. **7**, 150184–150202 (2019)

Huang, J., Zhou, K., Xiong, A., Li, D.: Smart contract vulnerability detection model based on multi-task learning. Sensors. **22**(5), 1829 (2022)

Ibba, G.: A smart contracts repository for top trending contracts. In: IEEE/ACM 5th International Workshop on Emerging Trends in Software Engineering for Blockchain (WETSEB), pp. 17–20. IEEE (2022)

Idé, T.: Collaborative anomaly detection on blockchain from noisy sensor data. In: IEEE International Conference on Data Mining Workshops (ICDMW), pp. 120–127. IEEE (2018)

Jayapal, C., et al.: An insight into NFTs, Stablecoins and DEXs in Blockchain. In: 2nd International Conference on Advancements in Electrical, Electronics, Communication, Computing and Automation (ICAECA) (2023). https://doi.org/10.1109/ICAECA56562.2023.10200121

Jiang, B., Liu, Y., Chan, W.K.: Contractfuzzer: fuzzing smart contracts for vulnerability detection. In: 33rd ACM/IEEE International Conference on Automated Software Engineering, pp. 259–269 (2018)

Juels, A., Kosba, A., Shi, E.: The ring of gyges: investigating the future of criminal smart contracts. In: ACM SIGSAC Conference on Computer and Communications Security, pp. 283–295 (2016)

Kalra, S., Goel, S., Dhawan, M., Sharma, S.: Zeus: analyzing safety of smart contracts. In: Ndss, pp. 1–12 (2018)

King, S., Nadal, S.: Ppcoin: peer-to-peer crypto-currency with proof-of-stake. Self-Published Paper. **19**, 1 (2012)

Kolluri, A., Nikolic, I., Sergey, I., Hobor, A., Saxena, P.: Exploiting the laws of order in smart contracts. In: 28th ACM SIGSOFT International Symposium on Software Testing and Analysis, pp. 363–373 (2019)

Kolvart, M., Poola, M., Rull, A.: Smart contracts. In: The Future of Law and Etechnologies, pp. 133–147. Springer (2016)

Kumar, N., Hossain, M.S., Jolfaei, A., Sangaiah, A.: Building resilient web 3.0 infrastructure with quantum information technologies and Blockchain: an Ambilateral view. IEEE Internet Things J. **10**(2), 1082–1090 (2023). https://doi.org/10.1109/JIOT.2022.3224343

Lashkari, B., Musilek, P.: A comprehensive review of blockchain consensus mechanisms. IEEE Access. **9**, 43620–43652 (2021)

Lattner, C., Adve, V.: LLVM: a compilation framework for lifelong program analysis & transformation. In: International Symposium on Code Generation and Optimization, pp. 75–86. IEEE (2004)

Li, Z., et al.: MuSC: a tool for mutation testing of ethereum smart contract. In: 34th IEEE/ACM International Conference on Automated Software Engineering, pp. 1198–1201. IEEE (2019)

Liao, Z., et al.: Large-scale empirical study of inline assembly on 7.6 million ethereum smart contracts. IEEE Trans. Softw. Eng. **49**(2), 777–801 (2022)

Liao, J.W., et al.: Soliaudit: smart contract vulnerability assessment based on machine learning and fuzz testing. In: 6th International Conference on Internet of Things: Systems, Management and Security (IOTSMS), pp. 458–465. IEEE (2019)

Lin, S.Y., et al.: A survey of application research based on blockchain smart contract. Wirel. Netw. **28**(2), 635–690 (2022)

References

Liu, H., et al.: S-gram: towards semantic-aware security auditing for ethereum smart contracts. In: 33rd ACM/IEEE International Conference on Automated Software Engineering, pp. 814–819 (2018)

Liu, Z., et al.: Combining graph neural networks with expert knowledge for smart contract vulnerability detection. IEEE Trans. Knowl. Data Eng. **35**(2), 1296–1310 (2021)

Liu, L., et al.: Blockchain-enabled fraud discovery through abnormal smart contract detection on Ethereum. Futur. Gener. Comput. Syst. **128**, 158–166 (2022)

Lys, L., Micoulet, A., Potop-Butucaru, M.: Atomic swapping bitcoins and ethers. In: IEEE International Conference on Blockchain, Paris, France (2024)

Mehra, D., et al.: Implementation of CBDC System for the Customized Development of Finance Service System. SRM Institute of Science and Technology (2023)

Mitrović, A., Vukmirović, S., Dalčeković, M., Nedić, N., Čapko, D.: Cross-chain general message passing protocol via eternal bridge. In: IEEE International Conference on Telecommunications Forum (TELFOR), Novi Sad, Serbia (2023). https://doi.org/10.1109/TELFOR2023.00032

Rao, I.S., Kiah, M.L.M., Hameed, M.M., Memon, Z.A.: Scalability of Blockchain: a comprehensive review and future research direction. Clust. Comput. **27**, 5547–5570 (2024). https://doi.org/10.1007/s10586-023-04257-7

Schueffel, P.: What colors are the bricks? Unboxing the DeFi model—a literature survey, empirical study, and taxonomy. J. Bank. Financ. Technol. (2025). https://doi.org/10.1007/s42786-024-00054-x

Sethaput, V., Innet, S.: Blockchain application for central Bank digital currencies (CBDC). Clust. Comput. **26**, 2183–2197 (2023). https://doi.org/10.1007/s10586-022-03962-z

Subhashini, P., Alekhya, J., Rana, A., Lakhanpal, S., V. G, Al-Allak, M.A.: Navigating Web3 evolution with Blockchain's role in shaping next generation internet semantics. In: IEEE International Conference on Communication, Computer Sciences and Engineering (IC3SE), Hyderabad, India (2024). https://doi.org/10.1109/IC3SE62002.2024.10593138

Vasconcelos, A., et al.: CBDC bridging between Hyperledger fabric and EVM-based Blockchains. In: IEEE ICBC, Emphasizes Bridging between Regulated Chains for Secure Asset Transfers (2023)

Wang, Y., Yan, Y., Liu, X., Gao, W., Wang, Z.: A technique for ensured cross chain IBC transactions using TPM. In: IEEE International Conference on Big Data and Privacy Computing (BDPC), Xi'an, China (2024). https://doi.org/10.1109/BDPC59998.2024.10649356

Xie, Z., et al.: Enhanced efficiency and security in cross-chain transmission of Blockchain internet of ports through multi-feature-based joint learning. Sci. Rep. **15**, 6199 (2025). https://doi.org/10.1038/s41598-025-85330-6

Yang, S., Zhang, G., Li, Y., Wang, P., Zhao, C., Feng, B., Shen, C., Zhang, Y.: Cross-chain architecture of Blockchain integrating notary mechanism and relay-chain technology. In: 2024 4th International Conference on Blockchain Technology and Information Security (ICBCTIS) (2024). https://doi.org/10.1109/ICBCTIS64495.2024.00014

Yang, S., Zhang, G., Li, Y., Wang, P., Zhao, C., Feng, B., Shen, C., Zhang, Y.: A secure cross-chain mechanism based on relay chain and smart contract encryption scheme. In: 2023 11th International Conference on Information Systems and Computing Technology (ISCTech) (2023). https://doi.org/10.1109/ISCTech60480.2023.00023

Zou, H., et al.: Decentralized and lightweight cross-chain transaction scheme based on proxy re-signature. In: IEEE 23rd International Conference on Trust, Security and Privacy in Computing and Communications (TrustCom), pp. 1201–1209 (2024). https://doi.org/10.1109/TrustCom63139.2024.00170

Chapter 4
Developer Guide

Contents

- 4.1 Introduction ... 95
  - 4.1.1 Cross-Chain Smart Contracts ... 95
  - 4.1.2 Scope of Development ... 96
- 4.2 Development Environment Setup ... 96
  - 4.2.1 Installing Node.js, Truffle and Ganache ... 97
  - 4.2.2 `Truffle` Project Creation ... 98
- 4.3 Foundations of Interoperability ... 100
  - 4.3.1 Programmable Logic for Interoperability ... 101
  - 4.3.2 Smart Contracts as Relayers ... 101
  - 4.3.3 Execution Boundaries ... 102
  - 4.3.4 State Dependencies ... 102
- 4.4 Implementing Interoperability ... 102
- 4.5 Programming Smart Contracts ... 103
  - 4.5.1 Cross-Chain Simulations on EVM ... 103
  - 4.5.2 Solidity Syntax Essentials ... 104
  - 4.5.3 Design Patterns ... 106
- 4.6 Cross-Chain Messaging Patterns ... 107
  - 4.6.1 `Lock-Mint`, `Burn-Mint` & Oracle-Based Flows ... 107
  - 4.6.2 Simulating Message Flow ... 108
  - 4.6.3 Events, Listeners, and JSON-RPC Calls ... 108
  - 4.6.4 Retry and Fallback Logic ... 109
- 4.7 LayerZero with Truffle ... 109
  - 4.7.1 Trustless Omnichain Communication with ULN ... 110
  - 4.7.2 Deployment ... 111
  - 4.7.3 Contract Code ... 111
  - 4.7.4 Deployment Scripts ... 112
  - 4.7.5 Deployment Walkthrough ... 113
- 4.8 Chainlink CCIP ... 118
  - 4.8.1 Oracle-Based Routing and Message Reliability ... 118
  - 4.8.2 Building with Chainlink CCIP ... 119
  - 4.8.3 Contract Code ... 120
  - 4.8.4 Deployment Walkthrough ... 122

© The Author(s), under exclusive license to Springer Nature
Switzerland AG 2025
P. Sarang, L. Nadkar, *Blockchain Without Barriers*, SpringerBriefs in Computer
Science, https://doi.org/10.1007/978-3-032-03413-7_4

4.9 Token Bridge... 124
    4.9.1 Prototype... 126
    4.9.2 Security Checklist... 130
4.10 Security Considerations.. 131
    4.10.1 Replay Protection and Nonce Tracking.............................. 132
    4.10.2 Oracle Manipulation and Verifiable Messaging.................. 133
    4.10.3 Circuit Breakers, Pause Mechanisms, and Role-Based Access................ 133
    4.10.4 Static Analysis and Deployment Verification...................... 133
4.11 Developer Tooling Summary.. 134
    4.11.1 Truffle: Foundation for Cross-Chain Simulation................. 134
    4.11.2 Web3.js for Simulating Cross-Chain Clients....................... 134
    4.11.3 APIs for Modular Testing and Future Upgrades.................. 135
    4.11.4 Project Structure Best Practices.. 135
4.12 Summary.. 136
References... 137

Abstract This chapter provides a complete developer-level guide on designing and analyzing cross-chain smart contract systems using Ethereum-compatible technologies. Before delving into basic blockchain interoperability concepts like state dependencies, execution boundaries, and smart contracts as message relayers, it provides a full setup guide for Node.js, Truffle, and Ganache. This chapter applies theory to practice by introducing developers to fundamental Solidity syntax and reusable design ideas.

The tutorial, which focuses on lock-mint and Oracle-based flows, retry logic, and JSON-RPC-based simulations, contains extensive implementation approaches for interoperable smart contracts. Two industry-leading interoperability protocols, Chainlink CCIP and LayerZero ULN, are simulated step-by-step together with contract code, deployment scripts, and interaction testing on simulated EVM chains. To illustrate sender–receiver logic, migration scripts, and security design principles, a token bridge prototype uses a lock-mint bridge.

Static analysis tools, circuit breakers, verified messaging, and nonce tracking are among the security best practices that have been discussed in the chapter. This chapter has covered a number of security best practices, including nonce tracking, circuit breakers, verified communications, and static analysis tools.

This chapter concludes with an overview of the tools and recommended project architectures, giving developers the confidence they need to create, test, and evolve cross-chain apps in safe environments.

Keywords Truffle · Ganache · Solidity · Ethereum · Cross-chain smart contracts · Lock-mint · Burn-mint · Chainlink CCIP · LayerZero ULN · Oracle-based messaging · Token bridge · EVM simulation · Secure cross-chain deployment

4.1 Introduction

You went through the regulations. You have gained knowledge of the governance models. It is time to move forward with practical application; engage in the testing of interoperability.

In the previous chapter, we examined the non-technical limitations which are regulatory barriers, institutional gatekeeping, and governance constraints that delineate the permissible activities within the domain of cross-chain systems. However, beneath those boundaries lies a more fundamental inquiry: what is achievable?

This chapter serves as your entry point to that exploration.

Imagine the capability to replicate a multi-chain exchange, oversee cross-chain communications in real time, or execute remote contract actions across distinct blockchains without incurring any mainnet gas fees. Imagine if the advanced interoperability protocols discussed in various whitepapers such as LayerZero, Chainlink CCIP, and token bridges could be replicated, tested, and refined on your personal workstation, using Truffle—a development framework for Ethereum, and Ganache—a local blockchain simulator for testing smart contracts.

We shall proceed to do precisely that.

In this context, you will not only gain an understanding of what makes up a cross-chain smart contract, but you will also engage in its implementation. You will emulate message relays, test fallback logic, investigate EVM (Ethereum Virtual Machine) characteristics, and replicate the behavior of high-level interoperability systems using common tools[1] such as Solidity, Truffle, and Ganache.

No complex jargon barriers. No unlimited pseudocode. This approach emphasizes practical logic, incorporates real-world examples, and provides hands-on tutorials that bridge the gap between theoretical concepts and tangible prototypes.

Let us transform theoretical concepts into practical applications.

4.1.1 Cross-Chain Smart Contracts

Imagine you are building a decentralized exchange that lets users swap ETH for Bitcoin without intermediaries. Or, picture a Web3 game where your in-game avatar, originally minted on Polygon, needs to buy a magical sword that's minted as an NFT on Avalanche. These are not distant-future visions, they're developer problems.

But here's the catch: how do these interactions occur seamlessly across incompatible blockchains without trusting a central server? This is where cross-chain smart contracts step in.

In both examples mentioned previously, you have two or more ecosystems that communicate in different languages. Cross-chain smart contracts are the

---

[1] Other tools like Hardhat, Foundry, Brownie (for Python), and Remix IDE can also be used depending on developer preference and use case complexity.

interpreters securing and running logic across several chains without compromising on decentralization. They're not an add on that promotes interoperability; they're essential to making Web3 ecosystems work as one coherent entity.

A study by Lys et al. [1] and Sönmez & Knottenbelt [2] highlights the significance of atomic swaps, cross-chain state commitments, and event-driven notification systems toward trustless interoperability. But come on, how many of those models have working code, downloadable developer toolkits, or even step-by-step instructions?

Hardly any.

That's why this chapter not only describes what cross-chain smart contracts are but demonstrates how to create them from scratch, test message passing, and debug real-world situations using Solidity, Truffle, and Ganache.

Theory is good, but working code is better.

4.1.2 Scope of Development

Let this chapter be your test kitchen for interoperability.

In this chapter, you won't just speculate on interoperability protocols, you'll model them locally, end to end. Without leaving your Truffle development environment, you'll model the Cross-Chain Interoperability Protocol (CCIP) flow of Chainlink, the ultra-light node messaging of LayerZero, and even token bridging patterns akin to those employed in Wormhole.

This is where cross-chain logic gets hands-on. You won't just learn about it, instead you will construct it, run it, and debug it. You will observe how smart contracts share state between chains, how oracles act as crypto notaries, and how message-passing patterns such as lock-mint, burn-mint, and oracle-based flows impose atomicity between systems that don't natively communicate.

The aim is not merely to get things working but to know how and why they work.

By the time you get to the simulation exercises on LayerZero and Chainlink CCIP, you'll be ready to step out of local development into testnets and production environments with ease. Migrating into real-world deployments whether with Chainlink nodes, LayerZero endpoints, or external relayers it is going to feel intuitive, not daunting.

But first, before we draft a single contract, let's get the foundations in place.

Next up, in the following section, we'll get your Development Environment ready which will be your gateway to cross-chain learning.

4.2 Development Environment Setup

You must first create a trustworthy local development environment before getting into the finer points of creating a cross-chain smart contract. Why is this required? Your most valuable assets when working with various blockchain settings are

4.2 Development Environment Setup

simulation and reproducibility. We create a sandbox for testing interoperability logic without deploying to actual networks, hence reducing complexity and gas costs.

4.2.1 Installing Node.js, Truffle and Ganache

"Why do I require Node.js?" is a question you may have. We use Solidity for development. Although Solidity is not a JavaScript language, most libraries in the Ethereum ecosystem, such as Truffle and Ganache, are built on Node.js. Node.js, the LTS version, is a must for using these libraries. Libraries like Truffle and Ganache are tested against LTS versions to ensure consistent behavior making them more reliable for development environments. It can be installed from the official website or using a version manager such as nvm (Node Version Manager) for ease of use.

Once Node.js is in place, install Truffle and Ganache globally using npm:

```
npm install -g truffle ganache
```

This command installs Truffle, a development framework for Ethereum that simplifies compiling, deploying, and testing smart contracts, and Ganache, a personal local blockchain for rapid testing. Ganache allows you to create and run multiple local Ethereum blockchain instances for testing and development. To simulate cross-chain communication on your computer, you will create one Ganache instance on port 7545 as "Chain A" and another instance on port 8545 as "Chain B," as shown in Fig. 4.1.

Without using **testnets** or **mainnet** forks, you can use this method to locally replicate contract interaction and cross-chain messaging. It is a reproducible, lightweight environment suitable for understanding the mechanisms of interoperability protocols such as LayerZero or Chainlink CCIP through simulated implementations.

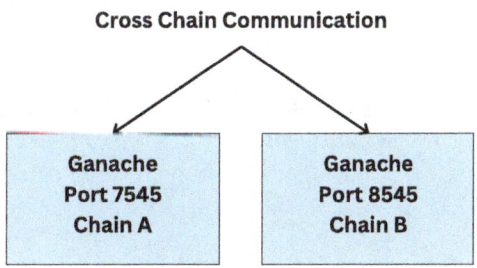

Fig. 4.1 Communication between different ganache instances

4.2.2 Truffle *Project Creation*

> For every project that we discuss in this chapter, the full project source is available on our GitHub (/CrossChainInteroperability) (There you will also find a link to a video demonstration of the running project.

Let us begin with our first Interoperability focused project using Truffle.

To initialize the truffle environment, create a working directory for your project in the command window on your computer and run the following command.

```
truffle init
```

This will create a basic project structure with directories for contracts, migrations, and tests in your working directory.

Your first step is to create mock contracts that mimic source and destination chains. To test cross-chain verification, create `ReceiverContract.sol` to receive and store incoming messages, and `SenderContract.sol` to emit or send those messages. Place both Solidity files in the contracts/ directory. This configuration enables the use of interoperability stubs, such as those derived from LayerZero or Chainlink CCIP, for emitting, relaying, or analyzing cross-chain signals, with each contract executing a portion of the logic within the Truffle sandbox.

To deploy contracts to two distinct chains (Chain A and Chain B), we will amend the truffle-config.js file to establish two custom networks, each corresponding to a Ganache instance operating on a separate port.

```
module.exports = {
  networks: {
    chainA: {
      host: "127.0.0.1",      // Localhost
      port: 7545,             // Ganache instance 1
      network_id: "*",        // Match any network ID
    },
    chainB: {
      host: "127.0.0.1",      // Localhost
      port: 8545,             // Ganache instance 2
      network_id: "*",        // Match any network ID
    }
  },

  compilers: {
    solc: {
```

4.2 Development Environment Setup

```
        version: "^0.8.20",    // Match Solidity version with contracts
    }
  }
};
```

You can start the two Ganache instances with these commands in two separate terminals:

```
ganache-cli --port 7545
ganache-cli --port 8545
```

In order to simulate cross-chain behavior deterministically, this configuration makes sure that both networks maintain separate blockchain and states while sharing the same deterministic wallet addresses.

When you execute the two ganache-cli commands on ports 7545 and 8545, each terminal window, as shown in Fig. 4.2, initializes a standalone local blockchain network. The screen output enumerates the available Ethereum accounts, their private keys, along with other information like chain ID, mnemonic, gas price, and block gas limit. Deterministic descriptions guarantee both chains begin with identical groups of test wallets, which is especially helpful in mimicking message transfers between contracts. In our example, these two networks will represent Chain A

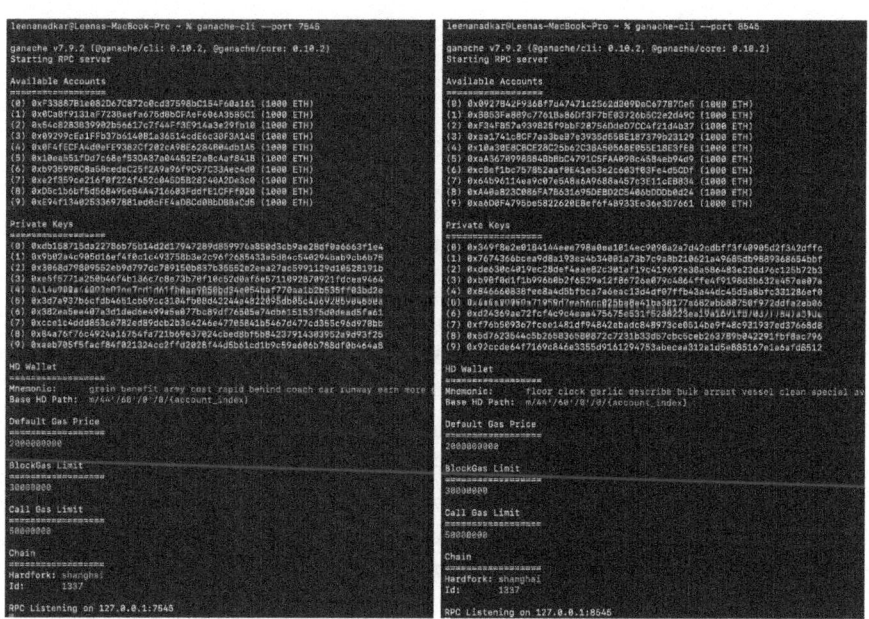

Fig. 4.2 Output of two ganache instances representing chain A and chain B

and Chain B, emulating two blockchains that are interoperable within a local environment.

We will now demonstrate how to enable interoperability between these two instances of blockchains. To begin, let us first learn the foundations of interoperability.

4.3 Foundations of Interoperability

Interoperability is more than just joining chains in a blockchain; it's about allowing logic, state, and trust to flow across decentralized boundaries. This foundation fundamentally relies on synchronized state transitions, well defined execution boundaries, and programmable smart contracts that function as relayers. As illustrated in Fig. 4.3, interoperability begins with smart contracts on each chain acting as senders or recipients of cross-chain messages. Standardized protocols are essential for regulating data flow, state updates, and dependency verification to ensure security and accuracy.

We will now examine the significance of the various blocks shown in Fig. 4.3.

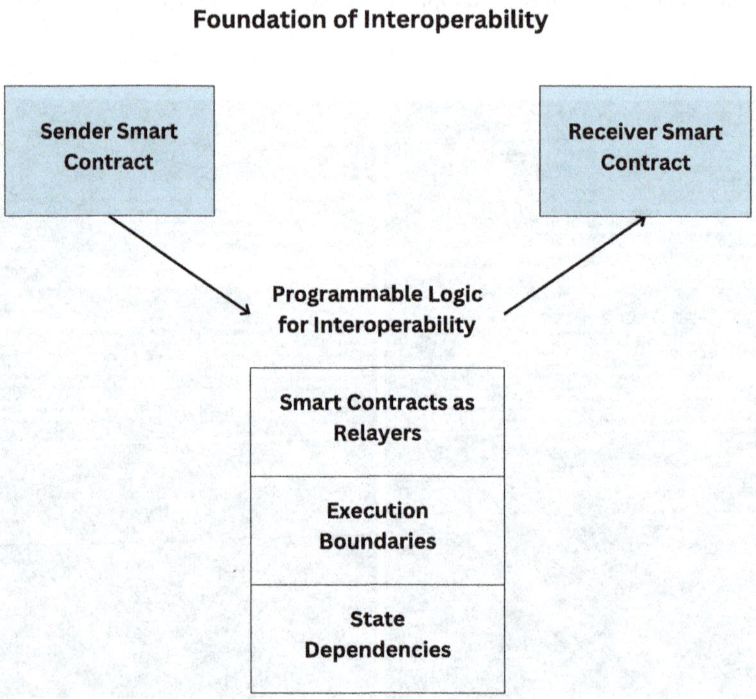

Fig. 4.3 Foundations of blockchain interoperability

4.3.1 Programmable Logic for Interoperability

Why can't blockchains use HTTP protocols and APIs to connect with each other like traditional internet services? The primary reason is that blockchain networks lack trust and are autonomous. A consensus, data structure, and state machine are unique to each chain. Verifiable, predictable, and programmable logic is essential for the transfer of assets or data between entities. It necessitates more than merely APIs. This is the point at which smart contracts become relevant.

Smart contracts are separate programs that run on decentralized nodes and provide immutability and consensus, unlike traditional backend programming that relies on centralized servers and runs off-chain. They act as a bridge connecting various blockchains to establish interoperable workflows. The protocol facilitating cross-chain communication, including token minting, status acknowledgment, and message verification, is contained within these contracts, allowing for independent verification on each participating chain. In the absence of such rationale, inter-chain communication relies on trust in intermediaries, which is incompatible with the decentralization concept. To guarantee atomicity and security, academic research such as Lys et al. [1] underscores the necessity of specific lock-and-release protocols for atomic swaps and cross-chain transfers. These limits can be solely defined by programmable smart contract logic [1].

Imagine a token bridge that links Avalanche and Ethereum. How can we ensure that when a sender sends Ethereum to a bridge contract, the token will be generated or unlocked on Avalanche correctly? The exchange may solely be sustained by implementing a smart contract on Ethereum to initiate a verifiable event and another on Avalanche to validate that event, likely using a dependable oracle. Programmable contract logic is an essential element of this intent-based communications architecture, included in protocols such as LayerZero [3] and Axelar [4].

4.3.2 Smart Contracts as Relayers

Different blockchains are comparable to sovereign states, each of which has its own set of laws, currency and standards for validating transactions. Transitioning between these networks involves not merely the transfer of data, but also the transmission of trust. Ambassadors in traditional diplomacy carry documents and messages that necessitate authentication. Like autonomous trust relayers, smart contracts encompass not only data but also verifiable intent about blockchain interoperability.

Consider a decentralized application (dApp) in which the loan is issued on the Avalanche network and the collateral is secured on the Polygon network. Upon the deposit of collateral, the Polygon smart contract is required to emit an event, which must thereafter be acknowledged and interpreted by another Avalanche smart contract. A research by Sönmez and Knottenbelt [2] asserts that such a procedure must ensure both logical coherence and cryptographic integrity, particularly when using native relayers such as IBC or third-party relayers like Chainlink [2].

Essentially, this is accomplished by means of linked contracts, one for every chain, which are intended to validate each other's actions. These contracts interact with one another using external oracles or relayers, exemplified by the decentralized routers of Chainlink CCIP or the Ultra-Light Node framework of LayerZero. These technologies maintain the decentralized nature of each blockchain zone by preventing either an oracle or a contract from determining the outcome. As cryptographic witnesses, they only permit activities once the source chain has produced evidence. This type of conduct has been examined in the role of trust boundaries in academic models and is now codified in modern interoperability protocols [4].

4.3.3 Execution Boundaries

One issue with cross-chain development that is commonly disregarded is execution boundaries. In Ethereum, a contract can use either a Solidity function called `call` or a `delegate call` to invoke another contract within the same chain. However, in no circumstance can it simultaneously trigger a contract on Solana or even on Polygon. The execution state of a single chain is inherently isolated, constituting a stringent limitation of the blockchain. Asynchronous and event-driven procedures are needed because state transition on one chain broadcasts events that are audited and acted upon.

4.3.4 State Dependencies

A token being burned before it is minted elsewhere is an example of how a transaction on one chain may be dependent on the verified state of another. To maintain authenticity, these dependencies necessitate strong assurances, including time-locked confirmation intervals, validator signatures, or cryptographic proofs. The IBC protocol uses a two-phase commit system within the Cosmos network, whereby messages are executed solely if their respective acknowledgments and proofs are valid [5]. Ethereum systems employ off-chain relay infrastructure, event logs, and Merkle Proofs to do this.

We will now demonstrate the implementation of these concepts to enable interoperability between our two blockchain instances.

4.4 Implementing Interoperability

Ethereum developers could use Truffle framework to emulate interoperability solutions. When using two Ganache networks to deploy mock contracts, a developer can configure one contract to emit an event, while another contract can read and verify the event through a hashed message or a predetermined signature pattern. Developers can learn how to describe atomic and non-linear, yet dependent and cross-referenced execution processes by emulating the behavior of production-level relayers. Kim et al. [6] investigate the latency and reliability problems this design presents for Cosmos IBC [6]. These limitations push developers to switch from sequential classical programming to a causal dependency graph design style, where an occurrence on one chain causes an event on another. We will mimic message handlers and check event flow using Truffle terminal commands.

4.5 Programming Smart Contracts

The most popular language for creating smart contracts is still Solidity, which serves as the foundation for Ethereum and many other blockchains that are compatible with Ethereum Virtual Machine (EVM). Understanding the subtleties of Solidity and the EVM is critical when developing smart contracts that simulate interoperability across several chains. The architecture of Solidity, however, strong for single-chain applications, necessitates particular patterns and structural comprehension to replicate multi-chain functionality in a local or testnet setting. This section lays the foundation for developing interoperability-aware smart contracts in Solidity 0.8.x, focusing on significant EVM limitations, syntax norms, and idioms such as proxies and upgradable contracts.

4.5.1 Cross-Chain Simulations on EVM

The original purpose of the Ethereum Virtual Machine was to provide strong transactional isolation and immutability while executing code deterministically on a single blockchain. To simulate cross-chain functionality in Ganache, such as moving data or state between Chain A and Chain B, developers must imitate external state validation, message integrity, and delayed consensus. Real bridge protocols like LayerZero or Chainlink CCIP typically handle these responsibilities. This is depicted in Fig. 4.4.

A primary restriction is that Ethereum contracts cannot inherently communicate with contracts on other blockchains. To simulate this, developers must abstract the notion of a relayer or oracle by using event emitters, off-chain scripts, or mock contracts as listeners. An event with encoded data may be produced by a sender contract on Chain A. The event data can then be supplied by a script or test listener on the developer's computer to simulate cross-chain communication in the receiver contract of Chain B.

Non-determinism and timestamp manipulations are two further drawbacks of the EVM architecture. In a conventional multi-chain setting, latency, block finality, and message sequencing might vary considerably. In Ganache or testnets, developers must mitigate asynchronous behavior by employing explicit control over mining

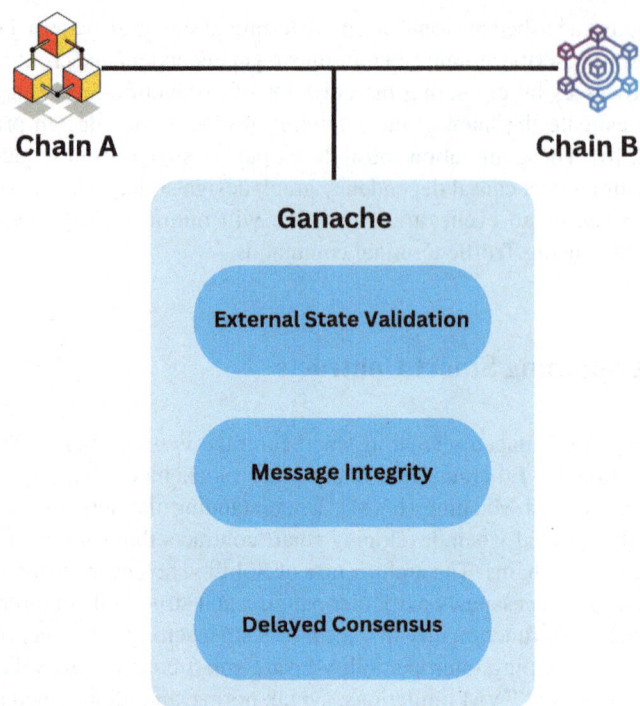

Fig. 4.4 Emulating cross-chain logic

(for example `evm_mine`) or time manipulation features (`evm_increaseTime`) while testing. The PoS (Proof of Stake) consensus of Ethereum is inapplicable to local test environments such as Ganache, which functions on a manual or instantaneous block mining paradigm.

4.5.2 Solidity Syntax Essentials

Solidity version 0.8.x added a set of usability and security enhancements that are fundamental to interoperable contract development. The standard for modern smart contract development is to use configurable error types, increase control flow, and have safe arithmetic built in (instead of SafeMath).

For interoperability simulation in this chapter, the developers need to learn firing events to emit correct off-chain data, and `abi.encode` / `abi.decode` for processing encoded data being exchanged between contracts. Custom struct types are also necessary for making cross-chain message payloads readable and trustworthy. Validation logic must use `require` or `revert` statements with custom errors to yield fine-grained control while processing messages. Lastly, knowing how to

4.5 Programming Smart Contracts

define interfaces will be essential in mocking cross-chain contract calls, particularly when emulating endpoint communication between different blockchains.

Here's a quick example: A basic contract that sends a message to be "relayed" on another chain. As mentioned earlier, the full project source is available on our GitHub (/sample code).

```
// SPDX-License-Identifier: MIT
pragma solidity ^0.8.20;

contract SenderContract {
    event MessageSent(address indexed sender, string payload);

    function sendMessage(string memory _message) external {
        emit MessageSent(msg.sender, _message);
    }
}
```

A simple technique for sending a message event is specified in this SenderContract. An event called MessageSent is triggered when the sendMessage function is called, logging the caller's address (msg.sender) and the string payload supplied as _message. This code mimics sending a message that is listened to by another chain through its receiver contract. This event will be picked up (simulated off-chain) and used to invoke a handler in ReceiverContract shown here:

```
contract ReceiverContract {
    string public lastMessage;

    function receiveMessage(string memory _message) external {
        lastMessage = _message;
    }
}
```

This contract uses a public state variable named `lastMessage` to store the most recent message received. In our simulation, we use the Truffle console to manually call `receiveMessage` on the receiver contract deployed on Chain B following an event produced by the sender contract on Chain A. This mimics how an actual cross-chain relay service would receive an event, call the handler, and deliver the message.

It acts as the receiving end of a simulated cross-chain interaction, where another contract (like `SenderContract`) triggers communication.

The event data is manually passed between Chain A and Chain B in order to simulate cross-chain communication. We will demonstrate this in the following sections where we look up the practical simulations.

Despite its crudeness, this serves as the foundation for understanding how message integrity, format, and verification function in a multi-chain context that lacks trust.

Having established a firm understanding of Solidity syntax, we now focus on design patterns such as minimal proxies and upgradable contracts, which guarantee that our cross-chain smart contracts stay modular, manageable, and adaptable over time.

4.5.3 Design Patterns

On many chains, cross-chain smart contracts are typically implemented as modules. In these situations, maintaining consistent logic while allowing for upgrades is paramount. Minimal proxy contracts, known as the EIP-1167 pattern [7], and upgradeable proxies, including OpenZeppelin's UUPS [8] or Transparent Proxy, are relevant in this context.

Minimal proxies delegate all logic to an implementation contract, using minimal gas. This method is especially relevant when implementing identical functionality across multiple chains while requiring modifications solely in one central contract.

The **@openzeppelin/contracts-upgradeable** library from OpenZeppelin [8] enables dynamic upgrades of upgradeable contracts by separating logic from state storage. This is particularly advantageous in multi-chain setups where faults or new features must be addressed in real time without impacting state.

```
// Initializer pattern
import "@openzeppelin/contracts-upgradeable
                    /proxy/utils/Initializable.sol";

contract UpgradeableReceiver is Initializable {
    string public message;

    function initialize() public initializer {
        message = "Init message";
    }

    function updateMessage(string memory _msg) public {
        message = _msg;
    }
}
```

The initializer pattern, which is crucial for upgradeable smart contracts implemented with proxy mechanisms, is used in the UpgradeableReceiver contract. It inherits from OpenZeppelin's Initializable contract and defines an `initialize` function that, in this case, creates the initial state by assigning a default string to the message variable, rather than using a constructor. Re-initialization attacks are prevented by the initializer modifier, which makes sure that this function can only be called once. Anyone can thereafter update the message using the `updateMessage` function. In proxy-based deployments, where constructors are not run and contract initialization needs to be done by hand after deployment, this approach is essential. This contract should be deployed via a Universal Upgradeable Proxy Standard (UUPS) [8].

The next section demonstrates how Solidity is used to encode, transmit, and mimic messages between chains using Truffle and Ganache, laying the foundation for building mock LayerZero or CCIP-type contracts. The subsequent phase involves studying the structure of Sender and Receiver contracts to replicate genuine cross-chain transactions through Truffle migrations and event decoding in the Truffle console.

4.6 Cross-Chain Messaging Patterns

Smart contracts on various blockchains can connect, sync, or transfer data and assets; thanks to cross-chain messaging, a low-level interoperability layer. To lock tokens on Ethereum and mint them on Avalanche, or to use oracles for integrating real-world price feeds into contracts on Polygon, the critical aspect is the communication framework between blockchains. However, with Truffle and Ganache in particular, how can we mimic these complex flows in a local developer environment?

4.6.1 *Lock-Mint, Burn-Mint & Oracle-Based Flows*

Among cross-chain communications patterns, lock-mint, burn-mint, and oracle-triggered relay are the most common. For instance, under the token bridge, one can secure 100 USDT[2] on Chain A and generate an equivalent quantity of wrapped USDT on Chain B. The burn-mint model entails the burning of the original token on the source chain and its subsequent reissuance on the destination chain to avert duplication. In both scenarios, the integrity of communications is crucial, as the inability to transmit the lock or burn message may lead to double issuance or financial loss.

Oracles are used when a decision must be made based on off-chain knowledge or inter-chain consensus. An oracle can verify an event on Chain A and subsequently notify Chain B via a reliable relay. Chainlink's Cross-Chain Interoperability Protocol (CCIP) exemplifies the role of oracles as validators of messages.

---

[2] USDT stands for Tether, which is a stablecoin—a type of cryptocurrency that is pegged to a stable asset, typically the U.S. Dollar.

Implementing this in a real system is, however, not straightforward. Without even requiring the operation of a complete oracle node, this chapter demonstrates how to replicate token flow and oracle validation in Truffle.

4.6.2 Simulating Message Flow

A SenderContract.sol and a ReceiverContract.sol are created in the same Truffle project and are configured to operate on separate chains in order to replicate this in a lab setting. Ganache is launched on two independent ports to emulate Chain A and Chain B, accompanied by individual deployments of these contracts. A JSON-RPC client or a customized script (Node.js/web3.js) can monitor events on one blockchain and execute transactions on another, thereby functioning as an off-chain relayer.

The SenderContract triggers an event, MessageSent (address receiver, string data), upon the fulfillment of a condition (Token locked). The Node.js listener acquires it and subsequently transmits a transaction to the Receiver Contract's receive Message (string data) method, simulating message delivery and processing. This configuration allows developers to comprehend the entire process of cross-chain communication: from emission, through off-chain monitoring, to event-driven activation.

4.6.3 Events, Listeners, and JSON-RPC Calls

Events from smart contracts serve as anchors to start off-chain processes. In the Truffle project, subsequent to deploying the mock contracts, you may either manually emit and observe events through the Truffle console or automate workflows using JavaScript listeners. This is a simplification of a simulation:

```
const sender = await SenderContract.deployed();
sender.MessageSent().on("data", async (event) => {
   const { receiver, data } = event.returnValues;
const receiverContract = new web3.eth.Contract
                      (receiverAbi, receiver);
   await receiverContract.methods.receiveMessage(data).send
         ({from: accounts[0] });
});
```

This code listens for a deployed `SenderContract` instance's `MessageSent` event. The event listener receives the data payload and recipient address from the returned event's `returnValues` when a message is sent (using `sendMessage`).

After that, it uses the receiver's address and[3]ABI to construct a new Web3 contract instance. It then instantly invokes the `receiveMessage` method on the receiver contract to transmit the message payload. In order to complete a simulated cross-chain message relay between sender and recipient on the same local setup, the transaction is sent from `accounts[0]`.

This emulates the behavior of LayerZero or Wormhole relays, wherein an off-chain node monitors emission events and transmits validated data to the target chain.

4.6.4 Retry and Fallback Logic

Message latency, network saturation, or oracle tampering can all cause established message flows to break in cross-chain events. Retry functionality must be implemented by re-entrant call gates, nonce-based idempotency checks, and off-chain retry queues. For instance, if the receiveMessage transaction fails due to gas-related complications or erroneous data, the listener script can capture the error and attempt a retry after a specified interval.

It's also possible to cache the hash of the most recent successful message in Solidity and compare it to a fresh one before applying it. This not only prevents replay attacks but also facilitates manual reconciliation for failed communications, a standard characteristic of operational bridges like Axelar and CCIP.

By emulating communications flows within Truffle and Ganache through local networks and simulated relayers, developers can prototype operational cross-chain architectures. This method facilitates hands-on participation with patterns such as lock-mint, burn-mint, and oracle messaging, as well as an understanding of failure management, retries, and state divergence. This not only prepares developers for more sophisticated tools like LayerZero's ULN or Chainlink CCIP but also introduces them to the principles of trustless, verifiable interchain communication.

4.7 LayerZero with Truffle

LayerZero is an omnichain interoperability protocol that makes messaging safe and easy. Unlike traditional cross-chain bridges that rely on centralized middlemen or complex validator networks, LayerZero introduces the concept of an Ultra-Light Node (ULN). ULNs use a decentralized oracle and relayer framework that significantly reduces on-chain verification costs while preserving message integrity and atomicity guarantees over several chains [9].

---

[3] Application Binary Interface (ABI) is a JSON representation that defines how smart contract functions and data structures can be called or interacted with from outside the blockchain, such as from web apps or other contracts.

4.7.1 Trustless Omnichain Communication with ULN

Omnichain is blockchain architecture or protocol design that enables seamless interaction across multiple blockchains simultaneously. The example here demonstrates the replication of LayerZero within a local Truffle context using two Ganache instances as distinct EVM-compatible chains, designated as "Chain A" and "Chain B." This eliminates real mainnet gas costs while allowing developers to navigate deployment, configuration, and transaction processes.

The fundamental concept of ULN is to transmit messages securely between blockchains without requiring comprehensive state awareness of external chains. The system consists of:

- **On-chain Endpoint Contracts**: Implemented on each participant chain to transmit and receive messages
- **Decentralized Oracle (Like Chainlink)**: Acquires block headers from source blockchains
- **User-defined Relayer**: Retrieves transaction proofs and submits them with headers
- **Proof Library**: Confirms the validity of a message and ensures it remains unaltered

The Proof Library plays a critical role by verifying that messages were truly committed on the source chain using Merkle Proofs and header data, thereby preventing replay or forged submissions. This added layer of verification, emphasized in red shown in Fig. 4.5, is central to ULN's assurances of atomic delivery, replay protection, and pluggable verification logic making it suitable for mission-critical cross-chain applications [10].

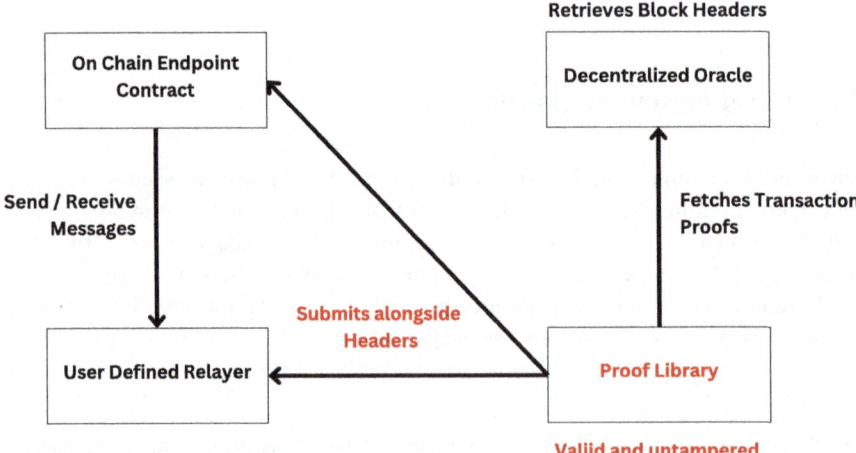

Fig. 4.5 Architecture of ULNs

4.7.2 Deployment

Let us walk through deploying LayerZero-compatible contracts using Solidity and Truffle. Refer Truffle Project creation section to create project folder for LayerZeroDemo and start Ganache CLI on two different ports. For a quick preview, you will find the full project source on our GitHub (/LayerZeroDemo).

4.7.3 Contract Code

Here's a minimal sender contract that simulates a LayerZero-style cross-chain message relay between Chain A and Chain B.

4.7.3.1 Sender Contract (on Chain A)

```
// SPDX-License-Identifier: MIT
pragma solidity ^0.8.20;

contract MockLayerZeroSender {
    event MessageSent(address indexed to, string message);

    function sendCrossChainMessage
(address receiver, string memory message) external {
        emit MessageSent(receiver, message);
    }
}
```

The sending side of a LayerZero-style cross-chain message is simulated by this contract. It defines an event called `MessageSent` that logs the message string being sent along with the address of the intended recipient. This event is sent by the `sendCrossChainMessage` function without actually calling another contract. In a real-world scenario, an ultra-light node or relayer would see this event and send the payload to a receiver contract on a different chain. This abstraction is helpful for testing or modeling LayerZero message flow.

The receiver contract would look like this:

4.7.3.2 Receiver Contract (on Chain B)

```
// SPDX-License-Identifier: MIT
pragma solidity ^0.8.20;
```

```
contract MockLayerZeroReceiver {
    string public lastMessage;

    function receiveMessage(string memory message) external {
        lastMessage = message;
    }
}
```

The most recent message received is stored in the contract's public state variable `lastMessage`. Any external sender, such as a test script or a mock LayerZero relayer, can call the `receiveMessage` function and pass a string payload. By simulating the behavior of cross-chain message delivery, this configuration can be used to confirm that a message sent from a simulated sender (on another Ganache instance) was successfully delivered and saved on the receiving contract.

These two contracts mimic the LayerZero `send` and `lzReceive` behavior but without invoking full protocol verification logic for simplicity.

4.7.4 Deployment Scripts

Truffle migration scripts are JavaScript files used to deploy smart contracts to a blockchain network in a specific sequence, managing deployment state and ensuring reproducibility.

Create a migration file for each contract:

4.7.4.1 Sender Contract

In order to maintain the dependency flow between smart contracts during deployment, truffle migration scripts are numbered (Like: 1_initial_migration.js, 2_deploy_contracts.js). By logging the most recent migration that was successfully completed, the Migrations.sol contract facilitates this process, enabling Truffle to monitor development and prevent the need to rerun finished scripts in further deployments.

`2_deploy_sender.js`

The code for the sender contract is available in the file 2_deploy_sender.js. This script tells Truffle how to deploy the MockLayerZeroSender contract to the configured blockchain network. It uses `artifacts.require` to load the compiled contract and then calls `deployer.deploy` to deploy it during the second step of the migration process.

4.7 LayerZero with Truffle

```
const Sender = artifacts.require("MockLayerZeroSender");

module.exports = function (deployer) {
    deployer.deploy(Sender);
};
```

4.7.4.2 Receiver Contract

The code for the receiver contract is available in the file 3_deploy_sender.js. This script handles the deployment of the MockLayerZeroReceiver contract. It imports the compiled contract using `artifacts.require` and deploys it using `deployer.deploy` as part of Truffle's third migration step, ensuring the receiver contract is available on the selected network.

```
3_deploy_receiver.js
const Receiver = artifacts.require("MockLayerZeroReceiver");

module.exports = function (deployer) {
    deployer.deploy(Receiver);
};
```

4.7.5 Deployment Walkthrough

4.7.5.1 Deploy on Chain A

To deploy the contracts on **Chain A**, we use the following Truffle command:

```
truffle migrate --reset --network chainA
```

This command instructs Truffle to deploy all contracts defined in the migration scripts to the network specified as chainA in the truffle-config.js file. The `--reset` flag ensures that all previous deployments are ignored and that the migration process restarts from the beginning. In this case, chainA corresponds to a Ganache instance running locally on port 7545, emulating a standalone blockchain environment.

As seen in the terminal output shown in Fig. 4.6, Truffle begins by checking the compilation status of the contracts. Since everything is already compiled and up to date, it proceeds directly to the migration steps. The first script executed is 2_deploy_sender.js, which deploys the `MockLayerZeroSender` contract. Truffle logs detailed information including the transaction hash, contract address, gas usage, block number, and deployment cost. In this instance, the sender contract is

```
leenanadkar@Leenas-MacBook-Pro LayerZeroDemo % truffle migrate --reset --network chainA

Compiling your contracts...
===========================
✓ Fetching solc version list from solc-bin. Attempt #1
> Everything is up to date, there is nothing to compile.


Starting migrations...
======================
> Network name:    'chainA'
> Network id:      1748887771133
> Block gas limit: 30000000 (0x1c9c380)


2_deploy_sender.js
==================

   Deploying 'MockLayerZeroSender'
   -------------------------------
   > transaction hash:    0xdbcbd4461f424335fa4f1fc4779e7d7f01d9528e95fddf2d352be2e8030c8229
   > Blocks: 0            Seconds: 0
   > contract address:    0x3F4B1aCc5D91b2F949Ed844dAc8a720eaebc2A2d
   > block number:        1
   > block timestamp:     1748887925
   > account:             0x457257aa3C57A44016483f3D93E2C2239D7dE8f4
   > balance:             999.999201124
   > gas used:            236704 (0x39ca0)
   > gas price:           3.375 gwei
   > value sent:          0 ETH
   > total cost:          0.000798876 ETH

   > Saving artifacts
   -------------------------------
   > Total cost:          0.000798876 ETH

3_deploy_receiver.js
====================

   Deploying 'MockLayerZeroReceiver'
   ---------------------------------
   > transaction hash:    0x3e5bea98ae7a68275c5622c8c6d31386f06041690728ed72cf95e8528ba4280b
   > Blocks: 0            Seconds: 0
   > contract address:    0x0Ca5a3e94C313d60ed516704A67f0AB91924a126
   > block number:        2
   > block timestamp:     1748887925
   > account:             0x457257aa3C57A44016483f3D93E2C2239D7dE8f4
   > balance:             999.997911529979483803
   > gas used:            394691 (0x605c3)
   > gas price:           3.267350967 gwei
   > value sent:          0 ETH
   > total cost:          0.001289594020516197 ETH

   > Saving artifacts
   -------------------------------
   > Total cost:     0.001289594020516197 ETH

Summary
=======
> Total deployments:   2
> Final cost:          0.002088470020516197 ETH


leenanadkar@Leenas-MacBook-Pro LayerZeroDemo %
```

Fig. 4.6 MockLayerZeroSender on port 7545

4.7 LayerZero with Truffle

deployed in block number 1, with a gas usage of 236,704 units and a total cost of approximately 0.00079 ETH.

4.7.5.2 Deploy on Chain B

Use the following command to deploy the receiver contract on chain B.

```
truffle migrate --reset --network chainB
```

Immediately following 2_deploy_sender.js, the 3_deploy_receiver.js script is executed, deploying the `MockLayerZeroReceivercontract`. This deployment occurs in block number 2 of the same local chain and consumes 394,691 gas units. The cost of this transaction is approximately 0.00128 ETH. Both deployments use the same Ethereum account provided by Ganache and maintain the chain's deterministic state.

At the end of the process, Truffle displays a summary indicating that a total of two contracts were deployed and the combined cost of deployment was around 0.00208 ETH. This successful execution confirms that both sender and receiver contracts are now live on the local Chain A environment and ready for interaction. These contracts can now be tested for cross-chain message simulation using event listeners and mock receivers in subsequent steps.

4.7.5.3 Interaction Simulation

With both the sender and receiver contracts deployed on Chain A, we proceed to simulate a LayerZero-style message transfer using the Truffle console. Enter the following command on the console to set up an interactive environment for manually testing the contract interactions.

```
truffle console --network chainA
```

We begin by fetching the deployed instances of both contracts using.

```
await MockLayerZeroSender.deployed()
```

and

```
await MockLayerZeroReceiver.deployed().
```

Once loaded, we simulate the message send operation by calling.

```
await sender.sendCrossChainMessage(receiver.address, "Hello LayerZero").
```

```
leenanadkar@Leenas-MacBook-Pro LayerZeroDemo % truffle console --network chainA

truffle(chainA)> let sender = await MockLayerZeroSender.deployed()
undefined
truffle(chainA)> let receiver = await MockLayerZeroReceiver.deployed()
undefined
truffle(chainA)> await sender.sendCrossChainMessage(receiver.address, "Hello LayerZero")
{
  tx: '0x2a9ddb4e29c1b0ea7ea9527da10a5a4b7feb9d425cc73517c27c97cf1753080a',
  receipt: {
    transactionHash: '0x2a9ddb4e29c1b0ea7ea9527da10a5a4b7feb9d425cc73517c27c97cf1753080a',
    transactionIndex: 0,
    blockNumber: 5,
    blockHash: '0xc05c43436ddbaa9af13059a92dde753c923ddfd25e631378db5a6f792c312e81',
    from: '0x73bdd97d9fb543031d221fd30b2829ed8efc46ca',
    to: '0x5e31645bfe06407b5dc12557e03a5084c0ac3908',
    cumulativeGasUsed: 76553,
    gasUsed: 76553,
    contractAddress: null,
    logs: [ [Object] ],
    logsBloom: '0x00000000000000000000000000000000100000000000000000000000000008000000000000000000
000000000000000000000000000000000000000000000010000000000400000000000000000000000000000000000
00000000000000000000000080000000000000000000000000000000000000000020000000000000000000000000000
    status: true,
    effectiveGasPrice: 3020420440,
    type: '0x2',
    rawLogs: [ [Object], [Object] ]
  },
  logs: [
    {
      address: '0x5E31645bFE06407B5Dc12557E03A5084c0Ac3908',
      blockHash: '0xc05c43436ddbaa9af13059a92dde753c923ddfd25e631378db5a6f792c312e81',
      blockNumber: 5,
      logIndex: 1,
      removed: false,
      transactionHash: '0x2a9ddb4e29c1b0ea7ea9527da10a5a4b7feb9d425cc73517c27c97cf1753080a',
      transactionIndex: 0,
      id: 'log_34864a5e',
      event: 'MessageSent',
      args: [Result]
    }
  ]
}
```

Fig. 4.7 Emitting MessageSent event from MockLayerZeroSender using truffle console

This triggers the MessageSent event and logs the transaction details on the blockchain, including the sender address, the receiver address, the string message, gas usage, and block metadata.

Figure 4.7 is the output showing sendCrossChainMessage execution with transaction and event log output.

Next, we verify whether the receiver contract has correctly stored the incoming message by accessing the public state variable lastMessage through.

```
let msg = await receiver.lastMessage()
```

The console returns "Hello LayerZero", confirming successful message relay. We also retrieve the last recorded sender and fetch past events emitted by the sender contract using getPastEvents("MessageSent").

Figure 4.8 is the screenshot showing lastMessage, lastSender, and the getPastEvents output from the sender.

To further validate the receipt of the message, we query the receiver contract's emitted events using.

4.7 LayerZero with Truffle

```
truffle(chainA)> let msg = await receiver.lastMessage()
undefined
truffle(chainA)> msg
'Hello LayerZero'
truffle(chainA)> let senderAddr = await receiver.lastSender()
undefined
truffle(chainA)> senderAddr
'0x5E31645bFE06407B5Dc12557E03A5084c0Ac3908'
truffle(chainA)> let events = await sender.getPastEvents("MessageSent", { fromBlock: 0, toBlock: "latest" })
undefined
truffle(chainA)> console.log(events)
[
  {
    address: '0x5E31645bFE06407B5Dc12557E03A5084c0Ac3908',
    blockHash: '0xc05c43436ddbaa9af13059a92dde753c923ddfd25e631378db5a6f792c312e81',
    blockNumber: 5,
    logIndex: 1,
    removed: false,
    transactionHash: '0x2a9ddb4e29c1b0ea7ea9527da10a5a4b7feb9d425cc73517c27c97cf1753080a',
    transactionIndex: 0,
    id: 'log_34864a5e',
    returnValues: Result {
      '0': '0xD8eD241c802210c2Ae8e42DA1D99FABF685a9723',
      '1': 'Hello LayerZero',
      to: '0xD8eD241c802210c2Ae8e42DA1D99FABF685a9723',
      message: 'Hello LayerZero'
    },
    event: 'MessageSent',
    signature: '0x0d7fccda06d6eb51c23cbd16d49b9b3f3ebafb002dba1b074896cbb35d0e8130',
    raw: {
      data: '0x000000000000000000000000000000000000000000000000000000000000000020000000000000000000000000000000
      topics: [Array]
    },
    args: Result {
      '0': '0xD8eD241c802210c2Ae8e42DA1D99FABF685a9723',
      '1': 'Hello LayerZero',
      __length__: 2,
      to: '0xD8eD241c802210c2Ae8e42DA1D99FABF685a9723',
      message: 'Hello LayerZero'
    }
  }
]
undefined
```

Fig. 4.8 Verifying message storage and retrieving MessageSent logs

```
receiver.getPastEvents("MessageReceived",
                        { fromBlock: 0, toBlock: "latest" }).
```

This confirms that the receiver contract emitted a `MessageReceived` event with the correct sender address and message payload.

Figure 4.9 is the screenshot showing the result of `getPastEvents("MessageReceived")` on the receiver contract.

This interactive console simulation confirms that both event emission and message storage are functioning correctly, mimicking LayerZero's message-passing behavior in a simplified local environment. While no actual cross-chain transport or oracle verification is performed, the structural logic and event flow offer a close approximation of LayerZero's `send` and `lzReceive` functions for educational and testing purposes.

In production, `send` invokes LayerZero's `Endpoint.send` method, while `lzReceive` is executed only after the message has been verified by Oracle and Relayer. This test configuration, however, remains beneficial in enhancing our understanding.

As demonstrated in [9], the assurance of message delivery can be formally validated by runtime verifiable metrics. Moreover, event relays and replay protection are emphasized by instruments such as CrossLink [10] and the security design

```
truffle(chainA)> let rxEvents = await receiver.getPastEvents("MessageReceived", { fromBlock: 0, toBlock: "latest" })
undefined
truffle(chainA)> console.log(rxEvents)
[
  {
    address: '0xD8eD241c802210c2Ae8e42DA1D99FABF685a9723',
    blockHash: '0xc05c43436ddbaa9af13859a92dde753c923ddfd25e631378db5a6f792c312e81',
    blockNumber: 5,
    logIndex: 0,
    removed: false,
    transactionHash: '0x2a9ddb4e29c1b0ea7ea9527da10a5a4b7feb9d425cc73517c27c97cf1753080a',
    transactionIndex: 0,
    id: 'log_2a7346de',
    returnValues: Result {
      '0': '0x5E31645bFE06407B5Dc12557E03A5084c0Ac3908',
      '1': 'Hello LayerZero',
      sender: '0x5E31645bFE06407B5Dc12557E03A5084c0Ac3908',
      message: 'Hello LayerZero'
    },
    event: 'MessageReceived',
    signature: '0x15340f1d3815fc99b59e3b9ed010321f64951d6ee6a43c97a9e92713e7cd6ad17',
    raw: {
      data: '0x000000000000000000000000000000000000000000000000000000000000002800000000000000000000000000000000
      topics: [Array]
    },
    args: Result {
      '0': '0x5E31645bFE06407B5Dc12557E03A5084c0Ac3908',
      '1': 'Hello LayerZero',
      __length__: 2,
      sender: '0x5E31645bFE06407B5Dc12557E03A5084c0Ac3908',
      message: 'Hello LayerZero'
    }
  }
]
undefined
truffle(chainA)>
```

Fig. 4.9 MessageReceived event with message payload

principles examined in [11]. The attack surface of smart contracts, especially those involving cross-chain data, remains an area of active investigation. Models based on deep learning, as referenced in [12], are being created to proactively identify such vulnerabilities.

The next section will use Chainlink with Truffle and Ganache simulation to show interoperability.

4.8 Chainlink CCIP

4.8.1 Oracle-Based Routing and Message Reliability

Chainlink Cross-Chain Interoperability Protocol (CCIP) uses decentralized oracle networks to ensure secure, validated, and reliable message delivery across blockchains. The goal of the CCIP is to standardize safe cross-chain messaging by using decentralized oracles for message routing and validation. Unlike bridges or relays that rely solely on smart contract verification, CCIP uses its extensive network of node operators for the validation and transmission of messages or token transfers across several chains, hence providing an enhanced assurance of trust and resilience [10].

Figure 4.10 illustrates the architecture of Chainlink CCIP, where a decentralized oracle network mediates cross-chain messages between smart contracts. The protocol ensures message integrity and reliability through Service Level Agreements (SLAs) enforced by CCIP Gateways and Routers, enabling seamless interaction across Layer 1 and Layer 2 blockchains [11].

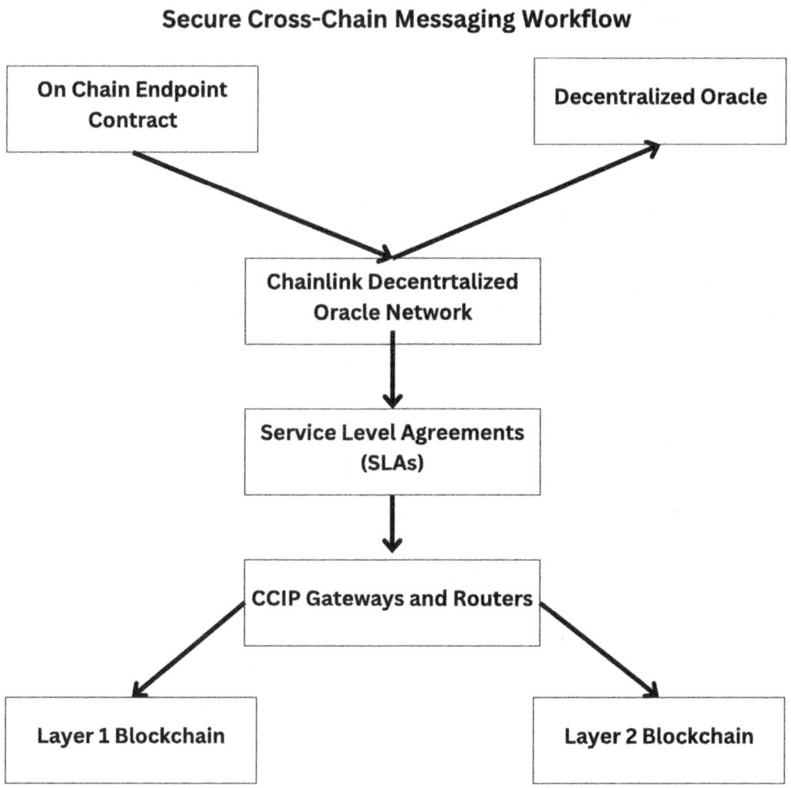

4.8 Chainlink CCIP

Secure Cross-Chain Messaging Workflow

```
┌─────────────────────┐           ┌─────────────────────┐
│  On Chain Endpoint  │           │ Decentralized Oracle│
│      Contract       │           │                     │
└──────────┬──────────┘           └──────────▲──────────┘
           │                                 │
           └──────────────┐   ┌──────────────┘
                          ▼   │
                ┌─────────────────────┐
                │ Chainlink Decentrtalized│
                │   Oracle Network    │
                └──────────┬──────────┘
                           ▼
                ┌─────────────────────┐
                │ Service Level Agreements│
                │        (SLAs)       │
                └──────────┬──────────┘
                           ▼
                ┌─────────────────────┐
                │ CCIP Gateways and Routers│
                └──────┬───────┬──────┘
                       │       │
              ┌────────▼──┐ ┌──▼────────┐
              │ Layer 1   │ │ Layer 2   │
              │ Blockchain│ │ Blockchain│
              └───────────┘ └───────────┘
```

Fig. 4.10 CCIP architecture

4.8.2 Building with Chainlink CCIP

As before, the full project source code is available on our GitHub (/ccip-demo).

Using mock contracts, we will model the transfer of cross-chain liquidity between two chains that are compatible with EVMs. Chain A and Chain B are represented by distinct ports in this demonstration, which assumes two local chains using Ganache.

Before proceeding further, it is important to install the necessary packages required for the Chainlink CCIP mock and interaction logic. These include the official Chainlink contract library, Ethers.js for encoding and interacting with contracts off-chain, and dotenv for securely managing environment variables. These can be installed via the following command:

```
npm install @chainlink/contracts ethers dotenv
```

This configuration and dependency setup provides the foundation for simulating oracle-based message routing using Chainlink-style contracts and flows entirely within a local Truffle and Ganache environment.

4.8.3 Contract Code

Refer Truffle Project creation section to create project folder for ccip-demo and start Ganache CL on different ports.

4.8.3.1 MockSender.sol

The MockSender contract simulates the behavior of a Chainlink CCIP sender by emitting an event that represents the act of sending liquidity to another blockchain.

This contract sends cross-chain messages.

```
// SPDX-License-Identifier: MIT
pragma solidity ^0.8.20;

contract MockSender {
    event LiquiditySent(address indexed from,
            uint256 amount, string destinationChain);

    function sendLiquidity(uint256 amount,
            string memory destinationChain) public {
        emit LiquiditySent(msg.sender, amount, destinationChain);
    }
}
```

The MockSender contract simulates the behavior of a Chainlink CCIP sender by emitting an event that represents the act of sending liquidity to another blockchain. It defines an event named `LiquiditySent`, which logs the sender's address (`msg.sender`), the amount of liquidity sent, and the name of the destination chain. The function `sendLiquidity` is publicly accessible and triggers this event when called, allowing off-chain services or mock receiver contracts to detect and respond to the message. While this mock does not implement actual token transfer or CCIP protocol logic, it effectively demonstrates how message emission from one chain can be tracked for cross-chain liquidity movement scenarios.

4.8.3.2 MockReceiver.sol

The `MockReceiver` contract acts as the receiving end of a Chainlink CCIP-style liquidity transfer simulation.

This contract mimics message reception.

```
// SPDX-License-Identifier: MIT
pragma solidity ^0.8.20;
```

4.8 Chainlink CCIP

```solidity
contract MockReceiver {
    uint256 public lastAmount;
    address public lastSender;

    function receiveLiquidity(address from,
uint256 amount) public {
        lastAmount = amount;
        lastSender = from;
    }
}
```

The contract includes two public state variables, `lastAmount` to store the most recently received liquidity amount, and `lastSender` to record the address from which the liquidity originated. The `receiveLiquidity` function accepts the sender's address and the amount as parameters and updates the state accordingly. This contract does not perform actual token handling but serves to demonstrate how a receiver on another chain might track incoming liquidity transfers, based on off-chain triggers or relayed data in a cross-chain setup.

4.8.3.3 Migration Scripts

Create separate migration files for each mock contract.

```javascript
// 1_deploy_sender.js
const MockSender = artifacts.require("MockSender");

module.exports = function (deployer) {
  deployer.deploy(MockSender);
};
```

The sender migration script is responsible for deploying the `MockSender` contract to the configured blockchain network during the first step of the Truffle deployment process. It uses `artifacts.require("MockSender")` to load the compiled contract artifact and then calls `deployer.deploy(MockSender)` to deploy it on-chain. When Truffle runs this script using the migrate command, it ensures that the `MockSender` contract is deployed to the specified network as defined in truffle-config.js.

```javascript
// 2_deploy_receiver.js
const MockReceiver = artifacts.require("MockReceiver");

module.exports = function (deployer) {
    deployer.deploy(MockReceiver);
};
```

The receiver migration script handles the deployment of the `MockReceiver` contract during the second step of the Truffle migration process. It first loads the compiled `MockReceiver` contract using `artifacts.require("MockReceiver")`, and then uses `deployer.deploy(MockReceiver)` to deploy it to the blockchain network specified in the Truffle configuration. When executed through truffle migrate, this script ensures that the `MockReceiver` contract is available on-chain, enabling it to receive simulated liquidity messages during the Chainlink CCIP mock interaction.

4.8.4 Deployment Walkthrough

To deploy the Chainlink CCIP mock contracts on each simulated chain, we use the following Truffle commands:

```
truffle migrate --network chainA
truffle migrate --network chainB
```

These commands deploy the MockSender and MockReceiver contracts to the respective Ganache instances running on ports 7545 and 8545, as configured in the `truffle-config.js` file. The deployment process and terminal output will closely resemble what was previously discussed in the LayerZero Deployment Walkthrough including contract compilation, execution of migration scripts, gas consumption, transaction hashes, and confirmation of deployed contract addresses. Once complete, both contracts will be ready for local testing of oracle-style cross-chain message simulation.

4.8.4.1 Interaction Simulation

To simulate a Chainlink-style liquidity transfer, we first deploy the MockSender contract on Chain A and invoke its `sendLiquidity` function with a sample value and destination chain string as shown in Fig. 4.11. This emits the LiquiditySent event and confirms the transaction's success, including gas usage and sender metadata.

We then inspect the event log from the returned transaction object using tx.logs as shown in Fig. 4.12. This confirms the event was emitted successfully, showing the sender's address, amount, and the destination chain.

On Chain B, we manually invoke the `receiveLiquidity` function on the deployed MockReceiver contract, simulating the role of an off-chain Chainlink Oracle or CCIP router as shown in Fig. 4.13. The function call succeeds, and the console confirms the transaction receipt with details such as block number and gas used.

4.8 Chainlink CCIP

Fig. 4.11 Emitting LiquiditySent event from MockSender on chain A

Fig. 4.12 Inspecting event log of sendLiquidity call

```
[truffle(chainB)> await receiver.receiveLiquidity("0x41e591272cD547515F1d3D8Bcbbc381731d97A1
5", 100)
{
  tx: '0x0bbb9bfbed5437a0d19afe247f48f3e8f19b1831bab6f7ec175d57337e7c5abd',
  receipt: {
    transactionHash: '0x0bbb9bfbed5437a0d19afe247f48f3e8f19b1831bab6f7ec175d57337e7c5abd',
    transactionIndex: 0,
    blockNumber: 3,
    blockHash: '0xb4c475c5f376698212f91531e9e68f168303f6edf32eeda5553003386aa6add2',
    from: '0xa2b9281135c1df8ea6d1c983a3d185017ea51c47',
    to: '0x1fd29142ef7c082e7226eb2fef45d51da0b86708',
    cumulativeGasUsed: 66449,
    gasUsed: 66449,
    contractAddress: null,
    logs: [],
    logsBloom: '0x000000000000000000000000000000000000000000000000000000000000000
0000000000000000000000000000000000000000000000000000000000000000000000000000000
0000000000000000000000000000000000000000000000000000000000000000000000000000000
0000000000000000000000000000000000000000000000000000000000000000000000000000000
0000000000000000000000000000000000000000000000000000000000000000000000000000000
000000000000000000000000000000000000000000000000000000000000000000000000000',
    status: true,
    effectiveGasPrice: 3172643419,
    type: '0x2',
    rawLogs: []
  },
  logs: []
}
```

Fig. 4.13 Simulating message reception using MockReceiver on chain B

To verify that the event was originally emitted on Chain A, we retrieve all past `LiquiditySent` events using `getPastEvents` as shown in Fig. 4.14. The log confirms that the message including the sender and liquidity value was correctly captured on-chain.

Finally, we validate the stored values on Chain B by calling the `lastSender` and `lastAmount` functions of `MockReceiver` as shown in Fig. 4.15. The console confirms that the receiver correctly stored the incoming liquidity and sender address, completing the full simulation of a mock Chainlink CCIP message flow.

Some of the most important flaws in traditional bridges are addressed by using oracles as routing and verification agents, which unbundle the trust model from individual contracts [3]. Token bridging and decentralized identity verifications are just two of the functions made possible by Chainlink CCIP modularity, which also paves the path for seamless DeFi and NFT interoperability across different blockchain platforms [11].

We will now show you how to achieve interoperability using a token bridge.

4.9 Token Bridge

This prototype establishes a lock-and-mint simulation between two EVM-compatible blockchains—two distinct Ganache instances representing "Ethereum" and "Polygon." By minting comparable wrapped tokens on the destination chain

4.9 Token Bridge

```
● ● ●    ccip-demo — node ~/.nvm/versions/node/v18.20.5/bin/truffle console --network chain...
truffle(chainA)> let logs = await instance.getPastEvents("LiquiditySent", { fromBlock: 0 })
;
undefined
truffle(chainA)> console.log(logs)
[
  {
    address: '0x11309b34C778506592B86632a6E7c41Ec0CFBc77',
    blockHash: '0xec1e2bf9bed17bca894d3b64f4b46009b3b718a6dda8040365feaaa29a793a74',
    blockNumber: 3,
    logIndex: 0,
    removed: false,
    transactionHash: '0x437520695fb371573e216988740760e8f7af035a877fc28d2cc0778897d65590',
    transactionIndex: 0,
    id: 'log_ee4f4f54',
    returnValues: Result {
      '0': '0x41e591272cD547515F1d3D8Bcbbc381731d97A15',
      '1': '500',
      '2': 'ChainB',
      from: '0x41e591272cD547515F1d3D8Bcbbc381731d97A15',
      amount: '500',
      destinationChain: 'ChainB'
    },
    event: 'LiquiditySent',
    signature: '0x92fc3a04fb4855951bfc999bd4ee4e6af9081f7a0b153dfeb70c00d10f9517b9',
    raw: {
      data: '0x0000000000000000000000000000000000000000000000000000000000001f4000000000000
00000000000000000000000000000000000000000000000000040000000000000000000000000000000000000000
000000000000000000006436861696e4200000000000000000000000000000000000000000000000000000000',
      topics: [Array]
    },
    args: Result {
      '0': '0x41e591272cD547515F1d3D8Bcbbc381731d97A15',
      '1': [BN],
      '2': 'ChainB',
      __length__: 3,
      from: '0x41e591272cD547515F1d3D8Bcbbc381731d97A15',
      amount: [BN],
      destinationChain: 'ChainB'
    }
  }
]
undefined
truffle(chainA)>
```

Fig. 4.14 Retrieving LiquiditySent event from chain A history

and locking up tokens on the source chain, the goal is to mimic the transfer of assets between two chains. To facilitate token transfer between ecosystems, this paradigm is used in production across a variety of cross-chain protocols, including Wormhole and Axelar [13].

In lock-mint bridging, what is the intuition? Let's say you want to use your Ethereum coins in a DeFi application that uses Polygons. The Ethereum chain locks your tokens in a bridge contract rather than sending the actual ETH. On the Polygon side, in the meantime, a synthetic equivalent which is often called wrapped ETH is produced. The wrapped token is now available in the Polygon ecosystem. These bridges guarantee that tokens are not lost or duplicated and that the circulating supply remains constant [14, 15].

```
leenanadkar@Leenas-MacBook-Pro ccip-demo % truffle console --network chainB
truffle(chainB)> let receiver = await MockReceiver.deployed()
undefined
truffle(chainB)> let tx = await sender.sendLiquidity("0xA2b9281135c1dF8ea6d1C983a3D185017EA
51C47", 100)
truffle(chainB)> await receiver.receiveLiquidity("0x41e591272cD547515F1d3D8Bcbbc381731d97A1
5", 100)
{
  tx: '0x0bbb9bfbed5437a0d19afe247f48f3e8f19b1831bab6f7ec175d57337e7c5abd',
  receipt: {
    transactionHash: '0x0bbb9bfbed5437a0d19afe247f48f3e8f19b1831bab6f7ec175d57337e7c5abd',
    transactionIndex: 0,
    blockNumber: 3,
    blockHash: '0xb4c475c5f376698212f91531e9e68f168303f6edf32eeda5553003386aa6add2',
    from: '0xa2b9281135c1df8ea6d1c983a3d185017ea51c47',
    to: '0x1fd29142ef7c082e7226eb2fef45d51da0b86708',
    cumulativeGasUsed: 66449,
    gasUsed: 66449,
    contractAddress: null,
    logs: [],
    logsBloom: '0x000000000000000000000000000000000000000000000000000000000000000
0000000000000000000000000000000000000000000000000000000000000000000000000000000000
0000000000000000000000000000000000000000000000000000000000000000000000000000000000
0000000000000000000000000000000000000000000000000000000000000000000000000000000000
0000000000000000000000000000000000000000000000000000000000000000000000000000000000
0000000000000000000000000000000000000000000000000000000000000000',
    status: true,
    effectiveGasPrice: 3172643419,
    type: '0x2',
    rawLogs: []
  },
  logs: []
}
truffle(chainB)> (await receiver.lastSender())
'0x41e591272cD547515F1d3D8Bcbbc381731d97A15'
truffle(chainB)> (await receiver.lastAmount()).toString()
'100'
```

Fig. 4.15 Verifying stored sender and amount in MockReceiver on chain B

4.9.1 Prototype

As mentioned earlier, the full project source is available on our GitHub (/tokenBridge).

We begin by starting two instances of Ganache, one on port 8545 (Chain B—Polygon) and one on port 7545 (Chain A—Ethereum). Our Truffle project will include two smart contracts: `MintContract.sol` on Chain B and `LockContract.sol` on Chain A. Tokens are sent to the LockContract, which then transmits an event. In response to this event, a mock relayer off-chain calls the `MintContract`'s mint method. This allows us to observe how events, messages, and state changes can resemble a cross-chain bridge.

```
// SPDX-License-Identifier: MIT
pragma solidity ^0.8.20;

contract LockContract {
    event TokenLocked(address sender, uint256 amount,
```

4.9 Token Bridge

```
                    string targetChain);

    function lockTokens(uint256 amount, bytes memory chain)
        public {
        emit TokenLocked(msg.sender, amount, string(chain));
    }
}
```

The LockContract simulates the "lock" side of a token bridge commonly used in cross-chain transfers. It defines an event `TokenLocked` that logs the sender's address, the amount of tokens being locked, and the name of the target chain. The `lockTokens` function accepts a uint256 amount and a bytes input for the chain name, which is cast to a string before emitting the event. This design mimics real-world bridge contracts where tokens are locked on one chain before being minted or released on another, and the use of bytes allows for encoding flexibility in cross-chain messaging systems.

And on the destination chain, the corresponding MintContract:

```
// SPDX-License-Identifier: MIT
pragma solidity ^0.8.20;

contract MintContract {
    event TokenMinted(address recipient, uint256 amount,
                      string sourceChain);

    function mintTokens(address recipient, uint256 amount,
                        bytes memory chain)
        public {
        emit TokenMinted(recipient, amount, string(chain));
    }
}
```

The `MintContract` represents the "mint" side of a token bridge in a cross-chain interaction, where tokens are issued on a destination chain after being locked on the source chain. It defines an event `TokenMinted` that logs the recipient's address, the amount of tokens minted, and the name of the source chain. The `mintTokens` function accepts the recipient's address, the token amount, and a bytes-encoded chain name which is converted to a string before emitting the event. This pattern is commonly used in lock-and-mint bridging mechanisms, enabling transparent tracking of cross-chain token transfers without actual asset movement.

This abstraction sets the foundation for simulating cross-chain flows, allowing us to now transition into writing migration scripts that deploy and connect these contracts across isolated test networks.

4.9.1.1 Migration Scripts

```
2_deploy_LockContract.js
const LockContract = artifacts.require("LockContract");

module.exports = function (deployer, network) {
  if (network === "chainA") {
    deployer.deploy(LockContract);
  }
};
```

The LockContract migration script conditionally deploys the LockContract only when the deployment is targeting the chainA network, as defined in the Truffle configuration file. It first loads the compiled contract using artifacts.require("LockContract"), and then checks the network argument. If the current deployment network is "chainA," it proceeds to deploy the LockContract using deployer.deploy. This setup is useful in multi-chain simulations, ensuring that specific contracts are only deployed to their intended chain, in this case, the lock-side contract is deployed exclusively to Chain A.

```
3_deploy_MintContract.js
const MintContract = artifacts.require("MintContract");

module.exports = function (deployer, network) {
  if (network === "chainB") {
    deployer.deploy(MintContract);
  }
};
```

The MintContract migration script, 3_deploy_MintContract.js, deploys the MintContract only when the Truffle migration is run on the chainB network. It begins by loading the compiled MintContract using artifacts.require, and then checks if the current deployment target matches "chainB." If so, it proceeds with deployer.deploy(MintContract). This approach ensures that the mint-side logic is isolated to Chain B, complementing the LockContract on Chain A, and enabling a clean simulation of a lock-and-mint cross-chain token bridge between two separate blockchain environments.

4.9.1.2 Interaction Simulation

After deploying the LockContract on Chain A and the MintContract on Chain B, we simulate the lock-mint interaction to demonstrate a basic token bridging pattern. Using the Truffle console on Chain A, we run LockContract's lockTokens function with the destination chain name and amount. By locking 1000

4.9 Token Bridge

```
leenanadkar@Leenas-MacBook-Pro tokenBridge % truffle console --network chainA
truffle(chainA)> let lock = await LockContract.deployed()
undefined
truffle(chainA)> let accounts = await web3.eth.getAccounts()
undefined
truffle(chainA)> await lock.lockTokens(1000, web3.utils.asciiToHex("chainB"), { from: accounts[0] })
{
  tx: '0xb5acd6ff04c1882f596f8116251366bac5629c9cd7e9b6420bb4f9f6a15a4c14',
  receipt: {
    transactionHash: '0xb5acd6ff04c1882f596f8116251366bac5629c9cd7e9b6420bb4f9f6a15a4c14',
    transactionIndex: 0,
    blockNumber: 3,
    blockHash: '0x4cb10ccab014f94af792e4dad2d9cfecdc8f590ccfad14dcd914ba8d1f438a85',
    from: '0xda1aae1487e4fc610e19fb4e3fd8a13792dd8716',
    to: '0x16665f19c34d9052e049200a528488349c5c789c',
    cumulativeGasUsed: 25576,
    gasUsed: 25576,
    contractAddress: null,
    logs: [ [Object] ],
    logsBloom: '0x000000000000000000000000000000000000000000000000000000000000000
0000000000000000000000000000000000000010000000000000000000000000000000000000000000
0000000000000000000000000000000000000008000000000000000000100000000000000000000000
0000000000000000000000000000000000000000000000000000000000000000008000000000000000
0000000000000000000000000200000',
    status: true,
    effectiveGasPrice: 3173113667,
    type: '0x2',
    rawLogs: [ [Object] ]
  },
  logs: [
    {
      address: '0x16665F19C34d9052E049200a528488349C5C789c',
      blockHash: '0x4cb10ccab014f94af792e4dad2d9cfecdc8f590ccfad14dcd914ba8d1f438a85',
      blockNumber: 3,
      logIndex: 0,
      removed: false,
      transactionHash: '0xb5acd6ff04c1882f596f8116251366bac5629c9cd7e9b6420bb4f9f6a15a4c14',
      transactionIndex: 0,
      id: 'log_4aabb6d9',
      event: 'TokenLocked',
      args: [Result]
    }
  ]
}
truffle(chainA)>
```

Fig. 4.16 Executing lockTokens on chain A with target chain B

tokens and triggering the `TokenLocked` event, this operation starts the cross-chain transfer by logging the sender's address, amount, and destination chain (Fig. 4.16).

Next, we move to the Truffle console on Chain B and invoke `mintTokens` on the `MintContract`, simulating a relayer delivering the proof of the lock event as seen in Fig. 4.17. This function mints 1000 tokens for the recipient and emits the `TokenMinted` event, confirming the source chain and token amount.

To verify the `TokenLocked` event, we retrieve the event log using `getPastEvents` from the `LockContract` on Chain A as shown in Fig. 4.18. The result confirms that the lock operation was recorded correctly, capturing the sender, amount, and `targetChain` value ("chainB").

Finally, we verify the `TokenMinted` event on Chain B using a similar call to `getPastEvents` on the MintContract as shown in Fig. 4.19. The log confirms that the recipient address, minted amount, and sourceChain ("chainA") were correctly stored and broadcasted as part of the mint operation.

To visually verify the transaction logs and state updates during simulation, developers can launch two Truffle consoles on separate terminals, one for each chain. The

Fig. 4.17 Executing mintTokens on chain B with Source chain A

log generated by `TokenMinted` on Chain B confirms that the message was accurately conveyed and the mint procedure was properly initiated.

4.9.2 Security Checklist

Developers must consider potential security flaws in such bridges, even though this is a simulation. Bridges are frequently targeted in real-world implementations, as seen by the 2022 attacks on Ronin and Wormhole. To prevent spoofing or double-minting, it is crucial to have event replay guards, reentrancy prevention, and signature validation [2].

Here is a general Security Review Checklist:

- Use message hashes or nonces to stop events from replaying between chains
- Logging sender and amount for auditability
- Only the relayer or validator can call mintTokens due to access restrictions for minting
- Circuit breaker (emergency pause modifier)
- Testing the retry and fallback procedures in case the relay fails

4.10 Security Considerations

Fig. 4.18 Retrieving TokenLocked event from chain A

We have now walked through the practical simulations of LayerZero's Ultra-Light Node, Chainlink CCIP's oracle-based messaging, and a lock-mint Token Bridge all using Truffle and Ganache for seamless local deployment and testing. These examples not only demonstrated how cross-chain messages are initiated, relayed, and consumed, but also laid the groundwork for understanding real-world interoperability. With the technical implementation in place, we now shift our focus to the critical aspect that underpins all of it that is the Security Considerations.

4.10 Security Considerations

Cross-chain smart contract developers must take into account more than just transaction coordination and message passing. Security becomes significantly more complex when multiple distinct chains operate, each possessing unique finality assumptions, consensus mechanisms, and temporal granularity. A hacked relay layer or replay message can stop the entire flow, even if the logic in each chain has

```
leenanadkar@Leenas-MacBook-Pro tokenBridge % truffle console --network chainB
truffle(chainB)> let mint = await MintContract.deployed()
undefined
truffle(chainB)> mint.getPastEvents("TokenMinted", { fromBlock: 0 }).then(console.log)
[
  {
    address: '0xCE6ca2134e91602dc4F3F588f5F4E2F7Fa485D27',
    blockHash: '0x461dc227768b42bb1d95197753154d841d13d4b869015c95080899c12f7e9c11',
    blockNumber: 3,
    logIndex: 0,
    removed: false,
    transactionHash: '0x1e7171f04085649f5466de5db3ae57b494e11c5c95e61586f5ea95db0af93e66',
    transactionIndex: 0,
    id: 'log_965a7ad3',
    returnValues: Result {
      '0': '0xD723C7e1F4297C031242E9fc9d6714bD683B4A2B',
      '1': '1000',
      '2': 'chainA',
      recipient: '0xD723C7e1F4297C031242E9fc9d6714bD683B4A2B',
      amount: '1000',
      sourceChain: 'chainA'
    },
    event: 'TokenMinted',
    signature: '0xdf92894dc4675a7333caa5903b69cf5d8e8ec0d3f361c88207b6688e525703bb',
    raw: {
      data: '0x000000000000000000000000d723c7e1f4297c031242e9fc9d6714bd683b4a2b00000000000000000000000000000000000000000000000000000000000003e800000000000000000000000000000000000000000000000000000000000000600000000000000000000000000000000000000000000000000000000000000006636861696e64100000000000000000000000000000000000000000000000000000',
      topics: [Array]
    },
    args: Result {
      '0': '0xD723C7e1F4297C031242E9fc9d6714bD683B4A2B',
      '1': [BN],
      '2': 'chainA',
      __length__: 3,
      recipient: '0xD723C7e1F4297C031242E9fc9d6714bD683B4A2B',
      amount: [BN],
      sourceChain: 'chainA'
    }
  }
]
undefined
```

Fig. 4.19 Retrieving TokenMinted event from chain B

integrity in isolation. Implementations of cross-chain interoperability must adopt strong patterns of replay protection, oracle trust reduction, and defensive coding disciplines in Solidity to address this.

4.10.1 Replay Protection and Nonce Tracking

Imagine that a user locks tokens on Chain A, and due to poor relaying or network slowness, the same mint message appears twice on Chain B. The mint function might be invoked again, repeating value on Chain B and inflating the token supply if replay protection was not present. Using nonces or one-time message IDs is the solution. A mapping of the IDs of processed messages must be used for each cross-chain action. A message's nonce must be marked as used once it has been processed and its outcome implemented. This facilitates idempotent execution and replicates optimal practices in atomic swap architectures [1]. Developers can replicate this technique by using mappings like `mapping(bytes32 => bool)` processedMessages; and implementing conditions with require(!proce ssedMessages[messageHash]).

4.10.2 Oracle Manipulation and Verifiable Messaging

Decentralized oracles act as message routers and validators in protocols like Chainlink CCIP. It is necessary for developers to code as though oracles are adversarial, even as these oracles minimize trust. ECDSA signature verification or confining oracles to tightly defined logic, such as routing messages without payload alteration, is an effective defense. Oracle-signed messages can be verified using hashed payload verification and Solidity's ecrecover function. Developers can imitate Truffle by using stubbed oracle contracts that emit signed payloads that the receiver checks before state changes [14].

4.10.3 Circuit Breakers, Pause Mechanisms, and Role-Based Access

Contracts that include controlled access and emergency stops offer even another degree of safety. The ability to halt activities as soon as a potential exploit or inconsistency is discovered is a prerequisite for cross-chain contracts. OpenZeppelin's Plausible contract is commonly employed for this purpose, as it maintains the addresses of privileges to temporarily suspend function executions. Similarly, only trustworthy individuals should be able to approve bridge activities like mint, unlock, or relayMessage, such as administrators, validators, or roles under DAO authority. This is provided by Solidity through the AccessControl module, which supports dynamically given and withdrawn roles such as BRIDGE_ADMIN_ROLE and RELAYER_ROLE.

4.10.4 Static Analysis and Deployment Verification

Code logic security is important, but tool-based analysis increases trust even more. Truffle provides a number of plugins that increase the auditability of contracts. Truffle-plugin-verify, for instance, enables developers to confirm the source of their contracts using Etherscan [16] or other compatible explorers, thereby making the released content publicly auditable. Despite Solidity 0.8.x's built-in overflow prevention, solhint [17], a Solidity linter, can identify dangerous constructs, unsafe math, and unused functions. By using them prior to deployment, especially in simulated cross-chain situations, developers are establishing a routine of writing audit-friendly code beforehand.

This part purposefully created a mint function vulnerability, like missing nonce tracking. Then, using a replayed message and a truffle exec script, the same function was attacked, reproducing a repeating mint on Chain B. It not only clarified the principles of replay attacks but also reaffirmed the reasons why cross-chain security is not the best course of action.

4.11 Developer Tooling Summary

Any cross-chain smart contract project's success is largely dependent on selecting the appropriate development tools and project structure in addition to having strong code logic. The main developer tools used in this chapter are examined in this section, along with their contributions to effectively replicating interoperability use cases.

4.11.1 Truffle: Foundation for Cross-Chain Simulation

Truffle is still the mainstay of smart contract development, especially when it comes to isolated environments and emulating multi-chain behaviors. Beyond contract generation and deployment, it can also be used for migrations, test automation, and debugging, which makes it perfect for simulating interoperability scenarios. In order to replicate message flow between networks, developers can deploy sender-receiver contract pairs and build two or more Ganache chains by operating them on separate ports. In truffle-config.js, the endpoints of each chain can be set up to differentiate deployments and mimic "Chain A" and "Chain B" interactions.

For instance, an event that is emitted by a sender contract running on Ganache port 7545 can be manually or by off-chain scripts picked up to initiate a receiver function running on port 8545. This simplified simulation mimics the potential behavior of LayerZero or CCIP message flow, providing engineers with a glimpse at protocol behavior without requiring the entire protocol stack or numerous live chains.

4.11.2 Web3.js for Simulating Cross-Chain Clients

Web3.js is something that developers frequently use to simulate off-chain actors like relayers or oracles. Both Ganache chains can be connected simultaneously because of this JavaScript library. An event listener can subscribe to MessageSent events on the source chain and, upon receipt, transmit a receiveMessage transaction to the destination chain. This type of scripting serves as the foundation for employing external actors to simulate cross-chain logic, which is an essential design

4.11 Developer Tooling Summary 135

element in LayerZero, Axelar, and Chainlink CCIP implementations. Web3.js provides tools for encoding and decoding message payloads, validating answers, and simulating failure and retry conditions.

4.11.3 APIs for Modular Testing and Future Upgrades

Applications developed on top of interoperability protocols must also change as these protocols do. Upgradability and flexibility are ensured by incorporating abstraction layers through APIs. It is recommended that developers separate the logic for relay interaction, message encoding, and decoding into modular JavaScript services. To replicate relay interfaces, these APIs can be made available as REST endpoints or incorporated into a Node.js backend for automated testing.

By using Truffle's `artifacts.require` combined with Web3 calls, developers can test new protocol behaviors (for example, LayerZero's retry mechanism or CCIP's oracle query fallback) without needing to change core smart contract code. Future updates will also be made easier because additional communications protocols can be added to the same client interface without changing the fundamental logic.

4.11.4 Project Structure Best Practices

Organizing the project correctly is crucial when working with multiple Truffle networks. A recommended structure includes:

```
/CrossChainInteroperability/
  /contracts/
    SenderContract.sol
    ReceiverContract.sol
  /migrations/
    1_deploy_sender.js
    2_deploy_receiver.js
  /test/
    sender_test.js
    receiver_test.js
    crosschain_flow_test.js
  /scripts/
    relayEvent.js
    oracleMock.js
  truffle-config.js
  package.json
```

Developers can independently test every component of the system because of its modular design. Network-specific contracts are implemented, cross-chain logic is simulated via scripts, and end-to-end message flows are tested. Maintaining this separation facilitates troubleshooting and is consistent with CI/CD pipeline architectures, which allow for the independent testing, upgrading, and deployment of each module.

Truffle, Web3.js, and modular APIs together ultimately give developers a strong platform on which to construct and test cross-chain smart contracts. By simulating intricate interoperability flows in a local environment, these tools help developers get ready for production deployments on real-world EVM-compatible blockchains like Ethereum, Polygon, and Avalanche.

4.12 Summary

In order to replicate LayerZero and Chainlink CCIP's messaging capabilities in a controlled testing environment, this chapter included implementation-focused, step-by-step instructions for cross-chain messaging using Solidity, Truffle, and Ganache. After outlining the architectural foundation for interoperable smart contracts, we wrapped off with workable prototypes for event verification, token bridging, and lock-mint procedures across virtual chains. We introduced the reader to the basic mechanisms of inter-chain communications using relay emulation, Truffle console simulations, and mock endpoints.

We discussed how developer-centric frameworks are provided by Chainlink's CCIP and LayerZero's ULN for creating secure, gas-efficient, and auditable communication across trust borders. With the help of the Token Bridge, it was demonstrated how token locking on one blockchain and minting on another could be integrated into well-thought-out Solidity workflows. These workflows included security features like emit-based validation and human relay triggers.

After exploring real-world simulations of LayerZero's ULN, Chainlink's CCIP, and a functional token bridge using Truffle and Ganache, we have seen how interoperability contributes out in practice, with developers creating message flows across separate blockchains, off-chain relays synchronizing states, and contracts emitting events. Beyond the theoretical, these practical implementations gave us a firm understanding of cross-chain messaging's operation and shed light on the backend complexities and dependability issues related to decentralized communication. Chapter 5 now turns our focus from development to reflection as we proceed, compiling insights, assessing trends, and projecting future events. It gathers data for researchers, politicians, and architects who want to influence the next generation of multi-chain ecosystems in addition to developers.

References

1. Lys, L., Micoulet, A., Potop-Butucaru, M.: Atomic swapping bitcoins and ethers. In: IEEE International Conference on Blockchain, Paris, France (2024)
2. Sönmez, F.Ö., Knottenbelt, W.J.: Cross-chain notification and awareness management. In: IEEE International Conference on Blockchain, London, UK, pp. 420–430 (2024). https://doi.org/10.1109/Blockchain62396.2024.00062
3. Kumar, V., Budhiraja, I., Jabbari, A., Garg, D., Singh, D., Mengani, N.: Efficient blockchain interoperability design for cross-chain transactions in future internet-of-value. Peer Peer Netw Appl. **18**(110), 1–21 (2025). https://doi.org/10.1007/s12083-025-01941-w
4. Zarick, R., Pellegrino, B., Banister, C.: LayerZero: Trustless Omnichain Interoperability Protocol, arXiv preprint arXiv: 2110.13871, 2021. [Online]. https://arxiv.org/abs/2110.13871
5. Morháč, D., Valaštín, V., Košťál, K., Kotuliak, I.: Enhancing XCMP interoperability across Polkadot Paraverse. In: IEEE International Conference on Blockchain, Bratislava, Slovakia (2023a). https://doi.org/10.1109/Blockchain50366.2023.00032
6. Kim, J., Essaid, M., Ju, H.: Inter-Blockchain communication message relay time measurement and analysis in cosmos. In: The 23rd Asia-Pacific Network Operations and Management Symposium (APNOMS) (2022). https://doi.org/10.1109/APNOMS60508.2022.00231
7. Murray, P., Welch, N., and Messerman, J.: "EIP-1167: Minimal Proxy Contract," Ethereum Improvement Proposals, Jun 22, 2018
8. OpenZeppelin.: UUPSUpgradeable.sol, available in OpenZeppelin Contracts v4.x, based on ERC-1822/1967
9. Ganguly, R., et al.: Distributed Runtime Verification of Metric Temporal Properties for Cross-Chain Protocols, arXiv preprint arXiv:2204.09796, 2022. [Online]. https://arxiv.org/abs/2204.09796
10. Hossain, T., et al.: CrossLink: A Decentralized Framework for Secure Cross-Chain Smart Contract Execution, accepted at 2025 IEEE ICBC Cross-Chain Workshop (ICBC-CCW 2025)
11. Azimi, S., Golzari, A., Ivaki, N., Laranjeiro, N.: A systematic review on smart contracts security design patterns. Empir. Softw. Eng. **30**, 95 (2025). https://doi.org/10.1007/s10664-025-10646-w
12. Gupta, N.A., et al.: Detection of vulnerabilities in Blockchain smart contracts using deep learning. Wirel. Netw. **31**, 201–217 (2025). https://doi.org/10.1007/s11276-024-03755-9
13. Mitrović, A., Vukmirović, S., Dalčeković, M., Nedić, N., Čapko, D.: Cross-chain general message passing protocol via eternal bridge. In: IEEE International Conference on Telecommunications Forum (TELFOR), Novi Sad, Serbia (2023). https://doi.org/10.1109/TELFOR2023.00032
14. Han, Y., Wang, C., Wang, H.: Research on Blockchain cross-chain model based on 'NFT + cross-chain bridge'. IEEE Access. **12**, 77065–77078 (2024a). https://doi.org/10.1109/ACCESS.2024.3401405
15. Han, J., Kim, J., Youn, A., Lee, J., Chun, Y., Woo, J., Hong, J.W.-K.: Cos-CBDC: design and implementation of CBDC on cosmos Blockchain. In: IEEE International Conference on Blockchain (2024b). https://doi.org/10.1109/ICBCTIS64495.2024.00014
16. Etherscan.: "Ethereum Blockchain Explorer," [Online]. https://etherscan.io. Accessed 21 June 2025
17. Protofire.: "Solhint: Solidity Linter," [Online]. https://github.com/protofire/solhint. Accessed 21 June 2025

Further Readings

Abdullahi, S.M., Lazarova-Molnar, S.: On the adoption and deployment of secure and privacy-preserving IIoT in smart manufacturing: a comprehensive guide with recent advances. Int. J. Inf. Secur. **24**, 53 (2025). https://doi.org/10.1007/s10207-024-00951-8

Augusto, A., et al.: CBDC bridging between Hyperledger fabric and permissioned EVM-based Blockchains. In: IEEE International Conference on Blockchain and Cryptocurrency (ICBC), pp. 1–8 (2023). https://doi.org/10.1109/ICBC56567.2023.10174953

"Blockchain Interoperability Guide," Cyfrin. [Online]. https://www.cyfrin.io/blog/blockchain-interoperability-guide. Accessed 14 Mar 2025. (2024)

Cai, J., et al.: A Blockchain-based privacy protecting framework with Multi-Channel access control model for asset trading. Peer Peer Netw Appl. **17**, 2810–2829 (2024). https://doi.org/10.1007/s12083-024-01732-9

Caprolu, M., Di Pietro, R., Lombardi, F., Onofri, E.: Characterizing Polkadot's transactions ecosystem: methodology, tools, and insights. In: 2024 IEEE International Conference on Decentralized Applications and Infrastructures (DAPPS) (2024). https://doi.org/10.1109/DAPPS61106.2024.00016

Choi, N., Kim, H.: Decentralized commit-reveal scheme to defend against front-running attacks on decentralized exchanges. In: IEEE International Conference on Blockchain and Cryptocurrency (ICBC) (2024). https://doi.org/10.1109/ICBC59979.2024.10634344

Ding, D., et al.: Privacy protection for Blockchains with account and multi-asset model. China Commun. **16**(6), 69–78 (2019)

Diallo, E.-h., Dieye, M., Dib, O., Valiorgue, P.: An agnostic and secure interoperability protocol for seamless asset movement. J. Netw. Comput. Appl. **230**, 103930 (2024). https://doi.org/10.1016/j.jnca.2024.103930

Dwivedi, R., Singla, T., Shukla, S.: Cross-chain atomic swaps without time locks. In: 2023 Fifth International Conference on Blockchain Computing and Applications (BCCA) (2023). https://doi.org/10.1109/BCCA58897.2023.10338878

Frauenthaler, P., Sigwart, M., Spanring, C., Sober, M., Schulte, S.: ETH relay: a cost-efficient relay for Ethereum-based Blockchains. In: IEEE International Conference on Blockchain, Vienna, Austria (2020). https://doi.org/10.1109/Blockchain50366.2020.00032

Guo, H., Liang, H., Huang, J., et al.: A framework for efficient cross-chain token transfers in Blockchain networks. J.O King Saud Univ. Comput. Inform. Sci. **36**, 101968 (2024). https://doi.org/10.1016/j.jksuci.2024.101968

Han, J., et al.: Cos-CBDC: design and implementation of CBDC on cosmos Blockchain. In: APNOMS 2021, Showcases Asset Mobility Via Cosmos IBC for Multi-Chain Integration (2021)

Hirai, Y.: Defining the ethereum virtual machine for interactive theorem provers. In: Financial Cryptography and Data Security: FC 2017 International Workshops, WAHC, BITCOIN, VOTING, WTSC, and TA, Sliema, Malta, vol. 7, pp. 520–535 (2017)

Hook, T.B., Brown, J.S., Breitwisch, M., Hoyniak, D., Mann, R.: High-performance logic and high-gain analog CMOS transistors formed by a shadow-mask technique with a single implant step. IEEE Trans. Electron. Devices. **49**(9), 1623–1627 (2002)

Hsien-De Huang, T., Kao, H.Y.: R2-d2: color-inspired convolutional neural network (cnn)-based android malware detections. In: IEEE International Conference on Big Data (Big Data), pp. 2633–2642. IEEE (2018)

Hu, K., Lei, L., Tsai, W.T.: Multi-tenant verification-as-a-service (VaaS) in a cloud. Simul. Model. Pract. Theory. **60**, 122–143 (2016)

Huang, Y., Bian, Y., Li, R., Zhao, J.L., Shi, P.: Smart contract security: a software lifecycle perspective. IEEE Access. **7**, 150184–150202 (2019)

Huang, J., Zhou, K., Xiong, A., Li, D.: Smart contract vulnerability detection model based on multi-task learning. Sensors. **22**(5), 1829 (2022)

References

Ibba, G.: A smart contracts repository for top trending contracts. In: IEEE/ACM 5th International Workshop on Emerging Trends in Software Engineering for Blockchain (WETSEB), pp. 17–20. IEEE (2022)

Idé, T.: Collaborative anomaly detection on blockchain from noisy sensor data. In: IEEE International Conference on Data Mining Workshops (ICDMW), pp. 120–127. IEEE (2018)

I., Sergey, I., Hobor, A., Saxena, P.: Exploiting the laws of order in smart contracts. In: 28th ACM SIGSOFT International Symposium on Software Testing and Analysis, pp. 363–373 (2019)

Jayapal, C., et al.: An insight into NFTs, Stablecoins and DEXs in Blockchain. In: 2nd International Conference on Advancements in Electrical, Electronics, Communication, Computing and Automation (ICAECA) (2023). https://doi.org/10.1109/ICAECA56562.2023.10200121

Jain, A.K., Gupta, N., Gupta, B.B.: A survey on scalable consensus algorithms for Blockchain technology. Cyber Secur. Appl. **3**, 100065 (2025). https://doi.org/10.1016/j.csa.2024.100065

Jiang, B., Liu, Y., Chan, W.K.: Contractfuzzer: fuzzing smart contracts for vulnerability detection. In: 33rd ACM/IEEE International Conference on Automated Software Engineering, pp. 259–269 (2018)

Juels, A., Kosba, A., Shi, E.: The ring of gyges: investigating the future of criminal smart contracts. In: ACM SIGSAC Conference on Computer and Communications Security, pp. 283–295 (2016)

Kalra, S., Goel, S., Dhawan, M., Sharma, S.: Zeus: analyzing safety of smart contracts. In: Ndss, pp. 1–12 (2018)

King, S., Nadal, S.: Ppcoin: peer-to-peer crypto-currency with proof-of-stake. Self-Published Paper. **19**, 1 (2012)

Kolluri, A., Nikolic, I., Sergey, I., Hobor, A., Saxena, P.: Exploiting the laws of order in smart contracts. In: 28th ACM SIGSOFT International Symposium on Software Testing and Analysis, pp. 363–373 (2019)

Kolvart, M., Poola, M., Rull, A.: Smart contracts. In: The Future of Law and Etechnologies, pp. 133–147. Springer (2016)

Kotey, S.D., Tchao, E.T., Ahmed, A.-R., Agbemenu, A.S., Nunoo-Mensah, H., Sikora, A., Welte, D., Keelson, E.: Blockchain interoperability: the state of Heterogenous Blockchain-to-Blockchain communication. IET Commun. **17**(8), 891–914 (2023). https://doi.org/10.1049/cmu2.12594

Kumar, N., Hossain, M.S., Jolfaei, A., Sangaiah, A.: Building resilient web 3.0 infrastructure with quantum information technologies and Blockchain: an Ambilateral view. IEEE Internet Things J. **10**(2), 1082–1090 (2023). https://doi.org/10.1109/JIOT.2022.3224343

Lashkari, B., Musilek, P.: A comprehensive review of blockchain consensus mechanisms. IEEE Access. **9**, 43620–43652 (2021)

Lattner, C., Adve, V.: LLVM: a compilation framework for lifelong program analysis & transformation. In: International Symposium on Code Generation and Optimization, pp. 75–86. IEEE (2004)

Lepore, C., et al.: A survey on blockchain consensus with a performance comparison of PoW, PoS and pure PoS. Mathematics **8**(10), 1782 (2020)

Li, Z., et al.: MuSC: a tool for mutation testing of ethereum smart contract. In: 34th IEEE/ACM International Conference on Automated Software Engineering, pp. 1198–1201. IEEE (2019)

Liao, Z., et al.: Large-scale empirical study of inline assembly on 7.6 million ethereum smart contracts. IEEE Trans. Softw. Eng. **49**(2), 777–801 (2022)

Liao, J.W., et al.: Soliaudit: smart contract vulnerability assessment based on machine learning and fuzz testing. In: 6th International Conference on Internet of Things: Systems, Management and Security (IOTSMS), pp. 458–465. IEEE (2019)

Lin, S.Y., et al.: A survey of application research based on blockchain smart contract. Wirel. Netw. **28**(2), 635–690 (2022)

Lisi, A., Lopardo, N., Tortola, D., Mori, P., Ricci, L., Severino, F.: A cross-chain rating system: bridging EVM-based Blockchains with Chainbridge. In: 2023 International Conference on Omni-Layer Intelligent Systems (COINS) (2023). https://doi.org/10.1109/COINS57856.2023.10189274

Liu, H., et al.: S-gram: towards semantic-aware security auditing for ethereum smart contracts. In: 33rd ACM/IEEE International Conference on Automated Software Engineering, pp. 814–819 (2018)

Liu, Z., et al.: Combining graph neural networks with expert knowledge for smart contract vulnerability detection. IEEE Trans. Knowl. Data Eng. **35**(2), 1296–1310 (2021)

Liu, L., et al.: Blockchain-enabled fraud discovery through abnormal smart contract detection on Ethereum. Futur. Gener. Comput. Syst. **128**, 158–166 (2022)

Mehra, D., et al.: Implementation of CBDC System for the Customized Development of Finance Service System. SRM Institute of Science and Technology (2023)

Morháč, D., Valaštín, V., Košťál, K., Kotuliak, I.: ParaSpell XCM SDK: a new protocol for interoperability in Polkadot Paraverse. In: 2023 Fifth International Conference on Blockchain Computing and Applications (BCCA) (2023b). https://doi.org/10.1109/BCCA58897.2023.10338906

Olivieri, L., Spoto, F.: Software verification challenges in the Blockchain ecosystem. Int. J. Softw. Tools Technol. Transfer. **26**, 431–444 (2024). https://doi.org/10.1007/s10009-024-00758-x

Park, S., Lee, J., Kim, H.: Efficient computation offloading for Ethereum DApps. J. Ind. Inf. Integr. **31**, 100411 (2023). https://doi.org/10.1016/j.jii.2022.100411

Rao, I.S., Kiah, M.L.M., Hameed, M.M., Memon, Z.A.: Scalability of Blockchain: a comprehensive review and future research direction. Clust. Comput. **27**, 5547–5570 (2024). https://doi.org/10.1007/s10586-023-04257-7

Rosa, G., Scalabrino, S., Mastrostefano, S., Oliveto, R.: Why and how developers maintain smart contracts. Empir. Softw. Eng. **30**, 84 (2025). https://doi.org/10.1007/s10664-025-10639-9

Schueffel, P.: What colors are the bricks? Unboxing the DeFi model—a literature survey, empirical study, and taxonomy. J. Bank. Financ. Technol. (2025). https://doi.org/10.1007/s42786-024-00054-x

Sengupta, A., Ranjan, R., Ghosh, A., Wang, L., Zomaya, A., Buyya, R.: DataHarbour: enabling decentralized AI data marketplace using Blockchain. IEEE Trans. Serv. Comput. **2024**, 1–4 (2023). https://doi.org/10.1109/TSC.2023.3256086

Sethaput, V., Innet, S.: Blockchain application for central Bank digital currencies (CBDC). Clust. Comput. **26**, 2183–2197 (2023). https://doi.org/10.1007/s10586-022-03962-z

Shukla, M., Verma, A., Kumar, N., Sharma, S.K., Hossain, M.S.: Advanced eHealth with explainable AI secured by Blockchain with AI-empowered block sensitivity for adaptive authentication. IEEE Trans. Industr. Inform. **19**(9), 9809–9817 (2023). https://doi.org/10.1109/TII.2022.3228264

Sonkamble, R.G., Bongale, A.M., Phansalkar, S., Dharrao, D.S.: A secure interoperable method for electronic health records exchange on cross platform blockchain network. MethodsX. **13**, 103002 (2024). https://doi.org/10.1016/j.mex.2024.103002

Sizan, N.S., Dey, D., Layek, M.A., Uddin, M.A., Huh, E.-N.: Evaluating Blockchain platforms for IoT applications in industry 5.0: a comprehensive review. Blockchain Res. Appl. **6**, 100276 (2025). https://doi.org/10.1016/j.bcra.2025.100276

Subhashini, P., Alekhya, J., Rana, A., Lakhanpal, S., V. G, Al-Allak, M.A.: Navigating Web3 evolution with Blockchain's role in shaping next generation internet semantics. In: IEEE International Conference on Communication, Computer Sciences and Engineering (IC3SE), Hyderabad, India (2024). https://doi.org/10.1109/IC3SE62002.2024.10593138

Thyagarajan, S.A., Malavolta, G., Moreno-Sanchez, P.: Universal atomic swaps: secure exchange of coins across all Blockchains. In: 2022 IEEE Symposium on Security and Privacy (SP), pp. 1299–1314 (2022). https://doi.org/10.1109/SP46214.2022.00063

Tortola, D., Lisi, A., Mori, P., Ricci, L.: Tethering layer 2 solutions to the Blockchain: a survey on proving schemes. Comput. Commun. **225**, 289–310 (2024). https://doi.org/10.1016/j.comcom.2024.07.017

Trozze, et al.: Detecting DeFi securities violations from token smart contract code. Financ. Innov. **10**, 78 (2024). https://doi.org/10.1186/s40854-023-00572-5

Tsai, W.-T., et al.: A multi-chain model for CBDC. In: 5th International Conference on Dependable Systems and their Applications (DSA), pp. 1–8 (2018). https://doi.org/10.1109/DSA.2018.00016.A

References

Vasconcelos, A., et al.: CBDC bridging between Hyperledger fabric and EVM-based Blockchains. In: IEEE ICBC, Emphasizes Bridging between Regulated Chains for Secure Asset Transfers (2023)

Virani, S.S.: Blockchain end user adoption and societal challenges: exploring privacy, rights, and security dimensions. IET Blockchain. **4**(S1), 691–705 (2024). https://doi.org/10.1049/blc2.12077

Vijayalakshmi, C., Florence, S.M.: Flameshift protocol: revolutionizing interoperability with dynamic asset recycling for cross-chain communications. SN Comput. Sci. **5**, 773 (2024). https://doi.org/10.1007/s42979-024-03116-5

Wang, Y., Yan, Y., Liu, X., Gao, W., Wang, Z.: A technique for ensured cross chain IBC transactions using TPM. In: IEEE International Conference on Big Data and Privacy Computing (BDPC), Xi'an, China (2024). https://doi.org/10.1109/BDPC59998.2024.10649356

Xie, Z., et al.: Enhanced efficiency and security in cross-chain transmission of Blockchain internet of ports through multi-feature-based joint learning. Sci. Rep. **15**, 6199 (2025). https://doi.org/10.1038/s41598-025-85330-6

Yang, S., Zhang, G., Li, Y., Wang, P., Zhao, C., Feng, B., Shen, C., Zhang, Y.: Cross-chain architecture of Blockchain integrating notary mechanism and relay-chain technology. In: 2024 4th International Conference on Blockchain Technology and Information Security (ICBCTIS) (2024). https://doi.org/10.1109/ICBCTIS64495.2024.00014

Yang, S., Zhang, G., Li, Y., Wang, P., Zhao, C., Feng, B., Shen, C., Zhang, Y.: A secure cross-chain mechanism based on relay chain and smart contract encryption scheme. In: 2023 11th International Conference on Information Systems and Computing Technology (ISCTech) (2023). https://doi.org/10.1109/ISCTech60480.2023.00023

Zou, H., et al.: Decentralized and lightweight cross-chain transaction scheme based on proxy re-signature. In: IEEE 23rd International Conference on Trust, Security and Privacy in Computing and Communications (TrustCom), pp. 1201–1209 (2024). https://doi.org/10.1109/TrustCom63139.2024.00170

Zou, H., et al.: Decentralized and lightweight cross-chain transaction scheme based on proxy re-signature. IEEE TrustCom. **2024**, 1201–1208 (2024). https://doi.org/10.1109/TrustCom63139.2024.00170

Chapter 5
Key Takeaways for Researchers

Contents

5.1	Summary of Key Lessons.	145
	5.1.1 Interoperability in Fragmented Ecosystems.	145
	5.1.2 Blockchain Interoperability Models.	145
	5.1.3 Practical Use Cases.	146
	5.1.4 Cross-Chain Security and Tooling.	146
5.2	Best Practices.	147
	5.2.1 Trustless Cross-Chain Messaging.	147
	5.2.2 Developer Abstraction.	147
	5.2.3 Rollup-Aware Interoperability.	148
	5.2.4 Enterprise Grade BlockChain Applications.	148
	5.2.5 Security Primitives.	149
	5.2.6 Governance Alignment.	149
5.3	Future Multi-Chain Ecosystems.	149
	5.3.1 Multi-Chain Paradigm.	150
	5.3.2 Hiding Complexity.	150
	5.3.3 Non-Monetary Applications.	151
	5.3.4 Interoperable dApps.	151
	5.3.5 DeFi in the Future.	152
5.4	The Next Phase of Interoperability.	153
	5.4.1 Modularization.	153
	5.4.2 Interdisciplinary Collaboration.	153
	5.4.3 Seamless Fluidity.	155
	5.4.4 Intelligent Wallets.	155
	5.4.5 Dynamic dApps.	156
	5.4.6 Rise of Supra-DAOs.	156
	5.4.7 Interoperability Beyond DeFi.	156
	5.4.8 Regulatory Harmonization Across Chains.	157
5.5	Final Thoughts.	157
	5.5.1 The Interoperability Trilemma.	158
	5.5.2 Security at the Crossroads.	158
	5.5.3 Reimagining Governance.	159
	5.5.4 A Vision: The Cross-Domain Trust Mesh.	160
	5.5.5 The Path Ahead: Standards, Verification, and Composability.	160
	5.5.6 The Last Word.	160

© The Author(s), under exclusive license to Springer Nature
Switzerland AG 2025
P. Sarang, L. Nadkar, *Blockchain Without Barriers*, SpringerBriefs in Computer
Science, https://doi.org/10.1007/978-3-032-03413-7_5

5.6 Conclusion and Future Directions for Research... 161
    5.6.1 The Future Is Composable... 161
    5.6.2 What Needs Reconsideration?.. 161
    5.6.3 For the Researchers... 162
References... 163

Abstract This chapter unifies the foundational understanding, practical solutions, and strategic vision needed for advancement of blockchain interoperability research. After summarizing the important technical and conceptual lessons learned, it goes into interoperability models appropriate for decentralized blockchain environments. This chapter provides a full overview of developing scalable, trustless, and modular cross-chain systems by examining security architectures, governance models, and developer abstraction layers.

Emerging concepts like smart wallets, seamless fluidity, and supra-DAOs are contrasted with real-world application scenarios such as rollup-aware interoperability and enterprise-level DApps. Future directions are discussed, with a focus on the challenge of attaining regulatory harmonization across chains, the emergence of dynamic dApps, and interdisciplinary collaboration. The Cross-Domain Trust Mesh (CDTM), a revolutionary framework for establishing verifiable and scalable interoperability without losing decentralization, is introduced.

This chapter finishes with practical recommendations for researchers, emphasizing the need to address the interoperability conundrum, combine cryptography and artificial intelligence methods, and standardize governance in multi-chain contexts. It emphasizes verifiability, composability, and open standards as the foundations for a fully interoperable Web3 future.

Keywords Multi-chain ecosystems · Trustless messaging · CDTM · AI-cryptography integration · Interoperability trilemma · Supra-DAOs · Modular blockchain design · Future DeFi · Regulatory harmonization · Intelligent wallets · Enterprise dApps · Research roadmap

We have now arrived at the most interesting section of this Research Brief. In this chapter, we will provide a brief overview of what you have studied so far and establish guidelines for future research on this trending subject. The following questions will be our primary focus.

What methods can be employed to enhance our comprehension of blockchain interoperability, encompassing both its structural components and practical applications? What insights can be derived from existing protocols, and in what manner are industry pioneers currently advancing the development of secure and scalable cross-chain systems? As the blockchain ecosystem continues to evolve, what opportunities arise for multi-chain systems, and in what ways will dynamic decentralized applications, modular networks, and intelligent cross-chain routing transform the architecture of decentralized applications?

This chapter aims to look into these concerns. We commence with a summary of the key concepts addressed in the preceding four chapters, defining the evolution of interoperability models, financial and identity use cases, as well as initial security frameworks. We present the prevailing best practices employed in production systems by prominent protocols and investigate the methods through which interoperability is reliably and securely attained in practical applications.

This chapter subsequently presents the future of multi-chain ecosystems, outlining key themes that are currently influencing the functionality of decentralized applications across various networks. We address challenges related to scalability, governance, and security. We will outline an advanced research framework for modular, resilient, and inclusive blockchain systems. The following sections aim to provide researchers with a comprehensive framework addressing unresolved issues, strategic opportunities, and design pathways for the advancement of the next generation of interoperable blockchain infrastructure.

5.1 Summary of Key Lessons

This section provides essential insights from the first four chapters of the book, highlighting the logical progression of blockchain interoperability from isolated ecosystems to secure, composable, and multifunctional cross-chain systems. We now review the specific aspects of the information that were covered in each chapter.

5.1.1 Interoperability in Fragmented Ecosystems

The first chapter introduced the issue of blockchain fragmentation, characterized by the existence of separate chains like Bitcoin, Ethereum, and Binance Smart Chain, which function as isolated entities lacking the ability to exchange data, assets, or logic. The isolation in design led to scaling challenges, restricted liquidity flow among markets, and hindered the composability of decentralized applications. This chapter established the book's theme that Web3 promotes a decentralized ecosystem where numerous blockchains can securely interoperate, coordinate, and build applications across networks without friction. It established interoperability as the technical and economic link between disparate blockchain ecosystems and the applications built upon them.

5.1.2 Blockchain Interoperability Models

Chapter 2 conducted a critical analysis of the existing architectural models that facilitate interoperability. The solutions were systematically categorized into relay-based models, hash time-locked contracts (HTLCs), and general message passing (GMP) frameworks. Each model was reviewed regarding its assumptions pertaining to trust, latency, security guarantees, and scalability. For example, Cosmos IBC was examined as a secure relay-based model using Tendermint consensus, whereas LayerZero proposed ultra-light clients that incur minimal overhead, but at the cost of finality guarantees [1, 2]. The Polkadot parachains [1, 2], Chainlink's CCIP [1, 2], and Axelar GMP [3] were reviewed as advanced solutions that abstract the intricacies of cross-chain messaging from developers. The chapter presented a technical framework for understanding the functionality of interoperability protocols, the types of attacks they are designed to mitigate, and the associated trade-offs involved.

5.1.3 Practical Use Cases

Chapter 3 transcended theoretical discussions by examining the ways in which interoperability enables practical applications across various industries. In decentralized finance (DeFi), interoperability plays a crucial role in enabling cross-chain lending, asset swapping, and liquidity pooling using platforms such as ThorChain [4] and SushiXSwap [5]. In identity systems, solutions such as self-sovereign identity (SSI) and verifiable credentials employ the issuance of credentials on permissioned chains, with verification conducted on public networks. The chapter also addressed NFT bridging, cross-chain gaming, and multi-chain governance, wherein users engage in voting and staking across multiple blockchains simultaneously. These examples suggest that interoperability serves as a catalyst for the development of more sophisticated and functional decentralized applications, rather than merely representing a technical advancement for asset transfer.

5.1.4 Cross-Chain Security and Tooling

Chapter 4 is designed for interoperability engineers and practical developers. The focus transitioned from theoretical models to the practical implementation of cross-chain smart contracts using Truffle and Solidity. This chapter commenced with the establishment of a full-stack development environment, guiding readers through the installation of Node.js, Truffle, and Ganache, and culminating in comprehensive sandbox simulations of lock-mint and oracle-based messaging patterns. The study examined the foundational elements of interoperability, encompassing programmable relayer logic, EVM-specific nuances, Solidity syntax fundamentals, and upgradeable design patterns. Comprehensive implementation walkthroughs were delivered for essential features such as LayerZero's Ultra-Light Node communication and Chainlink CCIP's oracle-driven message routing, accompanied by code snippets, deployment scripts, and verification through the Truffle console. Security considerations were also emphasized, encompassing nonce tracking, replay protection, and the utilization of static analysis tools. It also included Truffle Test and Debugger to simulate event-driven failures, ensure message integrity, and confirm transaction states across multiple chains.

The first four chapters collectively present an in-depth review of the existing landscape of blockchain interoperability. Considering its crucial function in isolated systems, in conjunction with technical solutions, practical implementations, and ongoing security challenges, it is clear that interoperability is imperative for the development of a decentralized, equitable, and scalable Web3. The chapters presented herein collectively provide the fundamental lessons and information necessary for any developer, architect, or researcher to make meaningful contributions to the future of cross-chain technology.

Next, we will describe the best practices in Blockchain Interoperability.

5.2 Best Practices

As interoperability protocols mature from theoretical designs to production-quality software, the blockchain industry has embraced a new generation of emerging best practices that combine security, usability, and modularity. These approaches not only liberate from centuries-old constraints of cross-chain design but also leverage lessons learned from real-world exploits and rapid protocol development.

5.2.1 Trustless Cross-Chain Messaging

A fundamental principle that has gained widespread adoption is trust-minimized cross-chain messaging. Instead of depending on centralized custodians or multisig bridges, which are vulnerable to single points of failure, modern interoperability designs employ light clients, oracle proofs, or cryptographic relays to authenticate cross-chain states.

One notable example is Cosmos IBC, which employs on-chain light client verification and secure packet relaying using Tendermint consensus, thereby eliminating the necessity for a trusted third party between zones [6]. In a comparable manner, LayerZero offers an "ultra-light client" architecture wherein two distinct entities, a relayer and an oracle, engage in the exchange and verification of messages without requiring independent trust in either party [1, 2]. This design modification enhances interoperability, moving toward a fully decentralized state verification, in line with the trustless nature of blockchain technology.

5.2.2 Developer Abstraction

Another effective practice involves abstracting complexity from developers, a necessity for widespread adoption. Technologies such as Axelar General Message Passing (GMP) empower decentralized application developers to create contracts that execute seamlessly across multiple blockchains, eliminating the need to navigate chain-specific bridge logic [7]. Rather than engaging in the manual conversion of code for Ethereum, Avalanche, or Cosmos, developers have the opportunity to author their code once, allowing Axelar to manage the routing and delivery seamlessly in the background. In a similar vein, Wormhole SDKs enhance the process of NFT and token bridging by abstracting shared logic into reusable components. This approach effectively reduces the cognitive load on developers and minimizes the potential for implementation errors. This technique of encapsulation and abstraction mirrors the evolution of cloud platforms through the implementation of APIs and SDKs, which facilitate the development of scalable, multi-cloud applications.

5.2.3 Rollup-Aware Interoperability

The recent proliferation of Ethereum rollups which is a Layer 2 scaling solutions that bundle transactions off-chain and post compressed proofs to Ethereum has established an innovative frontier in interoperability: inter-layer bridging between Layer 2 and Layer 1 networks. Initial designs focused primarily on token transfers; however, modern approaches now incorporate finality guarantees, fraud-proof delays, and gas optimization. For example, the Hop Protocol facilitates near-instantaneous transfers between rollups such as Optimism and Arbitrum by using liquidity providers and batched state commitments [6]. Alternatively, zkSync and StarkNet employ zero-knowledge proofs to securely verify execution and state transitions between rollups and the Ethereum Mainnet [8]. The design that is aware of rollups is currently regarded as essential for scaling Ethereum while maintaining both composability and decentralization.

5.2.4 Enterprise Grade BlockChain Applications

A new set of interoperability use cases have emerged, focusing on secure bridges between public and permissioned blockchains. This is particularly relevant in enterprise settings, which includes finance, supply chains, and healthcare. The focus in these circumstances is directed toward auditability, privacy, and the integrity of messages. Hyperledger Cactus is an open framework developed by the Hyperledger Foundation that offers plugin-based connectors designed to securely bridge disparate networks such as Fabric and Ethereum [9]. Wanchain [10] facilitates cross-chain transfers between private consortium chains and public blockchains using bridges that are governed by validators. These platforms are typically employed for cross-border compliance, digital identity exchange, and the regulated tokenization of assets for which standard DeFi bridges are inadequate.

5.2.5 Security Primitives

The implementation of security primitives at the interoperability layer is important. Rather than positioning verification as an external audit layer, new protocols integrate fraud detection, slashing, and redundancy directly into the foundational architecture. The Chainlink Cross-Chain Interoperability Protocol (CCIP) uses Decentralized Oracle Networks (DONs) to provide cryptographic guarantees regarding the authenticity of messages, in addition to offering fallback recovery mechanisms in the event of failure [11]. Wormhole V2 advances the technology by including Verifiable Action Approvals (VAAs), implementing replay protection, establishing rate limiting, and facilitating post-attack audit logging [12]. Security-oriented designs are increasingly becoming standard practice following high-profile incidents such as the Wormhole bridge hack, which highlighted the vulnerabilities associated with unregulated validator control [13].

5.2.6 Governance Alignment

As cross-chain infrastructure continues to expand, it is imperative that governance alignment and incentive compatibility are regarded as best practices in the current landscape. Protocols such as Cosmos Interchain Security enable consumer chains to "rent" the validator set of a provider zone, thereby securing themselves economically while ensuring that governance aligns with staking rewards [6]. In contrast, protocols such as Nomad [14] (prior to its exploit) employed optimistic message passing with bonded relayers that were subject to slashing for misconduct. This model is now evolving into more sophisticated DAO-governed relayer registries and permissionless slashing logic [14]. These systems guarantee that validators and message relayers across chains are financially motivated to maintain honesty, thereby establishing a vital foundation for long-term stability.

The top blockchain interoperability protocols, best practices they employ, and design focus categories—such as messaging, abstraction, rollup integration, security, and governance—are compiled in Table 5.1.

Now, we will present a preview of the multi-chain ecosystems that will emerge soon.

5.3 Future Multi-Chain Ecosystems

We will now go over a few features of a multi-chain ecosystem of the future.

Table 5.1 Blockchain interoperability protocols and their best practices

Category	Protocol/Platform	Best practice implemented
Trustless Messaging	Cosmos IBC	Trust-minimized relay via Tendermint light clients [6]
	LayerZero	Ultra-light clients with oracle-relayer split verification [1, 2]
Developer Abstraction	Axelar GMP	Cross-chain messaging abstraction layer (GMP APIs) [7]
	Wormhole SDK / V2	Developer SDKs, replay protection, rate-limiting [12]
Rollup Interoperability	Hop Protocol	Rollup-aware fast transfers using liquidity providers [6]
	zkSync / StarkNet	Zero-knowledge proofs for cross-rollup validation [8]
Public–Private Bridging	Hyperledger Cactus	Secure plugin-based public-private chain connectors [9]
	Wanchain	Validator-managed public/private token bridging
Security Embedded Design	Chainlink CCIP	Oracle-verified cross-chain message routing with fallback [1, 2]
	Wormhole V2	Replay protection, slashing conditions, audit logging [12]
Governance and Incentives	Cosmos Interchain Security	Validator leasing and economic alignment [6]
	Nomad (pre-exploit)	Optimistic messaging with bonded, slashable relayers [14]

5.3.1 Multi-Chain Paradigm

The interoperability observed so far has led to the emergence of a multi-chain paradigm. It has been observed that blockchain systems are facilitating the emergence of a multi-chain future, wherein various networks interconnect to provide specialized services free from monopolistic control. Sovereign networks, Layer 2 rollups, application-specific chains, and modular blockchains represent essential elements of a comprehensive decentralized infrastructure that is evolving within the Web3 landscape. Initiatives such as Celestia [15], Avalanche Subnets, and zkSync [8]. serve as prime examples of modularity that distinguishes and enhances data availability, execution, and consensus functions across various networks. Their design concept significantly improves scalability and stability, while simultaneously fostering innovation within targeted domains.

5.3.2 Hiding Complexity

A fundamental characteristic of forthcoming blockchain systems is user-centric interoperability. In the future, decentralized applications will provide a seamless user experience, effectively concealing the complexities associated with managing multiple chains behind the scenes. Wallets will facilitate transactions through interoperability protocols, including LayerZero endpoints [1, 2], or Axelar GMP [16], automatically, without users being aware of the specific underlying chain in use.

Within this framework, natively enabled cross-chain function calls will facilitate the seamless integration of decentralized applications across multiple blockchains. Moreover, user-facing technologies, including self-sovereign identity (SSI) systems [17], multi-chain NFTs, and universal asset portfolios [18], are undergoing standardization to facilitate seamless interaction for individuals within decentralized ecosystems. The transition to an interoperable blockchain framework serves as a prime example of a fundamental best practice: effective interoperability requires the concealment of complexity behind transparent, user-friendly interfaces that improve accessibility while maintaining the integrity of decentralization.

5.3.3 Non-Monetary Applications

The potential for blockchain interoperability extends beyond mere monetary applications. As outlined in the preceding chapters, the non-financial applications of interoperable blockchains are expected to experience significant growth.

Decentralized health networks represent a significant application that facilitates the transfer of sensitive patient data between private Hyperledger nodes and public Ethereum contracts, while preserving confidentiality and auditability. In a similar manner, governance systems undergo transformations, allowing users to make decisions regarding proposals by voting on staked assets distributed across various networks [19].

In educational contexts, the utilization of permissioned blockchains is expanding to facilitate the issuance of academic records, which will be verified against public attestations, thereby enabling global, tamper-proof credential validation.

These innovations emphasize that blockchain interoperability encompasses not only the exchange of trusted information but also the transfer of value, thereby broadening the potential for decentralized innovation across various industries.

5.3.4 Interoperable dApps

We will now present a layer-based architecture blueprint for decentralized systems, designed to facilitate the seamless development of cross-chain applications that are resilient to future challenges. This fundamentally involves an interoperability middleware layer, utilizing technologies such as LayerZero and Cosmos IBC to facilitate cross-chain messaging and asset transfer. This layer-based architecture blueprint facilitates the creation of an abstraction layer for smart contracts, allowing developers to build decentralized applications without the necessity of addressing the diverse formats or consensus algorithms present across multiple blockchains. To address the issue of privacy, a dedicated layer of zero-knowledge proofs (ZKPs) may be implemented to ensure confidentiality across multiple chains.

To enhance the security and resilience of interoperating systems, a reward layer system has been established that employs game-theory-friendly staking protocols to incentivize reliable cross-chain relayers and validators.

Fig. 5.1 Illustrates the layered architectural framework for next-generation interoperable decentralized applications (dApps)

5.3.5 DeFi in the Future

The application of blockchain interoperability in decentralized finance (DeFi) represents a significant advancement. Cross-chain composability is revolutionizing financial primitives and unlocking new opportunities for innovation. Platforms such as SushiXSwap [20] and ThorChain [6] have demonstrated the capabilities of multi-chain swaps, allowing users to exchange assets across different blockchains without reliance on centralized custodians. Building upon these foundations, the forthcoming phase of DeFi will encompass the creation of shared liquidity pools distributed

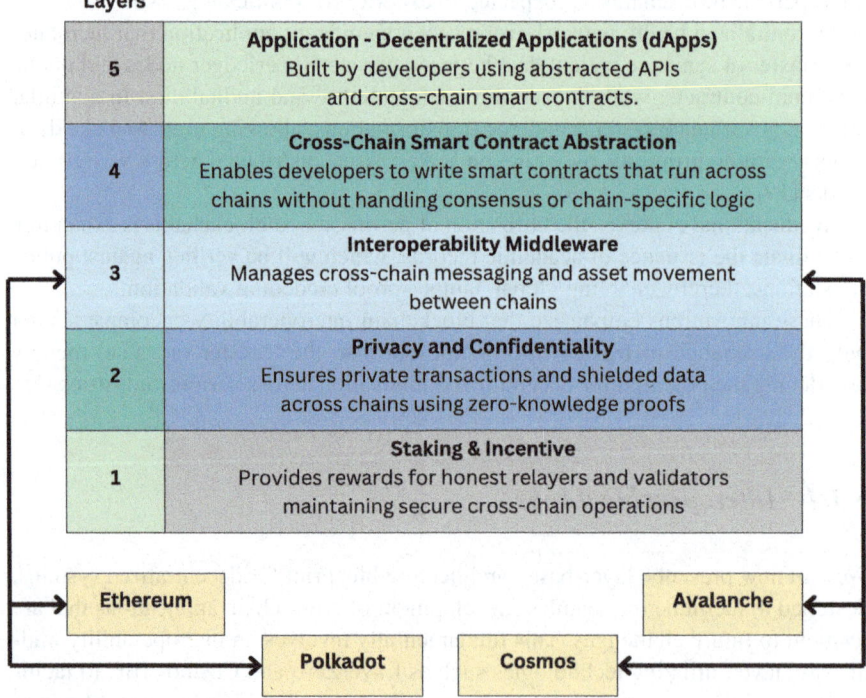

Fig. 5.1 Layered architectural framework for next-generation interoperable decentralized applications (dApps)

across multiple chains [21], composable collateralized debt positions (CDPs) that enable users to collateralize assets sourced from various blockchains [1, 2], and the implementation of integrated credit scoring systems that merge credit behavior across diverse networks [22].

While the interoperability of the future holds significant promise, encompassing modular Web3 infrastructures and interdisciplinary collaboration, realizing this vision will not be an effortless endeavor. The achievement of frictionless cross-chain operations necessitates the establishment of comprehensive technical standards, the creation of effective tooling, and the formulation of regulatory frameworks that can adapt to decentralized and borderless ecosystems. Above all, it is imperative that security is ensured.

Due to the interconnected nature of chains, new attack surfaces emerge, encompassing compromised validators, liquidity fragmentation, and risks associated with message relaying. In order to mitigate these risks, the forthcoming generation of cross-chain protocols should adhere to security-first design principles. The implementation of decentralized relayer networks, threshold signature schemes, and light client-based verifications must be established as standard practices to ensure trust-minimized [13], tamper-resistant [14] asset, and data transfers. These efforts will be essential in transforming interoperability into a concrete concept, serving as a secure, scalable, and operational foundation of Web3.

We'll now give you some pointers and study topics for the upcoming interoperability phase.

5.4 The Next Phase of Interoperability

5.4.1 Modularization

The recent trend of modularization within blockchain networks, exemplified by initiatives such as Celestia [15] and zkSync [8], suggests that the future infrastructure of Web3 will comprise highly specialized yet interoperable modules. Execution, consensus, and data availability will no longer reside within monolithic chains; rather, they will be distributed across services that are optimized for each layer. Interoperability will serve as the cohesive element that integrates these modules, enabling users to perform actions such as asset swapping, participating in governance proposals, or verifying identity credentials across various networks without requiring explicit understanding of the underlying processes.

5.4.2 Interdisciplinary Collaboration

The vision of a multi-chain and modular framework necessitates not only technical ingenuity but also collaboration across various disciplines. Collaboration among cryptographers, distributed systems engineers, governance theorists, and regulatory specialists is essential for the development of secure, scalable, and sustainable end-to-end interoperability frameworks. The implementation of open-source standards, the formal verification of cross-chain protocols, and the establishment of decentralized participation incentives will each play a crucial role in actualizing this vision.

Figure 5.2 explains the decoupling of execution, consensus, and data availability as distinct, yet interrelated modules. Interoperability protocols facilitate the collaboration of various blockchains across different layers, enabling end-users to communicate seamlessly across services on multiple networks, all without requiring knowledge of the underlying technical infrastructure.

As modular designs and interdisciplinary innovation commence to influence next-generation Web3 infrastructure, interoperability arises not merely as a technical solution, but as the definitive mark of a genuinely decentralized system. The future of blockchain lies not in isolated brilliance, but in collaborative convergence, where chains, protocols, and communities unite.

Blockchain interoperability should not be regarded as a secondary feature; rather, it constitutes the fundamental basis of a genuinely decentralized digital universe. It facilitates the collaboration of heterogeneous blockchains, thereby promoting global scalability, enhancing security, and fostering diverse application ecosystems

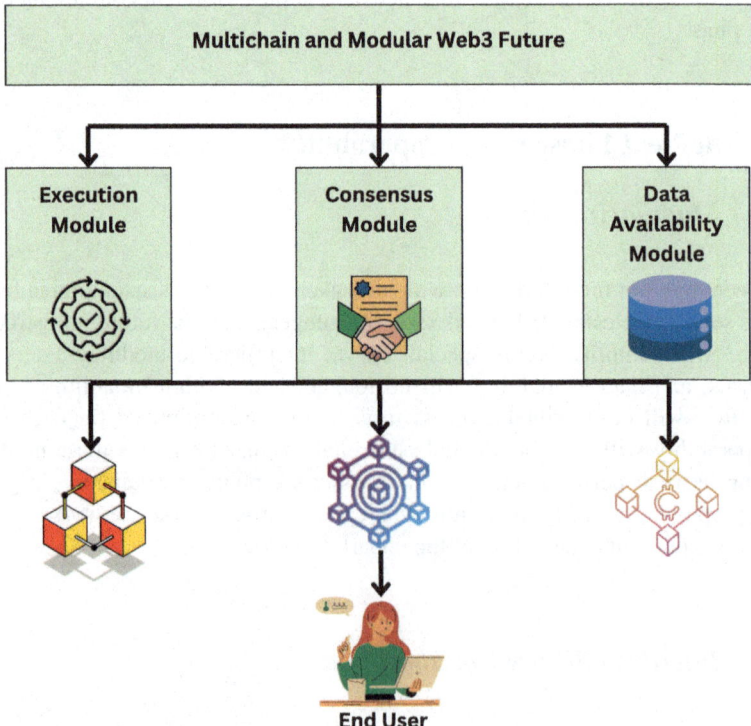

Fig. 5.2 Modular Web3 infrastructure powered by interoperability

across sectors such as finance, healthcare, governance, and beyond. As the blockchain ecosystem evolves, success will increasingly be characterized not by the dominance of a single chain, but by the seamless collaboration of multiple chains, all uniting to empower users, foster innovation, and uphold the essential principles of decentralization.

5.4.3 Seamless Fluidity

The future advancement of blockchain ecosystems will transcend basic interoperability, evolving into what can be characterized as seamless fluidity across networks. In the near future, users will not merely bridge assets or invoke functions between chains; rather, they will seamlessly coexist across multiple blockchains, experiencing no boundaries. This paradigm shift will transform decentralized application development, resulting in dApps that are inherently chain agnostic.

Celestia [15], Avalanche Subnets, and zkSync [8] advocate data availability, execution, and consensus among independent yet networked systems. Interoperability and composability between sovereign chains will prevail in such an ecosystem.

The goal is seamless fluidity, which requires intelligent routing, asset composability, and user state maintenance across chains. LayerZero [1, 2] and Axelar GMP [16] are early examples of a future where messaging standards and transaction finality will inherently function among ecosystems without user intervention. Universal smart contract interfaces will isolate chain identities, consensus processes, and block times from end-users.

5.4.4 Intelligent Wallets

Future multi-chain wallets will optimize network transactions like smart agents. Future wallets will dynamically choose the best chains based on latency, gas price, liquidity depth, and transaction success. A user's transaction may be routed between different networks to optimize cost and performance. LayerZero endpoint integrations [1, 2] and Axelar routing services [16] show early implementations of Future Wallets.

To manage self-sovereign identities between chains, smart wallets will be connected to decentralized identity (DID) systems [21]. Even with dApps on various base levels, users can maintain their reputation, credit rating, and access permissions. An individual chain optimizer and identity manager will simplify multi-chain interactions in the wallet.

5.4.5 Dynamic dApps

Most decentralized apps today are static blockchain deployments. Future dApps will switch chains to fulfill strategic needs like liquidity, governance engagement, or data localization. Due to market demands, a decentralized exchange can rebalance its liquidity pools from Polygon to Arbitrum without changing contracts.

Dynamic interoperability requires new cross-chain state synchronization protocols and execution proofs. Zk-rollups, optimistic relays, and shared security models are needed to realize this ambition. This will allow dApps to be mobile and flexible, switching between AWS [Amazon], Azure [Microsoft], and GCP [Google] for optimization. Applications will be free from blockchain constraints, optimizing efficiency, accessibility, and robustness.

5.4.6 Rise of Supra-DAOs

As governance progresses, cross-domain coordination will drive the establishment of Supra-DAOs: decentralized autonomous organizations whose governance processes operate concurrently across multiple blockchains. Rather than relying on isolated voting mechanisms associated with individual chains, these Supra-DAOs will consolidate proposals, votes, and policy enforcement across various ecosystems in a coordinated manner.

Supra-DAOs will employ cross-chain voting protocols, verifiable credentials, and federated governance layers to ensure that decisions made on one chain are securely and consistently implemented across others [19]. This holds particular importance for the governance of cross-chain liquidity pools, multi-chain DeFi platforms, and interoperability service protocols. As chains become progressively interconnected, governance must transition to a multi-layered structure capable of managing diverse assets and users across various domains, all while ensuring the security and fairness of participation are maintained.

5.4.7 Interoperability Beyond DeFi

In the upcoming years, interoperability will expand to new domains including the metaverse, gaming economies, and tokenization of real-world assets, while decentralized finance remains the original frontier of cross-chain technology. Users will be able to effortlessly transfer their achievements, digital goods, and avatars between worlds; thanks to the interconnection of isolated blockchain-based metaverses. Initial examples are already surfacing with multi-chain NFT standards and game bridges that coordinate character information and inventory items between games developed on different platforms [18].

Furthermore, the tokenization of real-world assets such as real estate, commodities, and intellectual property will establish cross-chain attestation and verification layers. The issuance of a property token on a private permissioned chain, for instance, necessitates the implementation of public attestation mechanisms to facilitate resale or collateralization in open DeFi markets [21]. This development will lead to the emergence of new hybrid systems in which permissioned and permissionless chains coexist through verifiable interoperability layers, thereby advancing Web3 technologies toward real-world economic and legal frameworks.

5.4.8 Regulatory Harmonization Across Chains

A developed multi-chain future necessitates a coordinated regulatory framework that spans various jurisdictions and ecosystems. Cross-chain asset transfer, decentralized lending markets, and sovereign identity systems will operate within a borderless, global ecosystem. Regulators must develop interoperability standards for compliance reporting, auditability, and KYC/AML enforcement, ensuring that the principles of decentralization and privacy inherent in blockchain technologies are not compromised.

Innovative solutions such as verifiable credentials associated with decentralized identities [17], decentralized oracles for compliance, and programmatic regulatory models embedded within smart contracts will be of significant importance. Regulatory harmonization will not seek to impose centralized control on decentralized systems; rather, it will serve to facilitate the establishment of reliable connections between conventional legal frameworks and decentralized, borderless economies.

An uninterrupted, perfectly linked network and service mesh will define the future rather than many blockchains functioning side by side. Users will no longer consciously "switch" between blockchains; rather, they will experience a continuous decentralized environment where services, assets, governance, and identity transition seamlessly across networks.

Making this vision a reality will require not only technological advancements but also improvements in governance, standards, and regulatory cooperation. As blockchain systems mature, the most successful initiatives will be those that emphasize modularity, cross-domain interoperability, and user-centric abstraction as their core principles.

5.5 Final Thoughts

As we conclude our exploration of blockchain interoperability, a series of essential questions remain that extend beyond the mechanics of protocols and delve directly into the establishment of robust multi-chain ecosystems. What strategies can be employed to enhance the scalability of interoperability protocols while maintaining a commitment to decentralization? Is there a method by which we can ensure security while avoiding congestion? And how do we create inclusive yet capture-resistant governance models?

This section will address several relevant concerns and offer concluding insights on the necessary actions to attain the objectives of Web3.

5.5.1 The Interoperability Trilemma

We start by examining the interoperability dilemma. This is when the question arises:

5.5.1.1 Can We Scale Without Breaking Trust?

The "interoperability trilemma," which refers to the delicate balancing act between decentralization, security, and scalability, is an ongoing battle. It seems that massive horizontal scalability is possible with modular blockchains and parallelized networks like Ethereum 2.0's sharding solution [23] and Polkadot's relay-parachains architecture [24]. But what if two chains are unable to synchronize states in time or agree on finality? This kind of misalignment may result in transactional orphaning, race situations, or introducing new attack surfaces.

Rollups offer a compelling future path by relieving Layer 1 of the execution burden without compromising mutual security, but they come with their own set of precautions. In the absence of strong zk-validity or fraud proofs, rollup-based interoperability runs are at risk of reverting to centralized checkpointing [25]. Scalability cannot be sacrificed for the moral of verifiable trust.

5.5.2 Security at the Crossroads

Here, we come with another major question:

5.5.2.1 Can AI and Cryptography Be Used Together?

It has become increasingly difficult to maintain security in blockchain interoperability, surpassing the capabilities of conventional encryption techniques. To guarantee secure communication between chains, modern systems make use of sophisticated cryptographic primitives such as threshold signature schemes, multi-signature logic, and zero-knowledge proofs (zk-SNARKs). Zk-SNARKs eliminate the need for trust assumptions by demonstrating knowledge of certain information without disclosing it [26]. At the same time, threshold signatures protect any private key from being

5.5 Final Thoughts

compromised by dividing up signing authority across several validators. Nevertheless, if cross-chain networks get increasingly complex, these solutions may be inadequate to protect against evolving and persistent attacks.

Artificial intelligence (AI) constitutes a substantial improvement to this security framework. These technologies may be integrated into blockchain protocols as machine learning models to oversee validator activity, identify consensus anomalies, and simulate real-time adversarial governance scenarios. A protocol for cross-chain bridges has the capability to autonomously identify abnormal voting patterns or transaction flows through the analysis of historical behavior. This technique enables the creation of adaptive security models that evolve in tandem with the network and respond dynamically to threats, rather than depending exclusively on static logic and predefined parameters.

This trend is supported by recent advancements. Enterprises such as Fetch.ai [27], Render [28], and BitTensor [29] illustrate the integration of AI with blockchain technology. These protocols intrinsically integrate AI agents into decentralized systems to maximize economic coordination, improve AI inference on-chain, or assess and encourage model performance via cryptographic staking. Rather than perceiving AI as an abstract concept, these initiatives aim to incorporate AI within the verifiable and trust-minimized structure of blockchain, thereby establishing systems that are both intelligent and accountable.

Blockchain's requirement for transparency and verifiability may be in conflict with the autonomous nature of AI systems, which could lead to transparency and non-determinism. Addressing this necessitates linking AI reasoning to verifiable cryptographic techniques, such as verifiable computing or auditable logs, to maintain confidence in self-learning contexts. The amalgamation of AI and cryptography is not merely feasible; it is becoming vital for the secure and scalable development of cross-chain protocols and decentralized infrastructure.

5.5.3 Reimagining Governance

Here comes another important question:

5.5.3.1 Who Owns the Cross-Chain World?

What is the use of decentralized interoperability if governance becomes centralized or obscure?

Such ecosystems as Terra-Luna's [30] stunning collapse and SushiSwap's leadership meltdown brought to light inherent flaws at the protocol-level governance. Neither possessed the necessary checks and balances to endure black swan events or leadership vacancies.

What, then, might governance look like in a multi-chain world? There are already experiments being conducted with slashing-based incentive alignment models [14], cross-chain DAOs, quadratic voting, and delegated staking. These approaches incentivize engagement and penalize malicious actors. Governance in a cross-chain environment must be as interoperable, verifiable, and composable as the chains it governs.

5.5.4 A Vision: The Cross-Domain Trust Mesh

This work proposes a new paradigm, the Cross-Domain Trust Mesh (CDTM), to advance robust interoperability. Envision smart contracts that are not just upgradable through multi-signature triggers but also validated by a hybrid oracle-validator consensus mechanism. The CDTM approach enables smart contracts to operate on both enterprise blockchains (like Hyperledger) and public chains (such as Ethereum) using semantic relay authentication, facilitating contextual validation of cross-chain data.

This multi-layered architecture enables multi-domain consensus, distributed policy enforcement, and modular upgrades, that is, a trinity of trust, scalability, and flexibility. CDTM is not just a design model; it serves as a framework for researchers to utilize when deploying at an industrial scale.

5.5.5 The Path Ahead: Standards, Verification, and Composability

How can this vision be put into practice? Standards such as CAIP [31] (Chain Agnostic Improvement Proposals) and APIs like EIP-5164 [32] allowing cross-chain function calls require broader adoption. Formal methodologies such as symbolic execution, fuzzing, and runtime verification should be integrated into the development cycle of all interoperability protocols [33].

Composability and upgradability should be preferred over secondary issues. A contract devoid of flexibility is destined for obsolescence or, more detrimentally, exploitation. A protocol that trails rather than progresses is one that cannot properly integrate with others.

5.5.6 The Last Word

In conclusion, we state the following.

5.5.6.1 It's Not Connecting Chains—It's Creating Ecosystems

Now, let us get back to the main query: What exactly is blockchain interoperability?

It's not about moving tokens back and forth or chaining bridges. The objective is to create robust, modular, and open ecosystems that facilitate harmonious coexistence among users, developers, and institutions. Polkadot's relay chain, Cosmos's hub-and-zone, LayerZero's ultra-light endpoints, and Chainlink's CCIP oracle verification each represent a progression toward a federated [6]. Web3.

The future will not consist of isolated smart contracts; rather, it will be driven by composable, interoperable apps that leverage the strengths of many chains to address global challenges.

5.6 Conclusion and Future Directions for Research

What if, instead of being a part of a single chain, the internet of the future develops into a harmonious orchestra of interoperable chains?

5.6.1 The Future Is Composable

The constantly growing field of blockchain interoperability has been explored in this brief not as a collection of tools or protocols but rather as a fundamental change that is reshaping the Web3 itself. In order to create robust, modular systems, we have investigated the architectures that facilitate cross-chain messaging, looked at real-world applications ranging from identification to banking, investigated security risks and governance stress testing, and developed architectural blueprints like the Cross-Domain Trust Mesh (CDTM). Every answer raises new issues, though, and every problem that is resolved shows its next level of complexity, as is the case with all of computer science's great adventures.

5.6.2 What Needs Reconsideration?

Blockchain interoperability is a vast and exciting horizon. Composability, upgradability, and cross-chain trust are not mere buzzwords; they represent open engineering frontiers that need precision, creativity, and experimentation. We need more than just better bridges, we need provably secure state channels, privacy-preserving composable logic, and middleware that can reason semantically across chains.

Interoperability cannot be seen as solely a technological issue by researchers. The systems we create have an impact on international regulatory cooperation, institutional acceptance, and user trust. The challenges of sovereign identification, algorithmic compliance, and decentralized arbitration will require not only cryptography solutions but also ethical frameworks and social modeling.

Imagine a scenario where a public Ethereum smart contract authenticates a scholarship certificate produced by a chain of universities with authorization, and it is immediately recognized as proof of employment across borders. No documentation, no notarization, no uncertainty. Consider a disaster relief DAO that uses stablecoin bridges to dynamically distribute funds to approved local relief organizations that have been verified via cross-chain governance. Although that is not the current reality, you possess the ability to actualize it.

What Needs Reevaluation? Is it possible to build cross-chain oracles that can deliver data, resolve conflicts, and carry out intent-based routing? How can the upgradability of officially decentralized cross-chain smart contracts be guaranteed? Can zero-knowledge proofs and artificial intelligence collaboratively authenticate behavior on networks and develop dynamic compliance systems? How can a decentralized Securities and Exchange Commission (SEC) function when it is composed of code?

Policymakers, academics, and developers are already confronted with these issues today; they are not matters of the future.

5.6.3 For the Researchers

For academics, this book serves as a starting point rather than a final destination. The standards for the next decade of decentralized innovation will be determined by your research, whether you are developing tokenized real-world asset (RWA) markets, cross-jurisdictional compliance layers, or interoperable voting platforms. Establish this as your primary strategy. Expand upon it. Fragment it. Improve it. Furthermore, establish a connection.

Table 5.2 presents a tripartite roadmap aimed at enhancing blockchain interoperability by means of three concurrent tracks: Security, Modularity, and Governance & Law. Track 1 highlights the importance of strong cryptographic foundations, including zero-knowledge based proofs and proxy re-signature schemes, in combination with AI-driven anomaly detection. Track 2 emphasizes composability and developer tooling by standardized cross-chain APIs (e.g., CAIP) and rollup-aware messaging. Track 3 delineates the legal framework for decentralized systems,

Table 5.2 Strategic tracks for blockchain interoperability development

Track 1 Security	Track 2 Modularity	Track 3 Governance and Law
• ZK-based proofs • Light client verifications • AI-driven anomaly detection • Proxy re-signature frameworks	• Standardized cross-chain • API interfaces (CAIP) • Composable middleware design for dApps • Rollup-aware messaging layers	• DAO meta-governance • Legal wrappers for DAOs • Jurisdiction-aware compliance tooling • Cross-chain dispute resolution layers

emphasizing DAO meta-governance, compliance tools, and mechanisms for cross-chain dispute resolution.

Whether you are a policymaker conceptualizing digital assets, an engineer creating zk-based cross-chain audits, or a research scholar designing a new consensus mechanism for earning a Ph.D., you are all a part of a larger picture. Success in interoperability requires not only coding but also collaboration across various disciplines, jurisdictions, and beliefs.

Ultimately, interoperability transcends the mere connection of blockchains. It pertains to the connection of future possibilities.

Proceed to Build It Now

References

1. Morháč, D., Valaštín, V., Košťál, K., Kotuliak, I.: Enhancing XCMP interoperability across Polkadot Paraverse. In: IEEE International Conference on Blockchain, Bratislava, Slovakia (2023a). https://doi.org/10.1109/Blockchain50366.2023.00032
2. Morháč, D., Valaštín, V., Košťál, K., Kotuliak, I.: ParaSpell XCM SDK: a new protocol for interoperability in Polkadot Paraverse. In: 2023 Fifth International Conference on Blockchain Computing and Applications (BCCA) (2023b). https://doi.org/10.1109/BCCA58897.2023.10338906
3. Mitrović, A., Vukmirović, S., Dalčeković, M., Nedić, N., Čapko, D.: Cross-chain general message passing protocol via eternal bridge. In: IEEE International Conference on Telecommunications Forum (TELFOR), Novi Sad, Serbia (2023). https://doi.org/10.1109/TELFOR2023.00032
4. ThorChain: Technical Documentation. [Online]. https://docs.thorchain.org
5. Sushi: SushiXSwap Cross-Chain AMM Bridge. [Online]. https://docs.sushi.com/docs/Products/SushiXSwa
6. Trozze, A., et al.: Detecting DeFi securities violations from token smart contract code. Financ. Innov. **10**, 78 (2024). https://doi.org/10.1186/s40854-023-00572-5
7. Choi, N., Kim, H.: Decentralized commit-reveal scheme to defend against front-running attacks on decentralized exchanges. In: IEEE International Conference on Blockchain and Cryptocurrency (ICBC) (2024). https://doi.org/10.1109/ICBC59979.2024.10634344
8. Park, S., Lee, J., Kim, H.: Efficient computation offloading for Ethereum DApps. J. Ind. Inf. Integr. **31**, 100411 (2023). https://doi.org/10.1016/j.jii.2022.100411
9. Shukla, M., Verma, A., Kumar, N., Sharma, S.K., Hossain, M.S.: Advanced eHealth with explainable AI secured by Blockchain with AI-empowered block sensitivity for adaptive authentication. IEEE Trans. Industr. Inform. **19**(9), 9809–9817 (2023). https://doi.org/10.1109/TII.2022.3228264
10. Chen, L., Yao, Z., Si, X., Zhang, Q.: Wanchain's cross-chain principle includes a hash-locking mechanism and a notary mechanism with threshold key sharing. Acad J Comput Inform Sci. **6**(7), 1–7 (2023)
11. Sengupta, A., Ranjan, R., Ghosh, A., Wang, L., Zomaya, A., Buyya, R.: DataHarbour: enabling decentralized AI data marketplace using Blockchain. IEEE Trans. Serv. Comput. **2024**, 1 (2023). https://doi.org/10.1109/TSC.2023.3256086
12. Schueffel, P.: What colors are the bricks? Unboxing the DeFi model—a literature survey, empirical study, and taxonomy. J. Bank. Financ. Technol. (2025). https://doi.org/10.1007/s42786-024-00054-x

13. Huang, Y., Bian, Y., Li, R., Zhao, J.L., Shi, P.: Smart contract security: a software lifecycle perspective. IEEE Access. **7**, 150184–150202 (2019)
14. Lepore, C., et al.: A survey on blockchain consensus with a performance comparison of PoW, PoS and pure PoS. Mathematics. **8**(10), 1782 (2020)
15. Li, Z., et al.: MuSC: a tool for mutation testing of ethereum smart contract. In: 34th IEEE/ACM International Conference on Automated Software Engineering, pp. 1198–1201. IEEE (2019)
16. Diallo, E.H., Dieye, M., Dib, O., Valiorgue, P.: An agnostic and secure interoperability protocol for seamless asset movement. J. Netw. Comput. Appl. **230**, 103930 (2024). https://doi.org/10.1016/j.jnca.2024.103930
17. Virani, S.S.: Blockchain end user adoption and societal challenges: exploring privacy, rights, and security dimensions. IET Blockchain. **4**(S1), 691–705 (2024). https://doi.org/10.1049/blc2.12077
18. Yang, S., Zhang, G., Li, Y., Wang, P., Zhao, C., Feng, B., Shen, C., Zhang, Y.: Cross-chain architecture of Blockchain integrating notary mechanism and relay-chain technology. In: 2024 4th International Conference on Blockchain Technology and Information Security (ICBCTIS) (2024). https://doi.org/10.1109/ICBCTIS64495.2024.00014
19. Kim, J., Essaid, M., Ju, H.: Inter-Blockchain communication message relay time measurement and analysis in cosmos. In: The 23rd Asia-Pacific Network Operations and Management Symposium (APNOMS) (2022). https://doi.org/10.1109/APNOMS60508.2022.00231
20. Jayapal, C., et al.: An insight into NFTs, Stablecoins and DEXs in Blockchain. In: 2nd International Conference on Advancements in Electrical, Electronics, Communication, Computing and Automation (ICAECA) (2023). https://doi.org/10.1109/ICAECA56562.2023.10200121
21. Wang, Y., Yan, Y., Liu, X., Gao, W., Wang, Z.: A technique for ensured cross chain IBC transactions using TPM. In: IEEE International Conference on Big Data and Privacy Computing (BDPC), Xi'an, China (2024). https://doi.org/10.1109/BDPC59998.2024.10649356
22. Lattner, C., Adve, V.: LLVM: a compilation framework for lifelong program analysis & transformation. In: International Symposium on Code Generation and Optimization, pp. 75–86. IEEE (2004)
23. Rao, I.S., Kiah, M.L.M., Hameed, M.M., Memon, Z.A.: Scalability of Blockchain: a comprehensive review and future research direction. Clust. Comput. **27**, 5547–5570 (2024). https://doi.org/10.1007/s10586-023-04257-7
24. Vasconcelos, A., et al.: CBDC bridging between Hyperledger fabric and EVM-based Blockchains. In: IEEE ICBC, Emphasizes Bridging between Regulated Chains for Secure Asset Transfers (2023)
25. Lashkari, B., Musilek, P.: A comprehensive review of blockchain consensus mechanisms. IEEE Access. **9**, 43620–43652 (2021)
26. Liu, Z., et al.: Combining graph neural networks with expert knowledge for smart contract vulnerability detection. IEEE Trans. Knowl. Data Eng. **35**(2), 1296–1310 (2021)
27. Fetch.ai Inc: Creating AI Platforms and Services that Let Anyone Build and Deploy AI Services at Scale, Anytime and Anywhere. Fetch.ai (2025)
28. Urbach, J., et al.: The Render Network Whitepaper. Render Network Foundation (2023) https://renderfoundation.com/whitepaper
29. Rao, Y., Steeves, J., Shaabana, A., Attevelt, D., and McAteer, M.: BitTensor: A Peer-to-Peer Intelligence Market. (2020). arXiv: 2003.03917
30. Miller, H., Melinek, J.: Terra $45 billion face plant creates crowd of crypto losers. Wall Street J. (2022)
31. Warta, S., Ligi., Gomes, P., Herzog, A., Tomalka, O., Ukustov, S, Haardik, I. G., Thorstensson, J., Malik, H., Bumblefudge, A. D.: Chain Agnostic Improvement Proposals (CAIPs), https://chainagnostic.org/. Accessed 19 June 2025
32. Asselstine, B., Turelier, P., Whinfrey, C.: EIP-5164: cross-chain execution [DRAFT]. Ethereum Improv Proposals. **5164**, 1 (2022)

References

33. Azimi, S., Golzari, A., Ivaki, N., Laranjeiro, N.: A systematic review on smart contracts security design patterns. Empir. Softw. Eng. **30**, 95 (2025). https://doi.org/10.1007/s10664-025-10646-w

Further Readings

Abdullahi, S.M., Lazarova-Molnar, S.: On the adoption and deployment of secure and privacy-preserving IIoT in smart manufacturing: a comprehensive guide with recent advances. Int. J. Inf. Secur. **24**, 53 (2025). https://doi.org/10.1007/s10207-024-00951-8

Augusto, A., et al.: CBDC bridging between Hyperledger fabric and permissioned EVM-based Blockchains. In: IEEE International Conference on Blockchain and Cryptocurrency (ICBC), pp. 1–8 (2023). https://doi.org/10.1109/ICBC56567.2023.10174953

"Blockchain Interoperability Guide":, Cyfrin, Feb. 2024. [Online]. https://www.cyfrin.io/blog/blockchain-interoperability-guide. Accessed 14 Mar 2025

Cai, J., et al.: A Blockchain-based privacy protecting framework with Multi-Channel access control model for asset trading. Peer Peer Netw Appl. **17**, 2810–2829 (2024). https://doi.org/10.1007/s12083-024-01732-9

Caprolu, M., Di Pietro, R., Lombardi, F., Onofri, E.: Characterizing Polkadot's transactions ecosystem: methodology, tools, and insights. In: 2024 IEEE International Conference on Decentralized Applications and Infrastructures (DAPPS) (2024). https://doi.org/10.1109/DAPPS61106.2024.00016

Ding, D., et al.: Privacy protection for Blockchains with account and multi-asset model. China Commun. **16**(6), 69–78 (2019)

Dwivedi, R., Singla, T., Shukla, S.: Cross-chain atomic swaps without time locks. In: 2023 Fifth International Conference on Blockchain Computing and Applications (BCCA) (2023). https://doi.org/10.1109/BCCA58897.2023.10338878

Frauenthaler, P., Sigwart, M., Spanring, C., Sober, M., Schulte, S.: ETH relay: a cost-efficient relay for Ethereum-based Blockchains. In: IEEE International Conference on Blockchain, Vienna, Austria (2020). https://doi.org/10.1109/Blockchain50366.2020.00032

Ganguly, R. et al.: Distributed Runtime Verification of Metric Temporal Properties for Cross-Chain Protocols, arXiv preprint arXiv:2204.09796, 2022. [Online]. https://arxiv.org/abs/2204.09796

Guo, H., Liang, H., Huang, J., et al.: A framework for efficient cross-chain token transfers in Blockchain networks. J King Saud Univ Comput Inform Sci. **36**, 101968 (2024). https://doi.org/10.1016/j.jksuci.2024.101968

Gupta, N.A., et al.: Detection of vulnerabilities in Blockchain smart contracts using deep learning. Wirel. Netw. **31**, 201–217 (2025). https://doi.org/10.1007/s11276-024-03755-9

Han, J., et al.: Cos-CBDC: Design and Implementation of CBDC on Cosmos Blockchain. In: APNOMS 2021, Showcases Asset Mobility Via Cosmos IBC for Multi-Chain Integration (2021)

Han, J., Kim, J., Youn, A., Lee, J., Chun, Y., Woo, J., Hong, J.W.-K.: Cos-CBDC: design and implementation of CBDC on cosmos Blockchain. In: IEEE International Conference on Blockchain (2024b). https://doi.org/10.1109/ICBCTIS64495.2024.00014

Han, Y., Wang, C., Wang, H.: Research on Blockchain cross-chain model based on 'NFT + cross-chain bridge'. IEEE Access. **12**, 77065–77078 (2024a). https://doi.org/10.1109/ACCESS.2024.3401405

Hirai, Y.: Defining the ethereum virtual machine for interactive theorem provers. In: Financial Cryptography and Data Security: FC 2017 International Workshops, WAHC, BITCOIN, VOTING, WTSC, and TA, Sliema, Malta, pp. 520–535 (2017)

Hook, T.B., Brown, J.S., Breitwisch, M., Hoyniak, D., Mann, R.: High-performance logic and high-gain analog CMOS transistors formed by a shadow-mask technique with a single implant step. IEEE Trans. Electron Devices. **49**(9), 1623–1627 (2002)

Hossain, T. et al.: CrossLink: A Decentralized Framework for Secure Cross-Chain Smart Contract Execution, accepted at 2025 IEEE ICBC Cross-Chain Workshop (ICBC-CCW 2025)

Hsien-De Huang, T., Kao, H.Y.: R2-d2: color-inspired convolutional neural network (cnn)-based android malware detections. In: IEEE International Conference on Big Data (Big Data), pp. 2633–2642. IEEE (2018)

Hu, K., Lei, L., Tsai, W.T.: Multi-tenant verification-as-a-service (VaaS) in a cloud. Simul. Model. Pract. Theory. **60**, 122–143 (2016)

Huang, J., Zhou, K., Xiong, A., Li, D.: Smart contract vulnerability detection model based on multi-task learning. Sensors. **22**(5), 1829 (2022)

Ibba, G.: A smart contracts repository for top trending contracts. In: IEEE/ACM 5th International Workshop on Emerging Trends in Software Engineering for Blockchain (WETSEB), pp. 17–20. IEEE (2022)

Idé, T.: Collaborative anomaly detection on blockchain from noisy sensor data. In: IEEE International Conference on Data Mining Workshops (ICDMW), pp. 120–127. IEEE (2018)

Jain, A.K., Gupta, N., Gupta, B.B.: A survey on scalable consensus algorithms for Blockchain technology. Cyber Security Appl. **3**, 100065 (2025). https://doi.org/10.1016/j.csa.2024.100065

Jiang, B., Liu, Y., Chan, W.K.: Contractfuzzer: fuzzing smart contracts for vulnerability detection. In: 33rd ACM/IEEE International Conference on Automated Software Engineering, pp. 259–269 (2018)

Juels, A., Kosba, A., Shi, E.: The ring of gyges: investigating the future of criminal smart contracts. In: ACM SIGSAC Conference on Computer and Communications Security, pp. 283–295 (2016)

Kalra, S., Goel, S., Dhawan, M., Sharma, S.: Zeus: analyzing safety of smart contracts. In: Ndss, pp. 1–12 (2018)

King, S., Nadal, S.: Ppcoin: peer-to-peer crypto-currency with proof-of-stake. Self-Published Paper. **19**, 1 (2012)

Kolluri, A., Nikolic, I., Sergey, I., Hobor, A., Saxena, P.: Exploiting the laws of order in smart contracts. In: 28th ACM SIGSOFT International Symposium on Software Testing and Analysis, pp. 363–373 (2019)

Kolvart, M., Poola, M., Rull, A.: Smart contracts. In: The Future of Law and Etechnologies, pp. 133–147. Springer (2016)

Kotey, S.D., Tchao, E.T., Ahmed, A.-R., Agbemenu, A.S., Nunoo-Mensah, H., Sikora, A., Welte, D., Keelson, E.: Blockchain interoperability: the state of Heterogenous Blockchain-to-Blockchain communication. IET Commun. **17**(8), 891–914 (2023). https://doi.org/10.1049/cmu2.12594

Kumar, N., Hossain, M.S., Jolfaei, A., Sangaiah, A.: Building resilient web 3.0 infrastructure with quantum information technologies and Blockchain: an Ambilateral view. IEEE Internet Things J. **10**(2), 1082–1090 (2023). https://doi.org/10.1109/JIOT.2022.3224343

Kumar, V., Budhiraja, I., Jabbari, A., Garg, D., Singh, D., Mengani, N.: Efficient blockchain interoperability design for cross-chain transactions in future internet-of-value. Peer Peer Netw Appl. **18**(110), 1–21 (2025). https://doi.org/10.1007/s12083-025-01941-w

Liao, J.W., et al.: Soliaudit: smart contract vulnerability assessment based on machine learning and fuzz testing. In: 6th International Conference on Internet of Things: Systems, Management and Security (IOTSMS), pp. 458–465. IEEE (2019)

Liao, Z., et al.: Large-scale empirical study of inline assembly on 7.6 million ethereum smart contracts. IEEE Trans. Softw. Eng. **49**(2), 777–801 (2022)

Lin, S.Y., et al.: A survey of application research based on blockchain smart contract. Wirel. Netw. **28**(2), 635–690 (2022)

Lisi, A., Lopardo, N., Tortola, D., Mori, P., Ricci, L., Severino, F.: A cross-chain rating system: bridging EVM-based Blockchains with Chainbridge. In: 2023 International Conference on Omni-Layer Intelligent Systems (COINS) (2023). https://doi.org/10.1109/COINS57856.2023.10189274

Liu, H., et al.: S-gram: towards semantic-aware security auditing for ethereum smart contracts. In: 33rd ACM/IEEE International Conference on Automated Software Engineering, pp. 814–819 (2018)

Liu, L., et al.: Blockchain-enabled fraud discovery through abnormal smart contract detection on Ethereum. Futur. Gener. Comput. Syst. **128**, 158–166 (2022)

Lys, L., Micoulet, A., Potop-Butucaru, M.: Atomic swapping bitcoins and ethers. In: IEEE International Conference on Blockchain, Paris, France (2024)

Mehra, D., et al.: Implementation of CBDC System for the Customized Development of Finance Service System. SRM Institute of Science and Technology (2023)

Olivieri, L., Spoto, F.: Software verification challenges in the Blockchain ecosystem. Int. J. Softw. Tools Technol. Transfer. **26**, 431–444 (2024). https://doi.org/10.1007/s10009-024-00758-x

Ou, W., Huang, S., Zheng, J., Zhang, Q., Zeng, G., Han, W.: An overview on cross-chain: mechanism, platforms, challenges and advances. Comput. Netw. **218**, 109378 (2022). https://doi.org/10.1016/j.comnet.2022.109378

Rosa, G., Scalabrino, S., Mastrostefano, S., Oliveto, R.: Why and how developers maintain smart contracts. Empir. Softw. Eng. **30**, 84 (2025). https://doi.org/10.1007/s10664-025-10639-9

Sethaput, V., Innet, S.: Blockchain application for central Bank digital currencies (CBDC). Clust. Comput. **26**, 2183–2197 (2023). https://doi.org/10.1007/s10586-022-03962-z

Sizan, N.S., Dey, D., Layek, M.A., Uddin, M.A., Huh, E.-N.: Evaluating Blockchain platforms for IoT applications in industry 5.0: a comprehensive review. Blockchain Res Appl. **6**, 100276 (2025). https://doi.org/10.1016/j.bcra.2025.100276

Sonkamble, R.G., Bongale, A.M., Phansalkar, S., Dharrao, D.S.: A secure interoperable method for electronic health records exchange on cross platform Blockchain network. MethodsX. **13**, 103002 (2024). https://doi.org/10.1016/j.mex.2024.103002

Subhashini, P., Alekhya, J., Rana, A., Lakhanpal, S., V. G, Al-Allak, M.A.: Navigating Web3 evolution with Blockchain's role in shaping next generation internet semantics. In: IEEE International Conference on Communication, Computer Sciences and Engineering (IC3SE), Hyderabad, India (2024). https://doi.org/10.1109/IC3SE62002.2024.10593138

Sönmez, F.Ö., Knottenbelt, W.J.: Cross-chain notification and awareness management. In: IEEE International Conference on Blockchain, London, UK, pp. 420–430 (2024). https://doi.org/10.1109/Blockchain62396.2024.00062

Thyagarajan, S.A., Malavolta, G., Moreno-Sanchez, P.: Universal atomic swaps: secure exchange of Coins across all Blockchains. In: 2022 IEEE Symposium on Security and Privacy (SP), pp. 1299–1314 (2022). https://doi.org/10.1109/SP46214.2022.00063

Tortola, D., Lisi, A., Mori, P., Ricci, L.: Tethering layer 2 solutions to the Blockchain: a survey on proving schemes. Comput. Commun. **225**, 289–310 (2024). https://doi.org/10.1016/j.comcom.2024.07.017

Tsai, W.-T., et al.: A multi-chain model for CBDC. In: 5th International Conference on Dependable Systems and their Applications (DSA), pp. 1–8 (2018). https://doi.org/10.1109/DSA.2018.00016

Vijayalakshmi, C., Florence, S.M.: Flameshift protocol: revolutionizing interoperability with dynamic asset recycling for cross-chain communications. SN Comput. Sci. **5**, 773 (2024). https://doi.org/10.1007/s42979-024-03116-5

Xie, Z., et al.: Enhanced efficiency and security in cross-chain transmission of Blockchain internet of ports through multi-feature-based joint learning. Sci. Rep. **15**, 6199 (2025). https://doi.org/10.1038/s41598-025-85330-6

Zarick, R., Pellegrino, B., Banister, C.: LayerZero: Trustless Omnichain Interoperability Protocol, arXiv preprint arXiv:2110.13871, 2021. [Online]. https://arxiv.org/abs/2110.13871

Zou, H., et al.: Decentralized and Lightweight Cross-Chain Transaction Scheme Based on Proxy re-Signature. IEEE TrustCom (2024). https://doi.org/10.1109/TrustCom63139.2024.00170

Zou, H., et al.: Decentralized and lightweight cross-chain transaction scheme based on proxy re-signature. In: IEEE 23rd International Conference on Trust, Security and Privacy in Computing and Communications (TrustCom), pp. 1201–1209 (2024). https://doi.org/10.1109/TrustCom63139.2024.00170

Made in the USA
Monee, IL
03 May 2026